The Pioneer Woman Cooks

COME and GET IT!

Mango-
Avocado Salad,
page 278

The Pioneer Woman Cooks

COME and GET IT!

SIMPLE, SCRUMPTIOUS RECIPES FOR CRAZY BUSY LIVES

REE DRUMMOND

WILLIAM MORROW
An Imprint of HarperCollinsPublishers

ALSO BY REE DRUMMOND

The Pioneer Woman Cooks: Recipes from an Accidental Country Girl

The Pioneer Woman Cooks: Food from My Frontier

The Pioneer Woman Cooks: A Year of Holidays

The Pioneer Woman Cooks: Dinnertime

The Pioneer Woman: Black Heels to Tractor Wheels—A Love Story

Charlie the Ranch Dog

Charlie and the Christmas Kitty

Charlie Goes to School

Charlie and the New Baby

Charlie Plays Ball

Little Ree

THE PIONEER WOMAN COOKS: COME AND GET IT! Copyright © 2017 by Ree Drummond. All rights reserved. Printed in the United States of America. No part of this book may be used or reproduced in any manner whatsoever without written permission except in the case of brief quotations embodied in critical articles and reviews. For information, address HarperCollins Publishers, 195 Broadway, New York, NY 10007.

HarperCollins books may be purchased for educational, business, or sales promotional use. For information, please email the Special Markets Department at SPsales@harpercollins.com.

FIRST EDITION

Designed by Kris Tobiassen of Matchbook Digital

Photographs on title page and pages 371 and 372 by Matt Ball
Food photography by Matt Ball and Ree Drummond
Photographs on pages 84–87 by Jay Gullion
Special editions: page 383 by Matt Ball and page 398 by Ree Drummond
All other photographs by Ree Drummond

Library of Congress Cataloging-in-Publication Data has been applied for.

ISBN 978-0-06-222526-9 (hardcover)
ISBN 978-0-06-283610-6 (BAM signed edition)
ISBN 978-0-06-283560-4 (B&N edition)
ISBN 978-0-06-283608-3 (B&N signed edition)
ISBN 978-0-06-283609-0 (B&N BF signed edition)
ISBN 978-0-06-283556-7 (Target edition)
ISBN 978-0-06-283554-3 (Walmart edition)

17 18 19 20 21   ID/LSC   10 9 8 7 6 5 4 3 2 1

TO LADD

Thank you for roping my heart.
It's yours forever. XO

CONTENTS

It's a Crazy Busy Life! viii
My 20 Favorite Pantry Items x
My 12 Favorite Freezer Staples..xii
My 15 Favorite Fridge Staples...xiv
My 10 (Okay, 12) Favorite Cuts of Beef...xvi

Breakfasts 1

Apps and Snacks 65

Lunches on the Go 33

Under 40 101

Under 20!...........................131

Sensational Sides.......................267

Take Your Time............................161

Bread, Baby!...............................299

Sheet Pan Suppers.....................211

Sweets, Glorious Sweets.........317

Acknowledgments 369
Recipes for All Occasions! 370
Universal Conversion Chart.............372
Index..373

Meatless Marvels.......................235

IT'S A CRAZY BUSY LIFE!

When I was in my early twenties, I thought I was busy. Then I married a cattle rancher and wondered what I ever did with my time when I was single.

When I married a cattle rancher, I thought I was busy. Then I had four babies and wondered what I ever did with my time before children.

When I had four babies, I thought I was busy. Then they became teenagers . . . and I found out what "busy" really meant. (Anyone who has lived with teenagers is nodding their head right about now.)

When I was married to a cattle rancher and had four babies who grew into teenagers, I thought I was busy. Then I opened a mercantile store and restaurant in our small town and . . .

Well, you get the idea! I feel like life has never been busier (I mean it this time), and you know what? Pretty much everyone I know feels exactly the same way! We humanoids manage to pack our days full to the brim with work, activities, errands, carpools, and obligations . . . and we're lucky if our heads hit our pillows by 10 p.m. We wake up with a to-do list a mile long, and it starts all over the next day. I feel like sales of Calgon should be spiking these days because relaxing bubble baths are so very, very needed.

But one thing I know: Our crazy busy lives should never edge out what's important. Quality time with our sweeties, our kids, our friends, our parents . . . *that's* the good stuff, Maynard. And there's no better way to make that happen than to prepare delicious food, whether it's breakfast, lunch, dinner, or snacks.

Bryce, 15

Todd, 13

Alex, 20

Paige, 18

Mama, ???

Good food on the stove, in the oven, or in the slow cooker will draw your loved ones toward you like a magnet. Don't get me wrong, occasional fast-food stops are unavoidable—we do it, too. (Sonic bacon cheeseburger, *por favor*.) But in my world, I tend to keep my sanity intact when I feel like I'm keeping the home-cooking machine plugging along. (And the occasional bubble bath doesn't hurt.)

The Pioneer Woman Cooks: Come and Get It! is my gift—well, my love letter—to everyone who finds themselves swept up in the crazy fun whirlwind of life, but who still wants to get home-cooked food on the table on a regular basis. I pulled out the most delicious recipes in my get-it-on-the-table repertoire, from gorgeously simple crostini bites to freezer-friendly French toast sticks to a lickety-split tortellini soup.

Grab-and-go lunches are included (indispensable with cowboys and kids!), as are 20-minute dinners, meatless meal ideas (don't tell all the cattle ranchers!), and sheet pan suppers—one of my favorite new ways to cook. And for the days you're not in a nutso rush, I also included things that take a little more time (but are still a total cinch): slow cooker favorites, simple soups, and comforting casseroles. And the icing on the cake: stress-free desserts you'll make again and again!

Because I'm a sucker for a good list, I couldn't resist throwing in a few for you: You'll find my top picks for freezer, fridge, and pantry staples, as well as a rundown of my most oft-used cuts of beef. Lists are natural, lists are good; not everybody does it, but everybody should!

I couldn't be more excited to share this cookbook with you, because it solves a very modern-day dilemma of how to keep feeding your loved ones (and yourself!) in the context of this increasingly harried and hectic world we live in. Some of my most beloved recipes are in these pages, along with some new, adventurous delights. I hope you love this book, and I hope it helps encourage and empower you to keep those home fires burning. ☺

I'm with ya!

Love,

Ree

MY 20 FAVORITE PANTRY ITEMS

Just for kicks, I stepped into my pantry and pulled out a few representative staples to show you. (These are the brands I had handy, but mix it up depending on what you can buy on sale and what's available in your region!)

Canned tomato products. Whole, diced, stewed, tomato sauce, tomato paste, tomatoes with green chiles. I can't survive without them.

Dried beans. White beans, pinto beans, black beans, navy beans. In most cases, you'll need to soak 'em overnight before cooking them. They're the perfect food!

Stocks and broths. Chicken, beef, vegetable, seafood. Low-sodium so things don't get too salty. Cans of beef consommé are good, too!

Potatoes. Keep them in an airy basket and rotate them if you won't use them very quickly. Bake them whole, slice and fry them, boil and mash them, cut and roast them. We love you, Idaho!

Onions and garlic. I keep them separate from the potatoes (it's a gas/fume thing) and I like to have 'em in abundance! I keep both white and yellow onions on hand, but truth be told, I think they're interchangeable.

Jarred marinara sauce. If I'm down to two or three jars, I start to get nervous. If you buy good-quality stuff, it's perfectly permissible as a stand-alone sauce for pasta or a dipping sauce for fried mozzarella or veggies. Or heat it up and spike it with cream for noodles . . . there's no limit to the deliciousness!

Canned beans. They're great in soups, stews, and meat mixtures for tacos when you don't have time to cook beans from scratch. Just be sure to rinse them first!

Pasta pasta pasta! All shapes, all sizes. Shells, spaghetti, linguine, fettuccine, penne, rigatoni, macaroni, lasagna sheets . . . and throw in a few fun or weird or interesting shapes to use here and there.

Syrups. Pure maple syrup, clear corn syrup, pancake syrup, even molasses. For pancakes, cookies, even sweetening up marinades.

Rice! Long-grain, medium-grain, short-grain, brown, wild, jasmine, basmati, Arborio . . . heck, I'm not against boil-in-bag rice in a pinch!

Breadcrumbs. Unseasoned, seasoned, panko . . . they're indispensable for topping casseroles, coating items to fry (see page 116), and even as a binder/filling for meatballs.

Jarred pesto. This jar of wonder is indispensable when it comes to adding a big basil flavor. Mix it with mayo for a sandwich spread. Dab it on crostini (page 95). Toss it with pasta and veggies. It's heaven!

Olives galore! I can't get enough. They're great for snacking, but I chop 'em up for olive cheese bread, spread 'em with Pimento Cheese (page 67), add 'em to the top of crostini (page 95), or lay 'em on pizza.

Salsas. They aren't just for dipping chips! I collect regular salsa, tomatillo salsa, chipotle salsa, peach salsa—the works. Spike soups, use them for layering enchiladas, add them to creamy dressings.

Jams and jellies. For toast . . . yes. But also for crostini (page 95), pancakes, and glazes (page 162), or pour it over cream cheese and serve with crackers for a tasty appetizer!

Oils and vinegars. Vegetable oil and white vinegar are no-brainers. But you also need olive oil, balsamic vinegar, apple cider vinegar, peanut oil, red wine vinegar, white wine vinegar, and rice vinegar. You'll thank me later!

Pickled jalapeños. What can I say? I'm addicted. They're an essential on burgers and pizza, in Mexican soups, and chopped up and stirred into scrambled eggs.

Roasted red peppers. What would I do without them? Cry, most likely. I layer them in grilled cheeses. I puree them for soups and pasta sauces. I add them to pot roast. I want to marry them!

Umami! Add that unmistakable flavor with soy sauce, hoisin sauce, teriyaki sauce, toasted sesame oil, and other pan-Asian-style sauces. I add a hint to sautéed green beans—yum!

Condiments. Ketchup, mustard (yellow, Dijon, country), mayo, barbecue sauce . . . you don't want to be caught without these standbys. And sometimes they can intermingle! Mix mayo, ketchup, and a little mustard for a fry-dipping sauce. (Mayo and BBQ sauce is a yummy mix, too!)

MY 12 FAVORITE FREEZER STAPLES

Aside from the obligatory gallon (or nine) of ice cream, I keep certain staples in my freezer so I'm never, ever, *ever* without options. Even if that option is sitting down with a gallon of ice cream and watching a movie. (Not that I would ever, ever, *ever* do that.)

Frozen peas. They're the next best thing to fresh! You can cook them in gently boiling water if you're just looking to use them as a side dish, but the best way to use them is to stir them straight into recipes in their frozen state. Add them frozen to simmering vegetable soup, pasta primavera (page 263), or any sauce that needs a little spring pea freshness.

Frozen corn kernels. Same as with peas: the next best thing to fresh. Keep it simple by simmering the corn in water until tender, then drain off the water and add butter, milk, salt, and pepper. That's a cowboy dish if I've ever seen one! You can fancy it up with diced green and red bell peppers, spice it up with diced jalapeños, flavor it up with diced green chiles, or turn it into a corn casserole and bake it topped with grated cheese. Frozen corn for prez!

Frozen green beans. Are we seeing a pattern here? I like to buy frozen vegetables that aren't quite as good in canned form; peas, corn, and green beans are at the top of that list. My favorite way to cook frozen green beans is to throw them in a pot with canned whole tomatoes, bacon, and onion and just let them cook like crazy. Makes a delicious side dish! But lightly simmered and tossed with olive oil, salt, and pepper is pretty darn good as well.

Frozen fruit. From berries to mangoes, you'll be able to make the smoothies (or muffins! Or pies!) of your dreams if you have a good stash of frozen fruit. Heck, once I found myself overrun with bags of frozen peaches, so guess what I did? I actually made a huge batch of peach jam and canned it for the pantry. Talk about two opposite ends of the preservation spectrum.

Freeze your own! By the way, you don't have to buy frozen fruit and veggies: You can freeze your own, whether it's excess from the produce section or from your own garden. To freeze fresh veggies and fruit, just flash freeze them on a sheet pan in a flat layer, then transfer them to larger bags. (Paige likes to put together her own smoothie bags with different mixes of fruit.)

Raw meats. Beef, pork, chicken, seafood—fill up the freezer and you'll never run out of dinner options! Make sure the meat is wrapped well in butcher paper or, if in plastic, make sure it's vacuum sealed before freezing. Well-packaged frozen meat will last a good six months or longer. (Always label the packaging with the date it goes into the freezer so there's no guesswork.)

Cooked meat "components." Grilled chicken breasts, boiled and shredded whole chicken, browned and crumbled ground beef . . . these are a busy home cook's dream! All you need is time to thaw the stuff, and everything from chicken Caesar salad to Spaghetti Sauce (page 169) is all yours.

Sauces, stews, and soups. Spaghetti sauce, chili, beef stew, chicken soup, the works! I generally like to freeze these things flat in large (gallon) plastic zipper bags. I'm happiest when I have stacks of options.

Casseroles. Naturally! With very few exceptions, most casseroles freeze beautifully, and here's a great trick: Before you add the casserole contents to the baking pan, line the pan with foil, leaving some foil to drape over the ends. After baking and cooling the casserole, freeze it, uncovered, until firm, then gently lift out the casserole using the overhanging foil. Then simply fold the foil over onto the top of the casserole, wrap the whole thing again in foil to make sure it's all sealed, and freeze these in stacks in the freezer (label them, of course). When you're ready to eat the casserole, place the form into the same baking pan, thaw, and bake! This keeps you from having to tie up scads of baking dishes in the freezer for months on end.

Bread dough. This stuff is magical. Oh, sure, you can thaw and bake the dough in loaf form as the package directions state. But the possibilities are much more fun! Thawed frozen bread dough makes a beautiful "homemade" pizza crust: Just roll or stretch it into a round, add the toppings, and bake. Or roll out the thawed loaf, brush with butter, herbs, and Parmesan, cut the dough into strips with a pizza cutter, and bake. Breadsticks!

Dinner rolls. Frozen little dough balls are perfect for calzones or meat pies (see page 202)! Thaw them and let them rise according to the package instructions, then roll them out, fill them with meat or cheese, seal, and bake. Or make them as regular dinner rolls, brushing them with melted butter and sprinkling them with minced fresh rosemary and sea salt before baking.

Puff pastry. Now we're getting fancy! Except no, we're not. Fancy would be making our *own* puff pastry,

which we don't have to do since the frozen stuff is so good. Dufour brand is great, but I also often use Pepperidge Farm brand. Puff pastry is a miracle. Make desserts (see page 319), puff pastry pizzas, cheese twists, sticky buns, or a million different appetizers . . . it opens up a universe of possibilities!

Pie crust. Yes, I make my own. Yes, I freeze my own! But the day always comes when I'm out of balls of homemade pie dough and I need to make a chicken potpie for dinner (or chocolate pie for the church potluck).

Aw, nuts! My father-in-law has a wonderful habit, but a habit nonetheless: He brings me bags and bags of pecans every fall. He loves visiting pecan farms and bringing back a bounty . . . but the problem is that I've always got more than I need for Thanksgiving dinner and beyond, and nuts go bad if left in the pantry too long. The freezer is the best place to park 'em, and I often just chop them from the frozen state and add them wherever I like. Always have walnuts, macadamias, pine nuts, and hazelnuts in the freezer so they'll be there when you need them.

Vive la freezer!

MY 15 FAVORITE FRIDGE STAPLES

Meat and produce aside, I try to keep longer-lasting staples in my fridge at all times so I never find myself without 'em.

Blocks of Cheddar cheese. Big blocks, little blocks, partial blocks, sharp Cheddar, extra-sharp Cheddar. Just gimme Cheddar, and I'll grate or slice it when I need it!

Feta cheese. Oh, feta. There's nothin' betta! It's long lasting in the fridge (you'll gobble it up before its expiration date!). Crumble it over salad, chunk it over pasta, cut it into cubes for Watermelon Feta Bites (page 68).

Cream cheese. Lasts a long time, too, and it's worth the peace of mind that comes from knowing you can make jalapeño poppers or cheesecake whenever you want! And it also makes for a super-fast appetizer: Pour a small jar of jalapeño jelly over a block and serve it with crackers.

Blocks of mozzarella (and Swiss . . . and Monterey Jack . . . and other white cheese). For dishes from lasagna to quesadillas, I love supermarket versions of white cheese. They melt marvelously!

Parmesan. This stuff will never get old—literally! Keep a big chunk handy for grating over pasta sauces and shaving over Parmesan-Panko Chicken (page 158). (And when you've grated off all the cheese, throw the rind into spaghetti sauce as it simmers!)

Bacon bacon bacon! For the purposes of restraint, I photographed only one of the nine million packages of bacon in my fridge. It's for frying and serving with eggs, of course, but also for BLT sandwiches, chopping and stirring into soups (see page 179) and sauces, wrapping meatloaf, and saving the world.

Eggs. Naturally! For scrambling and frying, but also for poaching and boiling! I keep uncooked eggs in the carton I buy them in and reserve hard-boiled eggs in a bowl so I can tell them apart.

Sour cream. Mix it into creamy salad dressings, use it as a fixin' for tacos and chili, use it in cakes . . . it's an essential!

Bowls of berries. When I buy berries at the store, I wash them and pour them into bowls as soon as I get home to make them ultra-accessible for smoothies, baked goods, or just snacking.

Peeled garlic cloves, aka lazy garlic! This stuff is a life saver. Sold in the produce section of supermarkets, these little pouches of whole cloves are great whether you're dicing them or roasting them whole (see page 301). I'm a believer!

Yogurt. Sweetened with vanilla, plain Greek, flavored with fruit—we have an entire yogurt shelf in our fridge, which means smoothies, muffins, and any other yogurt-containing recipes can happen whenever you need them.

Lemons and limes. Citrus lasts a long time in the fridge, and with a bounty of lemons and limes, you can make marinades, dressings, drinks, desserts, and salsas galore.

Half-and-half and cream. Coffee is my life, partially because of the caffeine (hello, legalized stimulants!) but partially because of the cream I pour into it. But also, these two dairy products show up in my cooking regularly, even if it's just a little splash to turn tomato sauce into tomato cream sauce.

Tortillas. Corn and flour. For any fajita, quesadilla, enchilada, or tostada that comes your way! They last much longer in the fridge.

Butter. No explanation required.

MY 10 (OKAY, 12) FAVORITE CUTS OF BEEF
(AND WHAT TO DO WITH THEM)

I start out with the two low-and-slow cuts; after that, the list is in no particular order!

Chuck roast. I don't just love it because Chuck is my father-in-law's name. Chuck roast is the best cut of roast there is, and will result in a decadent, moist, and tender pot roast every single time. Now, chuck is definitely a tougher meat and has to braise low and slow in a Dutch oven or slow cooker to let the connective tissue soften and get the meat slurpy-tender. But if you've got the time, you won't be sorry for one second.

Beef tenderloin. Sold in whole pieces or in shorter "butt" pieces (as above), this is the most tender cut of beef there is and is famous for the fact that it can often be cut with a fork! Season the outside very generously, because after you roast it whole (never past medium-rare, please!), you'll slice it into pieces, and the seasoned surface area will be proportionately small. Beef tenderloin is the priciest cut of meat there is, so we tend to save it for special occasions.

Skirt steak. I use this cut of meat for fajitas, grilling it whole and then slicing it (against the grain) right before serving. It's a beautifully flavorful cut of beef, but not very tender, so I always try to marinate it for a few hours before throwing it on the grill. Also, I make sure to grill it for only a couple of minutes on each side. You want to keep it on the rare side to maximize tenderness.

Beef short ribs. Imagine the most tender, succulent pot roast you could possibly taste, and you're getting close to the magic of a well-prepared short rib. They also fall under the umbrella of beef that has to cook over lower heat for a longer period of time (usually 3 hours or so), but again: definitely worth every slurp.

Filet mignon. Beef filet steaks, or filet mignon, are nothing more than slices of whole beef tenderloin that are cooked after slicing (rather than before)! The difference is that these are cooked as steaks rather than roasted whole, with more surface area hitting the heat. Wrap the sides of the filets in bacon before searing them and finishing them in the oven, or serve them plain with Wasabi Cream Sauce (page 156). Again: They ain't cheap! Save them for special occasions.

Flank steak. In the same general category as skirt steak, but less fatty. My mom always marinated hers for at least eight hours and quickly fried or grilled it so it was flavorful but still medium-rare. That way, it stays tender! Sliced very thin, it's perfect for fajitas or stir-fries.

Tenderized round steak. A very popular choice for dishes like Swiss steak or chicken-fried steak, tenderized round steak comes from the back side of the cow and is tough before it's pounded or run through the tenderizer. The flavor's great and it's lean, which means there won't be a lot of gristle . . . but that also means it's tough . . . and that's why it's best when it's tenderized.

Rib-eye steak. Also known as every rancher's favorite steak (and my favorite steak, for that matter!). Rib-eyes are beautifully marbled with fat (which is where the flavor comes from), and the meat is nice and tender, making them perfect for the grill, the skillet, or the broiler (page 232)! It's shown above with the bone still attached, but boneless is usually what we reach for. (Psst! If you have a wholesale source and can buy whole rib-eyes, you can slice the steaks yourself to any thickness you'd like. We do this once or twice a year, then vacuum seal and freeze the steaks. Saves money over time!)

T-bone steak. I'm fascinated by T-bone steaks, because they're two cuts of beef in one! One side (shown on top here) is a strip steak and the smaller side (shown below) is beef tenderloin—and the two sides are separated by a big honkin' T-shaped bone in the center. You may have heard the term "Porterhouse steak" as well, and that's simply a T-bone steak that's cut a little thicker and has a little more tenderloin than usual. T-bones are awesome on the grill!

Cube steak. Cube steak is tenderized round steak that's been extra tenderized, or run through the tenderizer twice, rotated 90 degrees before the second run. The result is a nice, flat piece of round steak that's beaten up to the point of becoming tender! If you don't want to add a thick breading, just dredge it in a little flour and fry it to serve with a salad or between two slices of white bread for a sandwich. Cube steak is a staple in our house!

Strip steak. Sold as New York strip or Kansas City strip (there is basically no difference!), this is a cut of steak from the short loin of a cow. It has great marbling like a rib-eye, and while the meat isn't quite as tender, it's a perfectly delicious choice for the grill any day of the week.

Top sirloin. When you get into tenderloins, rib-eyes, and T-bones, things can start to get pricey for basic, everyday dinners. For the times you want to take it easy on the ol' beef budget, I love a good piece of top sirloin steak. Grill or pan-fry them over super-high heat to get as much sear on the outside as possible, then slice them (or just serve them whole!). Since they're inherently a little tougher, you'll want to keep this rare to medium-rare—no futher than that. (Going beyond medium-rare is actually a felony in Osage County. Not really, but it should be.)

BREAKFASTS

A car won't go without gas, and a body won't go without breakfast! Even if it's just a small serving of oatmeal or a muffin-shaped egg casserole, I try to always eat a little something in the morning. My seventh-grade social studies teacher used to tell my classmates and me that we needed "a substantial breakfast," and I'm not about to let Ms. Bundren down!

Crunchy French Toast Sticks 2

Granola Bars 5

Chilaquiles 8

Amish Baked Oatmeal 10

Peachy Pancakes 13

Overnight Muesli 15

Mini Sausage Casseroles 20

Orange-Vanilla Monkey Bread 22

My Mom's Muffins 24

Waffle Iron Hash Browns 27

Orange-Blueberry Muffin Tops 30

CRUNCHY FRENCH TOAST STICKS

MAKES 36 STICKS

Ladies and gentlemen, I stand (actually, I'm sitting at my desk) before you now with irrefutable (actually, it's probably somewhat subjective) evidence that these crispy, crunchy, bake-as-needed French toast sticks (actually, they're slabs) are the Drummond children's current favorite thing in our freezer. The best thing about them (the French toast sticks, not the children) is that they're always ready to go in the oven and bake at a moment's notice. They're technically for breakfast, but I've seen them pass as lunch, dinner, and snacks as well. (Once you coat French toast in Cap'n Crunch, the rules are pretty much out the window.)

12 slices Texas toast

6 large eggs

½ cup half-and-half

½ cup sugar

1 tablespoon vanilla extract

1 teaspoon ground cinnamon

1½ cups panko breadcrumbs

1½ cups Cap'n Crunch cereal, crushed to fine crumbs

2 tablespoons butter, melted

Powdered sugar, for serving

Warm maple (or pancake) syrup, for serving

Fresh fruit, for serving

1. Cut the slices of Texas toast into three strips each.

2. Crack the eggs into a pie plate . . .

3. And add the half-and-half, ¼ cup of the sugar . . .

4. The vanilla, and ½ teaspoon of the cinnamon.

5. Whisk lightly until combined and set aside.

6. In a separate pie plate, stir together the breadcrumbs, crushed cereal, and remaining ¼ cup sugar and ½ teaspoon cinnamon.

7. Use a fork to stir in the melted butter, so that the crumbs are slightly moist. Crack up at the madness that is in this dish, then set it aside.

8. One by one, quickly dunk the bread strips in the egg mixture, turning them to coat . . .

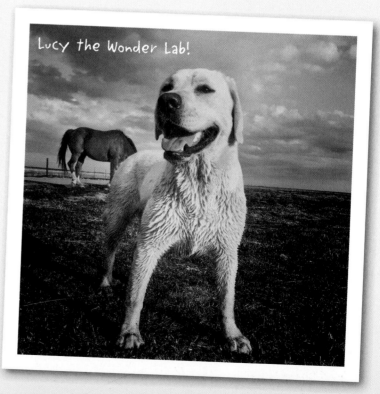

Lucy the Wonder Lab!

9. Then lay them in the dish with the crumbs and crushed cereal, turning them over, sprinkling and pressing so the crumbs totally cover the surface.

11. Then transfer to plastic zipper bags for storage in the freezer. I do smaller bags of 6 to 8 sticks each, but you can do larger batches if you prefer!

13. Sprinkle them with powdered sugar . . .

10. Place the sticks on a rack set in a baking sheet. Flash freeze for 30 minutes to set the surface . . .

12. To bake them from a frozen state, preheat the oven to 425°F. Bake on a rack set over a baking sheet until golden brown around the edges, 15 to 18 minutes.

14. And serve with warm syrup for dipping and fruit to make you feel good about life!

Skipping breakfast makes everyone cranky— even Walter!

GRANOLA BARS
MAKES 18 TO 24 BARS

It's a generally accepted fact that homemade foods are better than store-bought foods, but I have found this to be true with some things more than with others. I hope that made grammatical sense.

Case in point: granola. It isn't that store-bought granola can't be good. It's that homemade granola is just so perfect. The toastiness. The nuttiness. The freshness! Divine.

Here's my basic recipe for homemade granola in bar form, but note that you can change it to suit your fancy! Add different nuts, different grains, different cereals. This is the beauty of making your own granola bars: You can totally customize them according to what you like.

Let's *do* this thang.

4 tablespoons (½ stick) butter, melted

¼ cup vegetable or canola oil

6 cups old-fashioned rolled oats

1 teaspoon kosher salt

Cooking spray

1½ cups puffed rice cereal (such as Rice Krispies)

1 cup wheat germ

½ cup finely chopped pecans

¼ cup roughly chopped almonds

1 cup packed brown sugar

½ cup honey

¼ cup apple juice

¼ cup molasses

1 tablespoon vanilla extract

1. Preheat the oven to 350°F.

2. In a small pitcher or bowl, combine the melted butter and oil.

3. In a large bowl, mix together the oats and salt. Pour the butter-oil mixture on top . . .

4. And toss the oats until they're evenly coated.

5. Spread the oats onto two rimmed baking sheets (so they aren't crowded!) and bake them until toasted, 15 to 20 minutes. Shake the pans twice so they toast evenly. Set the oats aside to cool for 10 minutes, then put the oats back into the large bowl.

Reduce the oven temperature to 325°F, line one of the baking sheets with foil, and coat the foil with cooking spray.

6. Add the puffed rice cereal, wheat germ, pecans, and almonds to the oats and toss to combine. Set aside.

7. In a medium saucepan, combine the brown sugar, honey, apple juice, and molasses.

8. Heat the mixture slowly over medium heat, stirring until all is combined. Stir in the vanilla.

9. Pour the sugar mixture into the oat mixture, stirring as you go.

10. Keep tossing—it will be sticky!

11. Pour the oat mixture onto the prepared baking sheet.

12. Coat your hands with a little cooking spray and press the mixture lightly into the pan.

13. Bake until golden, 22 to 25 minutes. Set aside to let the baked granola cool completely. It'll seem soft when it first comes out of the oven, but will harden and become crispier as it cools.

14. Carefully peel the foil off, then set the slab on a cutting board.

15. Cut the granola into bars. You can do rectangles or squares . . . or both!

16. Or you can use a fork to break the granola into clusters. (These are fun to package in snack bags for your kids. Or your sweetheart. Or yourself!)

CHANGE THINGS UP!

In a shallow bowl, melt 12 ounces semisweet chocolate. Dip the bottom half of each granola bar in the bowl. (Or dip them entirely!) Put them on parchment to cool/set.

Cowboy Johnny and Cowboy Cameron, shooting the early-morning breeze.

CHILAQUILES

MAKES AS MANY SERVINGS AS YOU NEED!

Chilaquiles is pronounced *chee-lah-KEE-lays*, and it's an extremely fun word to say. It's also an extremely fun dish to eat, which can be said about most Mexican food. At its very root, chilaquiles is nothing more than crisp pieces of fried tortilla simmered (or covered) in sauce, which makes them slowly start to soften. They're usually topped with eggs or meat, and there's just nothing about them that isn't good.

Canned enchilada sauce!

Vegetable oil, for frying

Corn tortillas

Green enchilada sauce (I use Hatch) or tomatillo salsa

Eggs

Butter, for frying

Kosher salt and black pepper

Pico de gallo or salsa, for topping

1. In a skillet, heat 1 inch of vegetable oil over medium heat.

2. Cut the tortillas into quarters. I usually allow for about 2½ tortillas per person.

3. Carefully drop them into the hot oil . . .

4. And fry, turning them halfway through, until they are crisp but not yet browned, 1 to 1½ minutes.

5. Remove them to paper towels to drain. Set them aside. (I sometimes fry the tortillas the night before if I know I'm going to make chilaquiles; it saves a step in the morning!)

6. When you're ready to assemble, heat the green enchilada sauce until piping hot . . .

7. And in a skillet, cook the eggs in butter, seasoning them with salt and pepper. I allow 2 eggs per person, and I fry or scramble . . . depending on who will be eating them! Or depending on what mood I'm in . . . whichever force is stronger.

8. Lay a few tortilla chips in the bottom of a single-serving dish (or just on a regular plate!).

9. Pour on enough of the sauce to cover most of the chips, though you'll want to have a few bare spots sticking through so you can see what's under there.

10. Add a second layer of chips and another bit of sauce.

11. On go the eggs . . .

12. And a nice topping of pico. You'll love the flavors and the slight crunch.

CHANGE THINGS UP!

- *Instead of pouring the sauce over the chips, drop the fried chips into the pan with the sauce. Stir gently, and when they're halfway softened, serve them up.*
- *You can top the tortillas and sauce with cooked chicken or beef instead of eggs. Makes a great dinner!*
- *Use red enchilada sauce instead of green.*
- *Sprinkle on crumbled queso fresco at the end.*

AMISH BAKED OATMEAL

MAKES 8 TO 10 SERVINGS

I would love to boast that I was taught how to make this breakfast dish by my Amish friend three farms over, but that isn't the case. Instead, I learned how to make it from fellow homeschooling moms—which, if you don't happen to live near an Amish community, is the next best thing. Homeschooling moms are rich with ideas for recipes that are quick, easy, nutritious, and gol-darn delicious . . . and that just so happens to be the exact Merriam-Webster definition for Amish Baked Oatmeal!

This is pretty much an oatmeal cookie that decided to defect to the breakfast category, and I'm so very glad it did. It's super easy to make, too!

2 cups quick oats

¾ cup sugar

¾ cup whole milk

1 vanilla bean

1 teaspoon ground cinnamon

¼ teaspoon ground nutmeg

1 teaspoon kosher salt

1 teaspoon baking powder

8 tablespoons (1 stick) butter, melted

1 large egg

Heavy cream, brown sugar, nuts, and berries, for serving

1. Preheat the oven to 350°F. Grease a 9 x 13-inch baking dish.

2. In a medium bowl, combine the oats and sugar.

3. Pour in the milk.

7. Next comes the melted butter . . .

11. And spread it out. Bake until it's set, about 30 minutes.

4. With a small paring knife, split the vanilla bean lengthwise in half and use the back of the knife to scrape out all the vanilla caviar. (Tip: Put the empty pod in a container of sugar! It'll infuse it and make it a miracle.)

8. And the egg!

5. Add the vanilla caviar to the bowl . . .

9. Stir it together into a big delicious oaty mess of wonder . . .

6. Followed by the cinnamon, nutmeg, salt, and baking powder.

10. Plop it into the prepared baking dish . . .

12. Cut it into squares while still warm and serve it on a plate. (It will be slightly crumbly!) Pour a little cream on the plate, sprinkle the baked oatmeal with brown sugar and nuts, and serve with berries on the side.

PEACHY PANCAKES

MAKES 12 PANCAKES

Doctoring up a good pancake mix is one of the secrets to happiness when it comes to breakfast time in our crazy household. I don't feel guilty about it at all because there are so many great, wholesome pancake mixes available now, and also because once you add all the fun adornments, you'd never know it wasn't all 100 percent made from scratch.

Note: I used Bob's Red Mill whole-grain pancake mix here, and that mix calls for the eggs and oil as noted below. Adjust for whatever mix you use!

2 cups whole-grain pancake mix (see Note)

2 large eggs (or as called for in your mix)

2 tablespoons vegetable oil (or as called for in your mix)

2 tablespoons sugar

1 tablespoon vanilla extract

2 heaping tablespoons peach preserves, plus more for serving

2 peaches (use frozen if fresh aren't available!)

Butter, for frying and serving

Pancake syrup, warmed, for serving

1. In a bowl, combine the pancake mix, eggs, oil, sugar, and vanilla.

3. And 2 cups water . . .

5. Halve and pit the peaches . . .

2. Add the peach preserves . . .

4. And mix to combine.

6. And cut them into slices.

7. Dice half of the peaches . . .

11. And cook the pancakes until deep golden on both sides.

15. And warm syrup!

8. And add them to the batter. (Set the slices aside.)

12. Repeat with the rest of the batter.

9. Stir in the diced peaches just until combined. Don't overmix.

13. To serve, stack as many pancakes on a plate as you'd like. I chose four. I wanted five, but I'm all about restraint. Spread on a little peach preserves . . .

Peachy keen, jellybean!

CHANGE THINGS UP!

- *Use any pancake mix—buckwheat or buttermilk would be nice.*
- *Make a strawberry version instead: Use strawberry preserves and diced strawberries.*
- *A mixed berry version would be yummy, too! Try raspberry or blueberry jam, blueberries in the pancakes, and mixed berries on top.*

10. Heat a heavy skillet over medium-low heat and coat the surface with butter. Drop in ¼-cup portions of the batter . . .

14. Then add the sliced peaches and a pat of butter . . .

Make-ahead · Kid-friendly

OVERNIGHT MUESLI

MAKES ONE 1-PINT JAR (SO MAKE AS MANY AS YOU NEED!)

I fell in love with overnight muesli on a family trip to Colorado, and the only troublesome thing about it is that the ingredients are so wholesome and healthy that I am able to convince myself that eating a gallon at a time is okay. And I'm not really an oatmeal person—never have been! But that's how good this stuff is.

All you have to do is throw a bunch of stuff in however many jars you need and store them in the fridge overnight. In the morning you'll have the creamiest, dreamiest, slightly sweet whole-grain breakfast delight that you'll be tempted to eat for dessert because again: It's that good. (But the small jars keep you from eating a gallon!)

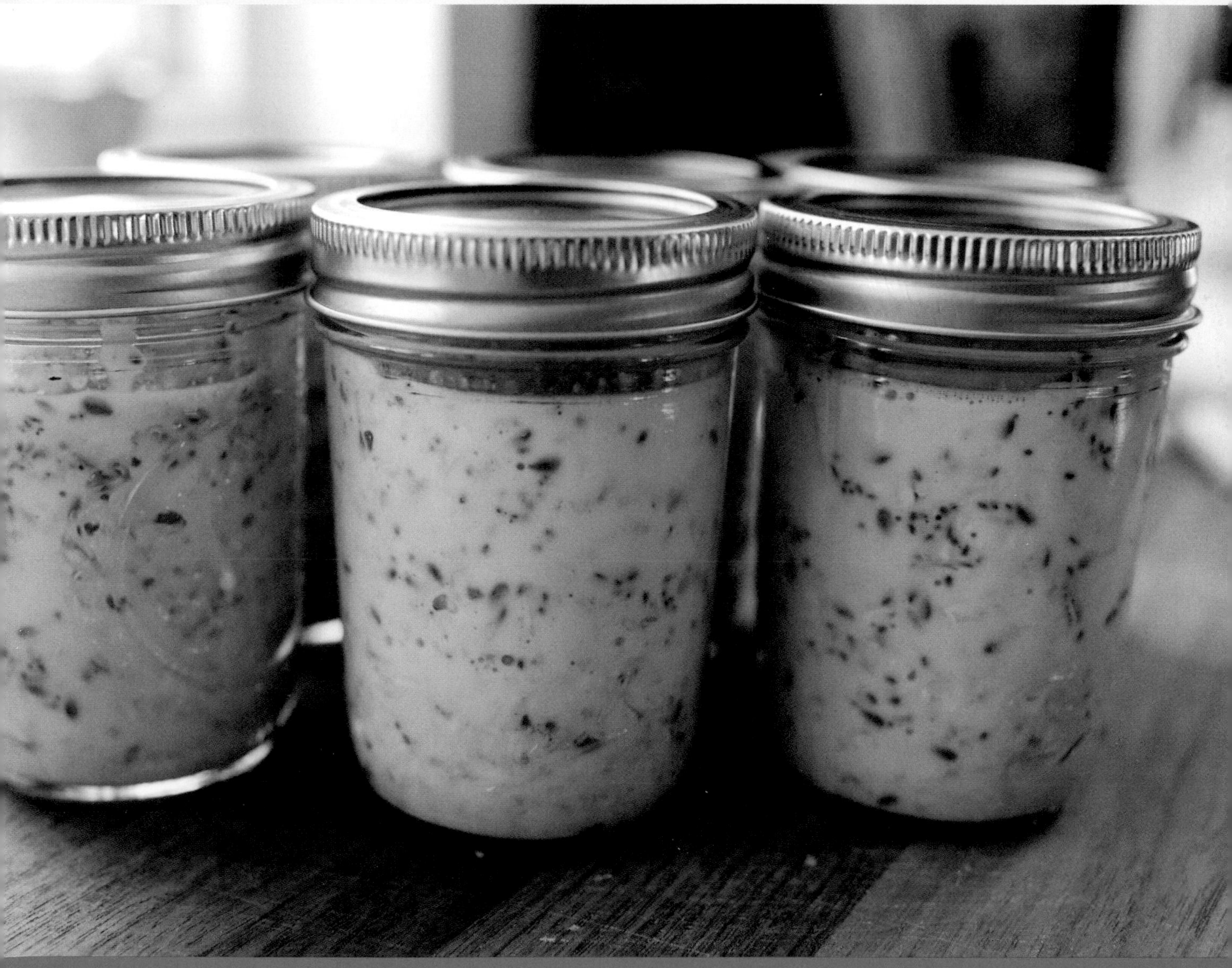

FOR EACH JAR

⅓ cup old-fashioned rolled oats

1½ teaspoons flaxseed

1½ teaspoons chia seeds

1 heaping tablespoon sweetened shredded coconut

2 tablespoons diced apple

1 tablespoon brown sugar (not packed)

½ cup whole milk

1 to 2 tablespoons half-and-half (or heavy cream, if you want extra richness)

¼ teaspoon vanilla extract

1. In each jar, layer the oats . . .

5. The apple . . .

9. Next, add the half-and-half . . .

2. The flaxseed . . .

6. And the brown sugar.

10. And the vanilla!

3. The chia seeds . . .

7. Pour in the milk very slowly . . .

11. Put the lid on the jar and give it a gentle shake.

4. The coconut . . .

8. So that it has a chance to work its way down into the oats and seeds.

12. Refrigerate for a minimum of 6 hours—overnight is best!

13. Look at how much it changes! The seeds and oats have absorbed a lot of the liquid, and . . . well, I can't wait another moment.

14. There should be just a little bit of liquid visible. If you like, you can splash in a little extra milk, to your taste.

Dig in and enjoy!

CHANGE THINGS UP!

• *Add chopped nuts: pecans, walnuts, even cashews!*
• *Substitute coconut milk for regular milk. Yum!*
• *Substitute regular or golden raisins for the apple.*
• *Substitute diced strawberries for the apple.*

Summertime on the Ranch!

When Ladd and I were engaged, my (normally optimistic and sweet) mother-in-law warned me that summer would one day become my least favorite season. I think she might have even used the word "hate" to describe how I would one day feel about the months of June, July, and August. As a child who spent summers at the pool playing Marco Polo in the deep end, I couldn't imagine what she possibly could have meant.

Well, I sure know now. Being the wife and mother of cowboys and cowgirls means getting up as early as 4 a.m. in the summer, if not to saddle the horses and gather cattle myself, then

to help four children and a husband find missing spurs, gloves, and hats before the sun even thinks about coming up. It means being on snack duty, lunch duty, mud duty, manure duty, and mood management duty as sleep deprivation slowly sets in and grabs hold. It means questioning country life, alarm clocks, and agriculture as a whole!

But it also means that we're there when the sun comes up. Right there, with front-row seats! And that makes summer instantly wonderful.

Such conflicting feelings! I guess that's what makes things exciting around here.

MINI SAUSAGE CASSEROLES

MAKES 18 CASSEROLES

There's no evading this simple truth of the universe: Sausage-and-egg casserole is one of the greatest breakfasts there is. It's retro (eighties bridal showers, anyone?), it's satisfying, it's flavorful, and, best of all, it's family friendly.

These are individual versions of the original, and I love making them for the Drummond kids. They're delicious fresh, of course, but they're also a good thing to keep in the freezer, in case of emergencies.

And they have cheese in them. Enough said.

Cooking spray

1 pound breakfast sausage

1 medium onion, finely diced

15 large eggs

Dash of kosher salt

¼ teaspoon black pepper

¼ teaspoon chili powder

1 cup freshly grated Cheddar cheese

1 medium green bell pepper, finely diced

1. Preheat the oven to 350°F. Generously coat 18 muffin cups with cooking spray.

2. In a large skillet, crumble and cook the sausage over medium-high heat until it's about three-quarters browned.

3. Add the onion, reduce the heat to medium-low . . .

7. When the sausage has cooled slightly, add it by the spoonful . . .

11. After they are out of the oven, the casseroles will start to flatten just a little bit within a minute or two. This is normal! Run a knife around the edge of each muffin cup . . .

4. And continue to cook the sausage, stirring occasionally, until the sausage is cooked and the onion is soft. Set the skillet aside to cool.

8. And stir until it's all mixed together.

12. And serve them warm.

5. Crack the eggs into a bowl and add the salt, black pepper, and chili powder. Whisk to combine.

9. Use a ⅓-cup measure to scoop the mixture into the muffin cups . . .

HELPFUL HINT
These casseroles freeze beautifully! Just seal them tightly in plastic zipper bags. Thaw and reheat in the microwave when you're ready to serve them.

6. Add the Cheddar and bell pepper and stir them in.

10. And bake them until they're puffy and just barely set, 20 to 22 minutes.

CHANGE THINGS UP!
- *Substitute finely chopped mushrooms for half the diced bell pepper.*
- *Add several dashes of hot sauce to the egg mixture for a little more spice.*
- *Substitute pepper Jack cheese for the Cheddar.*

ORANGE-VANILLA MONKEY BREAD

MAKES 12 SERVINGS

What kid doesn't love monkey bread? (And for that matter . . . what adult?) The original monkey bread is all about cinnamon sugar, which is great and all, but this super-sticky orange-vanilla version is just beyond everything. There won't be a single piece left over! Especially if I'm within a fifty-mile radius!

This is an incredibly easy recipe; have the kids help with the shaking!

Three 7.5-ounce cans refrigerated buttermilk biscuits

1 cup sugar

Zest of 2 oranges

Kosher salt

½ pound (2 sticks) butter

¾ cup packed brown sugar

1 tablespoon vanilla extract

1. Preheat the oven to 350°F.

2. Cut the biscuits into quarters.

3. Fill a large plastic bag with the sugar, orange zest, and a dash of salt.

4. Seal the bag and shake it around until the zest and the sugar are totally combined. Keep shaking until the clusters of orange zest are mostly broken up; the sugar should be a gorgeous, heavenly shade of light orange.

5. Add the biscuit pieces to the bag, then seal the bag and shake/toss/wig out until all the biscuit pieces are coated in the orange sugar.

6. Pour everything into a Bundt pan and set it aside.

7. In a medium saucepan, combine the butter, brown sugar, and vanilla.

8. Melt the mixture over medium heat, then pour it all over the biscuits, scraping the pan to get every last drop. Let it settle for a minute or two.

9. Bake the monkey bread until the tops of the biscuits are golden brown, about 25 minutes. Let the bread sit and cool in the pan for 8 to 10 minutes (not much longer!).

10. Turn the monkey bread out onto a cake plate. Some of the extra sweetness and goo will spill out, so be sure the plate has a little rim. Serve warm and enjoy being the most popular person in the room!

MY MOM'S MUFFINS

MAKES 12 MUFFINS

My mom made these blessedly beautiful muffins when she was visiting once, and I absolutely inhaled them. They're textural and flavorful and—bonus!—oil free and butter free, which to me is an invitation to slather on softened butter right before eating them.

But that's just me.

This recipe is particularly notable because it contains a banana. And this is only the second recipe containing a banana that I've ever shared in my ten-plus years of being a food blogger (and in my forty-eight years of being a human being, for that matter).

Bananas are terrible! But these muffins are amazing!

Softened butter, for greasing the pan and for serving

1 cup whole wheat flour

½ cup all-purpose flour

¼ cup ground flaxseed (flaxseed meal)

1 cup old-fashioned rolled oats

½ cup packed brown sugar

½ teaspoon kosher salt

1 teaspoon baking soda

2 teaspoons baking powder

½ teaspoon ground cinnamon

½ cup walnuts, roughly chopped

1 banana

1 cup buttermilk, plus more as needed

1 large egg

½ cup applesauce

¼ cup molasses

1 teaspoon vanilla extract

½ cup raisins (golden raisins are great, too!)

1. Preheat the oven to 350°F. Thoroughly grease 12 muffin cups.

2. In a large bowl, combine the flours, ground flaxseed, and oats . . .

3. Along with the brown sugar, salt, baking soda, baking powder, cinnamon . . .

4. And walnuts! Stir to combine.

5. Next . . . gulp . . . peel the banana . . .

6. And mash it up with a fork. (This is the hardest thing I've ever done in my life.)

7. In a separate bowl, mix together the buttermilk, egg, applesauce, and (gulp) banana. Stir it together . . .

8. Then add the molasses and vanilla . . .

9. And stir it around.

10. Pour the wet into the dry . . .

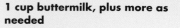

11. Stirring until it just barely comes together. The batter should be really wet and sticky; if needed, splash in a couple extra tablespoons of buttermilk.

14. And bake until the muffins are deep golden brown, 16 to 18 minutes.

"Hi, Mom!!!"

12. This is when you want to add the raisins, if that's your cup of tea! But even if it isn't, you have to add them because I stepped up to the plate and added a banana. And not just any banana—a mashed banana, which is the worst kind of banana there is!

13. Scoop ¼-cup measures of batter into the prepared muffin cups . . .

15. Serve with softened butter if you're a rebel like me. (A little honey or jelly is great, too!)

WAFFLE IRON HASH BROWNS

MAKES SIX 4-INCH WAFFLES

I'm beginning to think my waffle iron can do anything. It can make waffles, of course. It can make omelets (try it! Just whip up omelet ingredients and pour them in). It can make panini (whoa—game changer). And it can make quesadillas to beat the band.

(Oh, it can also sing "Jingle Bells" like no one's business. That's another story for another time.)

But did you know your waffle iron can turn frozen hash browns into the crispiest, butteriest taters you ever did see/hear/taste? It's true. And considering how long both frozen hash browns and waffle irons have been around, I'm amazed it took humankind this long to figure it out. (I'm so glad it did!)

One 30-ounce bag frozen shredded hash browns

4 tablespoons (½ stick) butter, melted

½ teaspoon black pepper

Cooking spray

½ cup chopped shaved ham

1 cup freshly grated Cheddar cheese

Ketchup, for serving

1. Thaw the hash browns at room temperature for about 3 hours, turning the package over occasionally. (Or you may place the frozen hash browns in the fridge overnight.) When they are thawed, preheat the waffle iron to medium-low heat.

2. Place half the hash browns in the middle of a stack of three or four paper towels.

3. Bunch up the potatoes and squeeze them to force out as much liquid as possible. Place the hash browns in a large bowl, then repeat with the rest of the hash browns.

4. Drizzle in the butter . . .

5. Then add the pepper and toss everything together.

6. Coat the surface of the waffle iron with cooking spray, then add ½ cup of the potato mixture to each well. (You should hear them start to sizzle!)

7. Sprinkle the chopped ham evenly over the potatoes . . .

8. Then add the cheese.

9. Sprinkle about ¼ cup of the potatoes over the top of each waffle . . .

10. Then close the lid and let 'em cook! How long the waffles take to cook depends on the heat of your waffle maker and the moisture of the potatoes. Lift the lid and check on the waffles from time to time to make sure they aren't burning.

11. The edges and the cheese will start to crisp up and get golden, but you'll want to keep it going until everything is deep golden.

12. Use a dull knife or spatula to remove the waffles. Serve them with ketchup . . .

And dig right in! These are absolutely addictive. Crispy and wonderful!

CHANGE THINGS UP!

- *For a simpler hash brown, omit the cheese and ham and just put ¾ cup potatoes in each well.*
- *Add diced onion and green bell pepper along with the ham and cheese.*

Tim Caleb Chuck Ladd Todd Bryce

The Drummond MEN! They clean up nice!

ORANGE-BLUEBERRY MUFFIN TOPS

MAKES 12 MUFFIN TOPS

There are two kinds of muffin tops in this world. One is caused by low-rise jeans, and we won't talk about them in this cookbook for obvious reasons.

The other kind of muffin top, which I will gladly talk about in this cookbook, is just what it sounds like: the delicious, perfect top from a muffin without all that annoying base. I have seen special muffin top pans in kitchen stores, but it isn't necessary to have one of those. All you need is a scoop and a sheet pan!

(I want that to go on my tombstone, by the way: "All she needed was a scoop and a sheet pan . . .")

(Right along with "Every bra she ever loved was discontinued . . .")

1 cup fresh blueberries

1½ cups all-purpose flour

12 tablespoons (1½ sticks) butter, softened

¾ cup sugar

1 large egg

¾ teaspoon baking soda

1 orange

¾ cup buttermilk

1 cup powdered sugar, sifted

1. Preheat the oven to 425°F. Line a baking sheet with a baking mat or parchment.

2. Place the blueberries in a bowl and toss with 1 tablespoon of the flour. Set aside.

3. In a mixer fitted with the paddle attachment, cream together the butter and sugar.

4. Add the egg and mix it well.

5. Add the rest of the flour along with the baking soda and mix until everything is just combined.

6. Zest the orange . . .

7. And add it to the bowl.

8. With the mixer on low, slowly pour in the buttermilk . . .

9. And stop when the dough has come together. (Don't overmix!)

10. Remove the bowl from the mixer, then add the blueberries and any excess flour around them . . .

11. And gently fold them in with a rubber spatula.

12. Use a ¼ cup scoop (a standard size ice cream scoop) to scoop out the dough onto the baking sheet.

13. Bake until the muffin tops are lightly browned, about 11 minutes. Let them cool slightly.

14. Meanwhile, make the glaze: In a medium bowl, combine the powdered sugar with the juice of the orange and whisk until smooth.

15. Generously drizzle the glaze over each muffin top. Enjoy them warm or at room temperature!

CHANGE THINGS UP!

- *For a tangier flavor, substitute lemon zest and lemon juice for the orange.*
- *Substitute semisweet chocolate chips for the blueberries: Orange-chocolate muffin tops!* What?!?

$\mathcal{L}$UNCHES ON THE GO

A long, leisurely lunch is nice and all, but doesn't it seem like the middle meal of the day is often the most hurried and hectic? Create your own "fast" food for those busy humans in your household (pssst—that includes you). These delicious lunchtime options are perfect to grab from the fridge on your way out the door in the morning.

Cowboy Bento Box 34

    BBQ Chicken Wings 36

    Lemon-Basil Potato Salad 38

    Apple-Celery Slaw 40

Pasta Salad in a Jar 43

Salad on a Stick 46

Beef Noodle Salad Bowls 48

Thai Chicken Wraps 54

Greek Feast to Go 57

Grilled Veggie and Cream Cheese Sandwiches 60

COWBOY BENTO BOX

MAKES AS MANY AS YOU NEED!

I am in love with preportioned meals packed in neat little sectioned trays, otherwise known as bento boxes. You can find them everywhere, and most of them have snap-on lids that keep everything contained until you're ready to chow down. It also happens to be a great way to deliver vittles to hungry cowboys! (I know one or two of 'em.)

**BBQ Chicken Wings (page 36),
with extra sauce for dipping**

**Lemon-Basil Potato Salad
(page 38)**

Apple-Celery Slaw (page 40)

Lemon Bars (page 358)

Fill each section with the different elements.

Best lemon bar ever! (A brownie is also totally perfect for this.)

It's a portable masterpiece of a feast!

Captain Forearms.

BBQ Chicken Wings

MAKES 24 WINGS

Sometimes I'm asked the hilariously cynical and pessimistic question (and don't get me wrong, I love answering hilariously cynical and pessimistic questions; I find it a nice, light challenge), "What is your least favorite thing to cook?" Well, I can absolutely answer that for you today: Buffalo chicken wings. I mean absolutely zero disrespect to residents of western New York, and I mean even less disrespect to the millions of football fans (my husband among them) who like to slurp on the things while watching their favorite game. And truth be told, I'll dive right in and slurp a few myself—I'm not ashamed!

It's just that I've made so darn many batches of them through the years of being married to a football lover and giving birth to four football lovers that I honestly worry sometimes that I'm going to be buried in a coffin full of Louisiana hot sauce. I just can't look at another Buffalo wing on some days.

Not that I'm bitter.

My point is this: Sometimes it's nice to change things up and throw a little curveball their way. These barbecue wings are the bomb. (The secret's in the sauce!) And they're an awesome thing to make ahead of time, as they reheat beautifully. Heck, they taste great cold right out of the fridge!

Just a warning: If you haven't ever whipped up a batch of your own barbecue sauce, your life as you know it is about to change.

Canola oil

½ onion, diced

2 garlic cloves, minced

1 cup ketchup

⅓ cup molasses

⅓ cup packed brown sugar

¼ cup minced chipotle peppers in adobo sauce

¼ cup white vinegar

1 tablespoon Worcestershire sauce

24 chicken wing parts (12 wings separated into 2 pieces, wing tips removed)

2 tablespoons sliced green onions, for serving

1. First make the barbecue sauce. In a medium saucepan, heat 2 tablespoons canola oil over medium-high heat and sauté the onion and garlic until soft, 4 to 5 minutes.

2. Turn the heat to low, then add the ketchup . . .

3. Followed by the molasses, brown sugar, chipotle peppers, vinegar, and Worcestershire. So simple!

4. Stir it around, letting it cook gently until thickened slightly, about 20 minutes.

6. For the wings: Pour about 3 inches canola oil into a heavy pot and heat over medium-high heat until a deep-fry thermometer registers 375°F. Add half the chicken pieces to the oil . . .

8. Drain on paper towels, then repeat with the other half.

Preheat the oven to 325°F.

5. Turn off the heat and set the pan aside.

7. And fry until golden brown and fully cooked, about 5 minutes.

9. Put the wings in a baking dish, then pour the sauce over the top . . .

10. And toss to coat. Bake the wings to set the sauce, about 15 minutes. (If you can't wait, you can dive right in and skip the oven step!) Sprinkle with the green onions and serve.

These are wondrous! Great by themselves or as part of a big ol' picnic.

Lemon-Basil Potato Salad

MAKES 6 TO 8 SERVINGS

Potato salad, if one is not *extremely* careful, can easily devolve into something of a deli case calamity! And I'm not trying to be judgmental! It's just that I know how downright delicious a good potato salad can be, and I want all potato salads in the world to live up to that same potential.

I sound judgmental, don't I? Argh . . . I hate it when I do that! I swear I didn't mean it. Deli case potato salad must be a hot button issue for me.

As potato salads go, this is low on effort and really big on flavor. My favorite combo of factors!

3 pounds small potatoes

¼ cup pine nuts

½ cup mayonnaise

3 tablespoons olive oil

2 tablespoons prepared pesto

1 large lemon

Kosher salt and black pepper

Basil leaves, for serving

1. In a pot of boiling water to cover, cook the potatoes fully. Drain and set aside. Don't worry, potatoes! We'll be back!

2. Meanwhile, toast the pine nuts in a skillet over low heat, stirring often, until just light golden, 3 to 4 minutes.

3. Now it's on to the dressing: In a bowl, combine the mayonnaise, olive oil, and pesto . . .

6. And stir until it's all combined. (This dressing, by the way? So good! Makes a great dip for raw veggies, a yummy spread for sandwiches . . . you get the idea.)

9. Then stir until the potatoes are all coated and combined! Cover and refrigerate for a few hours. To really get ahead, you could make it up to 48 hours in advance and keep it in the fridge.

4. Then zest the lemon right into the bowl to make it lovely and citrusy (leave a little zest for the garnish).

7. Cut the potatoes in half (or in quarters if they're a little larger).

5. Since the lemon is naked and afraid, go ahead and squeeze in the juice, then add salt and pepper . . .

8. And throw them into the dressing bowl along with the pine nuts . . .

10. Serve it with some extra zest and basil leaves all over the top.

Apple-Celery Slaw

MAKES 6 TO 8 SERVINGS

Slaw really is one of those perfectly versatile foods. You can treat it as a salad alongside meat. You can treat it as a fixin' for tacos. You can even pile it on top of hot dogs! This slightly sweet-spicy slaw uses traditional ingredients as well as a not-so-traditional one: julienned apple! The sweet crunchiness will rock your world.

½ cup olive oil

1½ teaspoons Dijon mustard

1 tablespoon sugar

1 teaspoon white vinegar

¼ teaspoon cayenne pepper

⅛ teaspoon kosher salt

⅛ teaspoon celery salt

4 celery stalks, cut into matchsticks

2 green apples, unpeeled, cored, and cut into thin matchsticks

1 jalapeño, thinly sliced

½ head green cabbage, thinly sliced

½ head red cabbage, thinly sliced

1. In a medium bowl, mix the olive oil, mustard, sugar, vinegar, cayenne, kosher salt, and celery salt. Tasty as all get-out!

2. Combine the celery, apples, jalapeño, green cabbage, and red cabbage in a bowl. The colors are gorgeous, and I love everything cut into sticks!

3. Pour three-quarters of the dressing over the top. I do this to make sure the slaw doesn't get too wet. You can add more later if it needs it.

4. Toss everything together well . . .

5. Then serve it immediately *or* cover with plastic wrap and refrigerate for a few hours.

Todd's (almost) always got a smile on his face!

PASTA SALAD IN A JAR

MAKES 4 TO 6 QUART-SIZE JAR SALADS

Salads in jars are sweeping the nation! Aside from being nifty and beautifully organized (especially if you obsess over arranging the layers neatly), they also happen to be poifectly poitable! (That's "perfectly portable" for all you normal, nonweird types out there.)

DRESSING

1 cup olive oil

6 garlic cloves, minced

½ teaspoon kosher salt

1 teaspoon black pepper

½ cup balsamic vinegar

1 tablespoon grated lemon zest

1 tablespoon chopped basil

1 tablespoon chopped parsley

SALAD

1 bunch kale, thinly sliced (remove the tough stems first)

4 ounces Parmesan cheese, shaved

Kosher salt and black pepper

¼ cup pine nuts

3 cups halved cherry tomatoes

8 ounces bow-tie pasta (farfalle), cooked according to package directions

8 ounces small mozzarella balls

1. First, make the dressing: In a large skillet, heat the olive oil over low heat and add the garlic.

4. Then pour the oil mixture into a small mason jar.

2. Let the garlic cook for about a minute. When it begins to sizzle, stir it around so it doesn't get too brown.

5. Add the balsamic, lemon zest, basil, and parsley . . .

3. When the garlic starts to turn golden, add the salt and pepper and stir. Set aside for 5 minutes . . .

6. Then put the lid on and shake like crazy! Set it aside.

We love pasta salad!

7. Make the salad: Return the same skillet to medium-high heat (don't wash all that flavor out!). Add the kale . . .

8. And cook until it's partly wilted, about 5 minutes. Remove it from the heat and let it cool for about 5 minutes . . .

9. Then add the Parmesan shavings . . .

10. And toss. Season with salt and pepper.

11. Put the pine nuts in a small skillet over low heat. Toast slowly for 3 to 4 minutes, tossing them often. Remove from the skillet and set aside. (Don't let 'em get too brown!)

12. Assemble the salads: To a quart jar, add some dressing . . .

13. Some of the cherry tomatoes . . .

14. A nice handful of pasta . . .

15. Some pine nuts . . .

16. A small amount of kale . . .

17. A handful of mozzarella balls . . .

18. And finally, another little bunch of the kale. Repeat with the other jars, screw on the lids, and refrigerate until ready to eat. When that time comes, give the jar a healthy shake while the lid is still on, then dig right in with a fork!

Paige, Paige on the range . . .

SALAD ON A STICK

MAKES 6 TO 8 SERVINGS

The big selling point of this salad is that it's F-U-N, fun! I mean, sure . . . it might be just as easy (okay, easier) to throw salad ingredients into a bowl and toss them with the dressing. But I ask you: What mark are we trying to make here on the world, people?!? Are we men or are we mice?!? Are we bold and courageous or are we standard and predictable?!? I think you need to spend some time taking a good, hard look at yourself and evaluating whether or not you really want to be here!!!!!!

Sorry. I sound like a high school football coach.

¼ cup olive oil

2 tablespoons red wine vinegar

1 teaspoon Italian seasoning

Kosher salt and black pepper

½ head iceberg lettuce, cut into small chunks

12 cherry tomatoes

8 ounces mild Cheddar cheese, cut into cubes

½ cucumber, cut into chunks

1. Make the dressing! Drizzle the olive oil into a bowl . . .

4. Next, use wooden skewers to build the salads.

5. Place the skewers on a platter and brush the dressing all over them. Then the stick salads will be all ready to eat!

2. And add the vinegar, Italian seasoning, and salt and pepper to taste.

Go in any order you want! (And change up the ingredients to suit your fancy.)

3. Whisk until it's all totally combined.

You can snip off the sharp end of the skewers if you're serving them to youngsters.

6. Serve immediately (or pack them up for a picnic).

CHANGE THINGS UP!

Try:

- *Small white mushrooms*
- *Whole black olives*
- *Chunks of zucchini or summer squash*
- *Asparagus tips*
- *Radish halves*
- *Thin-sliced ham or turkey, folded into wedges*
- *Cooked bow-tie pasta*

Salads + evening walks = jeans fit

BEEF NOODLE SALAD BOWLS

MAKES 4 SALAD BOWLS

There's so much going on in this bowl that it would be difficult for me to describe it in mere mortal terms. There's the slightly spicy peanut-curry sauce. There's the seasoned steak, grilled to perfection and sliced. And there are noodles—lots and lots and lots and lots of noodles. To top it off, it all comes together to make the most delightful portable lunch!

Lots of moving parts here, but nothing complicated at all. To save time, make the peanut sauce and/or grill the steak well in advance and keep them in the fridge until you need to assemble the salad.

One ¾- to 1-pound sirloin or rib-eye steak

Kosher salt

DRESSING

¾ cup ponzu sauce or regular soy sauce, plus more for drizzling

3 tablespoons toasted sesame oil

2 tablespoons olive oil

2 tablespoons rice vinegar

2 tablespoons packed brown sugar

2 teaspoons minced fresh ginger

1 teaspoon hot chili oil

2 garlic cloves, finely minced

NOODLES AND FIXINS

8 ounces thin noodles, cooked and drained

½ cup sliced green onions

PEANUT SAUCE

1 tablespoon vegetable oil

1 tablespoon curry powder

1 shallot, minced, or 2 tablespoons minced onion

2 garlic cloves, minced

One 1-inch piece fresh ginger, peeled and minced

½ cup coconut milk

¼ cup soy sauce

2 tablespoons packed brown sugar

1 tablespoon smooth peanut butter

½ teaspoon hot chili oil

Juice of 2 limes

Kosher salt

1. Prepare a grill or heat a grill pan over medium-high heat. Season both sides of the steak with salt. Grill the steak on one side for about 2 minutes . . .

2. Then cook it on the other side for another 2 to 2½ minutes for medium-rare. Remove it to a plate to cool.

3. Make the dressing: Combine the ponzu sauce, sesame oil, olive oil, vinegar, brown sugar, ginger, hot chili oil, and garlic in a bowl.

4. Whisk to combine, then taste and adjust the flavors and seasonings. Add a little more hot chili oil if you like to walk on the wild side!

5. When the steak is cool enough, place it in a large plastic zipper bag. Add 3 tablespoons of the dressing, setting aside the rest for later. Seal the bag tightly and place in the fridge until needed. This is sort of the "quick marinade" method: Instead of marinating the meat before grilling, you do it after!

6. For the noodles: Place the noodles in a bowl, pour in the remaining dressing, and toss to combine.

7. Add the green onions and toss them in. Cover the bowl with plastic wrap and refrigerate for at least a couple of hours, or until cool.

8. Meanwhile, make the peanut sauce: In a small skillet, heat the vegetable oil over low heat. Add the curry powder . . .

9. The shallot . . .

10. And the garlic and ginger . . .

11. And cook until the aromatics soften, about 5 minutes.

The flavah! The flavah! It's amazing.

12. Scrape the mixture into a blender and add the coconut milk . . .

13. Along with the soy sauce, brown sugar, peanut butter, hot chili oil, lime juice, and a pinch of salt.

14. Blend the sauce, adding hot water as needed to thin it and make it silky and smooth. (Again: Feel free to make this ahead of time! It holds really well in the fridge for up to a week.)

15. Now it's time to assemble this craziness! Remove the steak from the bag and slice it against the grain into thin strips.

16. Divide the noodles among four portable bowls and arrange several strips of beef on the top of each one.

17. Pour a little peanut sauce into a small container with a lid . . .

18. And pop it right in the center of the bowl. The sauce gets poured over everything, and you'll pretty much go crazy for the end result.

Happy noodles!

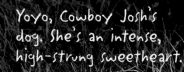

Yoyo, Cowboy Josh's dog. She's an intense, high-strung sweetheart.

Don't Blink!

The Drummond kids are growing up! I swear this photo was taken two weeks ago.

Look at them now! Somebody please stop time. My heart can't take this anymore.

THAI CHICKEN WRAPS

MAKES 4 SERVINGS

I just love a good wrap! And this chicken-and-veggie version is definitely a good one. You can make these all the way through and eat the wraps while the chicken is still warm. Or, my personal favorite, you can make up a batch of the chicken (and delectable peanut sauce) ahead of time and just assemble the wraps throughout the week.

(I kept these pretty pared down for simplicity . . . but see how many of the extra/optional ingredients you can add. There's no limit to the deliciousness!)

MARINADE/SAUCE

1 tablespoon rice vinegar

¼ cup soy sauce

1 teaspoon toasted sesame oil

1 teaspoon hot chili oil

Juice of 2 limes, squeezed halves reserved

1 tablespoon minced fresh ginger

2 tablespoons packed brown sugar (optional)

1 teaspoon cornstarch

2 tablespoons honey (or more brown sugar)

CHICKEN

2 tablespoons peanut or canola oil, for frying

3 boneless, skinless chicken breasts, cut into bite-size pieces

PEANUT SAUCE

½ cup peanut butter (crunchy/chunky is good!)

Juice of 2 limes

3 tablespoons soy sauce

3 tablespoons honey

½ teaspoon hot chili oil

1 teaspoon red pepper flakes

WRAPS

4 whole wheat tortillas (soft taco size)

Green-leaf or other lettuce, leaves left whole or shredded

1 large carrot, cut into thin strips or julienne

½ cucumber, seeded and cut into thin strips

Peanuts

OPTIONAL ADDITIONS

Bean sprouts

Alfalfa sprouts

Baby spinach leaves

Thinly sliced red onion

Sliced green onions

Blanched asparagus

Sriracha sauce

1. First, make the marinade/sauce: In a bowl, combine the vinegar, soy sauce, sesame oil, hot chili oil, lime juice, ginger, and brown sugar (if using). Whisk it together . . .

2. Then pour off half the liquid into a separate bowl.

3. Add the cornstarch and honey to the bowl, then stir it with a fork. Set the sauce aside.

4. Marinate and cook the chicken: Put the chicken into the bowl you used to make the marinade. Throw in the squeezed lime halves and stir the chicken around. Let it sit for a bit.

5. In a heavy skillet, heat the peanut oil over high heat. Add the chicken in a single layer and let cook on one side, undisturbed, for about 1 minute. Then stir the chicken around and cook until it's totally done, 3 to 4 minutes.

6. Reduce the heat to low and pour in the sauce with the cornstarch. Stir it around; the sauce will immediately start to thicken.

7. Cook over low heat for 1 minute, then set aside to cool slightly. If you want to serve the wraps cold, refrigerate the chicken until you're ready to assemble them.

8. Make the peanut sauce: In a small bowl, mix together all the ingredients, stirring in teaspoons of water until it gets to a nice drizzle-friendly consistency. Taste and add more of what it needs: spice, sweetness, whatever you like! Set aside.

9. Assemble the wraps: Lay a tortilla on a cutting board. Add the lettuce leaves (or shredded lettuce) . . .

10. Some of the chicken . . .

11. And some of the carrot and cucumber strips . . .

12. Drizzle on a good amount of the peanut sauce, then sprinkle on some peanuts. (If you want to add any of the optional ingredients, do it now.)

13. Roll up the tortilla tightly, then slice in half and serve!

So fresh! So delicious!

Soooooo good.

HELPFUL HINT: *You can save even more steps and grab some store-bought peanut sauce!*

Are they weeds or wildflowers? When they're bloomin' and beautiful, it doesn't really matter.

GREEK FEAST TO GO

MAKES 4 SERVINGS

I can't think of much that makes me happier than a portable lunch with a bunch of nibble-friendly options. Enter: this super-fun Greek Feast to Go. There's color, crunch, and flavor everywhere you turn, from a chunky salad to homemade hummus to flavorful chicken to olives to pita bread, which brings the whole delicious mess together! Pack up smaller portions if it's just you, or a little more if you're meeting a friend.

A peanut butter sandwich is going to have to seriously step up its game to keep up with this.

ROASTED RED PEPPER HUMMUS

Three 14.5-ounce cans chickpeas, drained and rinsed

2 jarred roasted red peppers

⅓ cup plus 1 tablespoon tahini (sesame paste)

3 garlic cloves, chopped, or more to taste

½ teaspoon ground cumin, or more to taste

Juice of ½ lemon

¼ cup olive oil

Kosher salt

CHICKEN AND MARINADE/ DRESSING

½ cup olive oil

¼ cup red wine vinegar

1 teaspoon sugar

1 teaspoon dried oregano

½ teaspoon red pepper flakes

Kosher salt and black pepper

2 boneless, skinless chicken breasts, cut into strips

GREEK SALAD

1 cucumber, cut into wedges

1 pint cherry tomatoes, halved

½ red onion, thinly sliced

4 ounces feta cheese, cut into ½-inch cubes

ACCOMPANIMENTS

Pita bread

1 cup pitted kalamata olives

1. Anytime up to a day or two before you need the feast, make the hummus: Add the chickpeas to a food processor . . .

2. Then add the roasted red peppers, the tahini . . .

3. The garlic, cumin, lemon juice, olive oil, and some salt.

4. Pulse until the mixture is smooth and combined. Add up to ½ cup water as necessary to facilitate blending (the moisture level of chickpeas can be an unpredictable thing).

5. Soak wooden skewers in water while you prepare the marinade/ dressing.

6. Make the marinade/dressing: In a mason jar, combine the olive oil, vinegar, sugar, oregano, red pepper flakes, and some salt and black pepper . . .

7. And shake the jar to combine. Mason jars are my boyfriend!

8. Place the chicken strips in a bowl and pour half the dressing on top . . .

9. Then toss them to coat thoroughly. Let them sit while you prepare the Greek salad.

10. Make the salad: In a separate bowl, combine the cucumber, tomatoes, and red onion. Pour the remaining dressing over the top . . .

11. And, using clean tongs, toss the salad until it's all coated. (The salad is best when it's tossed a little while before serving!)

12. Meanwhile, back at the chicken: Heat a grill pan (or a grill, if ya feel like it!) over medium-high heat. Thread the chicken strips onto the skewers . . .

13. And grill the chicken until it's cooked through and charred, 3 to 4 minutes per side. Remove the skewers to a large piece of foil to cool.

14. Place the Greek salad in a to-go container and top the salad with the feta cheese.

15. Then pack everything up, including the pita and olives, nice and neat!

This is definitely a favorite of mine!

TIP: *All the elements hold well in the fridge, so prepare up to a day or two before you need it! Or make the full quantities, then grab smaller portions throughout the week as you need them.*

GRILLED VEGGIE AND CREAM CHEESE SANDWICHES

MAKES 4 SANDWICHES

There's not much I love more than grilled vegetables. As delicious as a vegetable already is, something happens during the grilling process that makes me want to propose. And not to a man! To the grilled veggies themselves.

Grilled vegetables are a great sandwich filler, and you won't even think about the fact that there's no meat anywhere in sight. I love this make-ahead sandwich because . . . well . . . you can make it ahead of time. Ha ha! Actually, it's *better* if you make it ahead of time and let it get more and more wonderful. By the time lunch rolls around, you've got a little miracle on your hands.

I mean *in* your hands.

I mean in your *mouth*!

1 large zucchini, cut lengthwise into thin slices

1 medium onion, cut into ½-inch-thick rings

1 red bell pepper, seeded and cut into 4 slabs

1 yellow bell pepper, seeded and cut into 4 slabs

Olive oil, for brushing

¾ cup cream cheese mixed with chives

Kosher salt and black pepper

8 slices good sandwich bread, lightly toasted

1. Heat a grill pan over medium-high heat. Place the veggies on the hot surface . . .

4. Make sure everything has brownish/blackish bits. That's where the flavor is!

7. Sprinkle on salt and black pepper to taste . . .

2. And let the first side cook without oil, so it gets great grill marks on the surface. After that, turn them over . . .

5. Remove the veggies to a plate and let them cool completely.

8. Then lay on one of each color of bell pepper . . .

3. And brush them with a little bit of olive oil.

6. Spread a heaping tablespoon of cream cheese on one piece of the toasted bread.

9. Two slices of zucchini (trim them to fit the bread) . . .

10. And a slice of onion.

11. Spread the other piece of bread with cream cheese . . .

12. And put it on top.

13. And now—this is the kicker!—wrap the sandwich in plastic wrap and refrigerate it for a few hours (or overnight). Just the thing to grab on your way out the door in the morning.

14. Mmmm. This is many hours later. Great things have happened! I can feel it in my soul.

15. Time to dig in. (Pssst: The onions are absolutely miraculous.) Portable lunch has never tasted so good!

CHANGE THINGS UP!

- *Grill slices of eggplant to replace (or go alongside) the zucchini.*
- *Sliced poblano chiles are a delicious replacement for the bell peppers.*
- *Spread one of the slices of toast with pesto, Dijon mustard, or any spread of your choice.*
- *Press some fresh basil leaves on the cream cheese before you add the veggies.*
- *Use bagels, a baguette, or any bread of your choice.*

My niece Halle is one of the best cowgirls around!

APPS AND SNACKS

I think appetizers and pop-in-your-mouth snacks are my favorite food group, because you can nibble on them while standing up in the kitchen, which means the calories won't count! And the presence of apps and snacks usually means you're watching a movie, cheering on your favorite sports team, having friends over, or throwing a cocktail party. Good times!

Pimento Cheese..67

Watermelon Feta Bites...68

Stuffed Pizza Crust (Without the Pizza!)...........................70

Hot Corn Dip...74

Tortilla Pinwheels...76

Bacon-Wrapped Almond-Stuffed Dates...........................79

Pretzel-Coated Fried Goat Cheese..................................80

Rosemary Skewers...82

The Merc's Queso..89

Zucchini Roll-Ups...92

Cheese Lover's Crostini..95

Slow Cooker Beef Enchilada Dip....................................97

PIMENTO CHEESE

MAKES 12 SERVINGS

I grew up strongly disliking pimento cheese, and that's because my mom and dad weren't eaters of the stuff and the only pimento cheese I ever tried was the kind sold in a plastic tub in supermarkets. And that pimento cheese is . . . well, to put it very politely . . . *grody!*

This homemade version is a completely different ballgame. It is beyond miraculous. You'll make it time and time again.

4 ounces cream cheese, at room temperature

½ cup mayonnaise

1 tablespoon Dijon mustard, or more to taste

1 tablespoon adobo sauce (from canned chipotles), or more to taste

½ teaspoon black pepper

2 teaspoons chopped dill

8 ounces sharp Cheddar cheese, grated and kept cold

8 ounces Monterey Jack or mozzarella cheese, grated and kept cold

4 ounces jarred sliced pimentos, drained

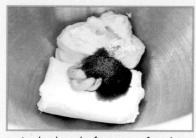

1. In the bowl of a mixer fitted with a paddle attachment, combine the cream cheese, mayonnaise, mustard, adobo sauce, and black pepper.

2. Add the dill, cheeses, and pimentos . . .

3. Then mix it on low speed until it's just combined. Use a rubber spatula to scrape the sides, then give it a taste. Add more of whatever flavor you need! (I almost always add more adobo, because spice is my life.) Then refrigerate it for at least 2 hours before serving.

4. Pile it into a bowl and serve with olives, crackers, and hollowed-out mini peppers.

5. Look at the texture!

6. Oh, and warning: Pimento cheese definitely *will* become habit-forming.

WATERMELON FETA BITES

MAKES ABOUT 24 BITES

This is a beautiful and oh-so-tasty appetizer that was born in a land called Pinterest. For years, I have considered watermelon and feta to be a perfect pairing in salads . . . but these clever bites are relatively new to my world. They're in that fantastic category of recipes that look *waaaaaay* more difficult than they actually are, and you can seriously impress some guests with these babies.

½ small seedless watermelon

One 12-ounce block feta cheese

3 tablespoons balsamic glaze, homemade (page 82) or store-bought

12 large basil leaves, plus some smaller leaves for garnish

1. You only need half of the watermelon, so use a sharp knife to carefully (and slowly!) cut the watermelon in half lengthwise.

2. Put one half of the watermelon cut side down, then slice it crosswise. (Wrap the other half in plastic wrap and store it in the fridge for another use.)

3. Cut off the rind so you're left with random pieces.

6. Cut the feta into cubes that are a little smaller than the watermelon cubes.

9. Place them on a serving plate and drizzle the balsamic glaze all over the top.

4. Cut the watermelon into equal-size strips . . .

7. To assemble the bites, set a piece of feta on top of a piece of watermelon and secure it with a toothpick.

10. Stack and roll up the basil leaves, then cut the roll into thin strips.

5. Then cut the strips into equal-size cubes. Use the sharp end of the knife to remove any stray seeds you see. (News flash: Seedless watermelons do still actually have seeds! They just aren't mature seeds like those in regular watermelons, so they are softer and much smaller.)

8. Continue until you've used all the watermelon and feta!

11. Arrange the basil all over the bites, garnishing with some smaller basil leaves.

CHANGE THINGS UP!

- *Alternate honeydew melon and cantaloupe for a pretty presentation.*
- *Forgo the toothpicks and turn this into a big salad in a bowl!*
- *Use cubes of fresh mozzarella for a milder cheese.*

STUFFED PIZZA CRUST (WITHOUT THE PIZZA!)

MAKES 6 TO 8 SERVINGS

This is one of the best things I've ever seen. It's a cross between stromboli and calzone, but really, it's cheese baked inside of bread. And the fact that it's thrown together with frozen bread dough and string cheese makes it even more delightful. This is a super-fun thing to serve at parties. Impress your friends! (Or, better yet, impress yourself.)

One 1-pound loaf frozen bread dough (such as Rhodes)

2 tablespoons olive oil, plus more for greasing the pan

Kosher salt and black pepper

⅓ cup marinara sauce, plus more for serving

10 pieces string cheese

1 egg

Fresh basil leaves, for serving

1. Set the loaf of frozen dough on the counter and cover it with a dishtowel. Let it thaw according to package directions, usually around 3 to 4 hours. (You can also set the loaf in a plastic bag in the fridge and thaw it over a 24-hour period!)

2. When it's totally soft and just starting to rise, 'tis ready! Preheat the oven to 475°F.

3. On the countertop or large board, roll out the dough to about 30 inches long, keeping it as narrow as possible. (Go long, not wide, in other words!)

4. Drizzle the dough with the olive oil and sprinkle it with salt and pepper.

5. Spread on the marinara sauce, leaving a clear ¼-inch rim around the edge.

6. Lay the string cheese, 2 pieces at a time, all the way down the dough, leaving a small edge at either end.

7. Gather the two sides together . . .

8. Pinching the seam to seal it well.

9. Grabbing the center of the rope with two hands, carefully transfer it to a baking sheet, placing the seam side down.

10. Bring both ends around to connect, pinching the ends together. Make sure the seam stays underneath.

11. Looks a little funny right now . . . but wait until you bake it!

12. Make an egg wash by lightly whisking the egg and a couple of tablespoons of water.

13. Brush the egg wash generously over the crust, making sure to get the seal holding the two ends together.

14. Bake for 13 minutes, or until it's dark golden brown.

15. Transfer to a serving platter . . . or just serve it right on the baking sheet! Place a dish of marinara sauce garnished with basil in the center of the crust.

16. Use a small serrated knife to cut slices . . .

17. Then dig right in.

This won't last long at all!

CHANGE THINGS UP!

- *Sprinkle finely diced pepperoni or cooked, crumbled Italian sausage over the string cheese before sealing the crust.*

- *Add finely diced black olives, green peppers, or any other pizza topping you like.*

- *Of course you may use your favorite homemade pizza dough recipe instead of the frozen bread dough if you prefer!*

- *For a beautiful serving idea, fill the center hole with a big green salad or sliced tomatoes!*

Make-ahead

HOT CORN DIP

MAKES 12 TO 16 SERVINGS

Hot corn dip is one of those things that can cause me to completely embarrass myself at parties, as if putting my leg behind my head to show off my residual ballet flexibility isn't embarrassing enough. This dip is positively to die for, and you can make it ahead of time and keep it in the fridge before baking it if that works better for your schedule.

5 ears of corn

Vegetable oil, for brushing

Kosher salt

2 tablespoons butter

½ red onion, finely diced

2 garlic cloves, minced

1 red bell pepper, seeded and finely diced

1 green bell pepper, seeded and finely diced

1 jalapeño, finely diced (scrape out half the seeds and membranes)

One 8-ounce package cream cheese, at room temperature

½ cup mayonnaise

½ cup sour cream

1 pound Monterey Jack cheese, grated

2 green onions, thinly sliced

One 4-ounce can diced green chiles, undrained

Chili powder, for sprinkling

Tortilla chips, for serving

1. Heat a grill pan over medium heat (or heat an outdoor grill).

2. Brush the corn with vegetable oil, sprinkle with a little salt . . .

3. And cook it on a grill pan (or outdoor grill), turning it occasionally, until nice grill marks form, about 10 minutes. Set it aside to cool.

4. In a large skillet, melt the butter over medium heat. Add the onion, garlic, bell peppers, and jalapeño . . .

5. And stir and cook the veggies until they're soft and golden, about 5 minutes. Set aside to cool slightly.

6. Cut the kernels off the cobs; I stand the cob in the center of a Bundt pan to keep kernels from winding up all over the universe!

7. In the bowl of a mixer fitted with a paddle attachment, combine the cream cheese, mayo, sour cream, and two-thirds of the Monterey Jack. Mix on low until combined.

8. Add the green onions, veggie mixture, corn, and green chiles in their liquid . . .

9. And mix on low until just combined. (And if you think this isn't the most delicious cold dip of your life, you've got another think coming. Just grab a spoonful of the stuff and you'll see what I mean! Actually, don't. Once you start, it's hard to stop that train.)

10. Spread the mixture in a 9 x 13-inch baking dish . . .

11. And sprinkle with the rest of the cheese and a little chili powder. (At this point, you can cover the pan with foil and keep it in the fridge for up to 2 days! When you're ready to bake it, just let it sit at room temperature for 30 minutes, then proceed as below.)

12. Preheat the oven to 350°F. Bake the dip until bubbling and golden, 20 to 22 minutes.

13. Remove from the oven and serve warm with tortilla chips!

CHANGE THINGS UP!

- *Add 4 slices bacon, finely diced, to the skillet with the veggies. Drain any excess grease before you add the mixture to the mixer.*
- *Use frozen corn kernels for a shortcut!*

TORTILLA PINWHEELS

MAKES ABOUT 40 PINWHEELS

Why, hello, 1994! It's wonderful to see you again. I've missed you so much, and I'd really like my small waist back. Thank you. And while you're at it, could you please send me some of those crazy easy tortilla roll-ups that people used to make for casual get-togethers? Because life has gotten rather complicated here in the new millennium and people think these are out of style. Which they are. But I don't care.

And never mind, no need to send. I'll just make a batch myself!

Love ya. Say hi to my size 6 jeans!

Two 8-ounce packages cream cheese, at room temperature

One 1-ounce package dry ranch dressing mix

½ teaspoon black pepper

5 large (burrito-size) flour tortillas

1 red bell pepper, seeded and finely diced

1 green bell pepper, seeded and finely diced

5 green onions, thinly sliced

1. In a bowl, combine the cream cheese, three-quarters of the packet of ranch dressing mix (add more to taste), and the black pepper.

2. Stir it with a wooden spoon until totally combined.

3. Divide the mixture equally among the tortillas . . .

4. And spread it into an even layer all over the surface of each tortilla, making sure to get it all the way out to the edge.

5. Sprinkle on the red and green bell peppers and the green onions.

6. Roll the tortillas up nice and tight . . .

7. Then wrap them individually in plastic wrap.

8. Store in the fridge for at least 2 hours or up to 12 hours. I make them well in advance of when we need them!

9. Before serving, cut into 1-inch slices . . .

10. And serve them on a platter.

CHANGE THINGS UP!

- *Sprinkle ¼ cup chopped olives over each tortilla along with the peppers and green onions.*
- *Add shaved ham or turkey to the roll-ups.*
- *Add canned green chiles (well drained) to the cream cheese mixture.*

You can't eat just one!

BACON-WRAPPED ALMOND-STUFFED DATES

MAKES 35 TO 40 DATES

Anything wrapped in bacon is going to be divine, but there's something about this salty, smoky, crunchy, sweet combo that causes these dates to completely disappear any time I serve them. They're not difficult to make at all, especially if you have assembly line help. Yum!

35 to 40 pitted dates

Salted roasted almonds (enough to stuff each date)

2 pounds thin bacon slices, halved crosswise

1. Preheat the oven to 425°F.

2. Stuff each date with 1 or 2 almonds depending on the size of the date (since they're pitted, they are already split down the middle).

3. Wrap each date with a piece of bacon and secure with a toothpick.

4. Place the nuggets on a wire rack set on a rimmed baking sheet . . .

5. Then bake until the bacon is sizzling and slightly crisp, 15 to 18 minutes, turning them halfway through so the bacon is evenly cooked.

6. Serve warm or at room temperature. These can be made ahead of time, frozen in a plastic zipper bag, then thawed and warmed in a 250°F oven for 8 to 10 minutes.

Todd selfies are the best selfies.

PRETZEL-COATED FRIED GOAT CHEESE

MAKES ABOUT 4 SERVINGS

Once upon a time, I wanted to make fried goat cheese. I'd seen it on a reality show and, like most things I see on reality shows, I couldn't get it out of my head. So I resolved to make it before the day was through.

Then I went to the pantry to fetch my breadcrumbs—an essential component of the crispy outer coating—and found I didn't have any! It was a tragedy of reality show proportions.

I cried.

And then I cried again.

And then . . . I glanced at another shelf in the pantry and saw a bag of pretzels. And my day got a whole lot brighter. Let me show you why!

2 cups mini pretzels

2 large eggs

½ cup all-purpose flour

Two 4-ounce logs goat cheese

Olive oil, for frying

Marinara sauce, warmed, for serving

Minced parsley, for garnish

1. The pretzels are the coating! Place them in a food processor . . .

2. And grind them to a very fine crumb.

3. Place the pretzel crumbs in a bowl. In a separate bowl, lightly whisk the eggs with 2 tablespoons water. Place the flour in a third bowl.

4. Unwrap the goat cheese logs and slice each log into quarters for a total of 8 goat cheese slices. (If the cheese is too soft to slice neatly, place the logs in the freezer for 20 minutes first.)

5. Grab one slice and dredge it in the flour, shaking off the excess . . .

6. Then dip it in the egg wash, turning it a couple of times to make sure it coats the flour.

7. Finally, drop it in the pretzel crumbs and turn it over to coat thoroughly.

8. Repeat with the rest of the slices.

9. In a skillet, heat ½ inch of olive oil over medium heat. Gently lay in 4 of the goat cheese slices and fry them for about 45 seconds. Turn them over with a slotted spoon and fry the other side until golden and crisp, 30 to 45 seconds.

10. Remove them to paper towels to drain. Repeat with the remaining 4 slices.

11. Serve with marinara sauce and a sprinkling of parsley.

ROSEMARY SKEWERS

MAKES AS MANY AS YOU NEED

My sister-in-law, Missy, who loves experimenting with pretty, inventive party food ideas (whereas I can sometimes work my way into chips-and-salsa ruts) first taught me the fun of using rosemary sprigs in place of wooden skewers. I think they're pretty much the most gorgeous appetizers you can serve, and while there are a million combos of things you can include on the skewers, this simple tomato-mozzarella version is my favorite.

BALSAMIC GLAZE

1 cup balsamic vinegar

One 15-ounce jar plum preserves

2 tablespoons packed brown sugar

SKEWERS

Mozzarella balls (I used the smaller size, but any will do)

Olive oil

Red pepper flakes

Kosher salt and black pepper

Rosemary sprigs (long enough to allow for a 2-inch "skewer" on the end)

Grape tomatoes

1. Well in advance, if you like, make the balsamic glaze: In a blender, combine the balsamic vinegar, plum preserves, and brown sugar . . .

2. And puree it until it's totally smooth.

3. Pour it into a medium saucepan . . .

We're going to change his name to Rafter.

4. And bring to a boil over medium-high heat. Reduce the heat to a simmer and cook until the mixture has reduced by half, about 10 minutes.

5. It should be fairly thick and will thicken further as it cools. When cool, put it in a jar or squeeze bottle and keep it in the fridge. (Shortcut! You can now buy balsamic glaze in larger supermarkets! It is a revelation. Pick up a bottle and you can skip this step.)

6. When you're ready to assemble the skewers, place the mozzarella balls in a bowl with the olive oil, red pepper flakes, and salt and black pepper to taste . . .

7. And stir to coat.

8. Use your fingers to strip the leaves off the bottom 2 inches of the rosemary sprigs. Skewer on one or two mozzarella balls, then a tomato.

9. Drizzle on some of the balsamic glaze, reserving the rest for future salads!

CHANGE THINGS UP!

- *Fold salami slices into wedges and spear them on the skewers.*
- *Cut artichoke hearts in quarters and spear them, too!*
- *If you can't find mozzarella balls, just cut a chunk of mozzarella into cubes.*

The Pioneer Woman Mercantile!

Several years ago, Ladd and I had a temporary moment of insanity and purchased an old building on Main Street in our hometown of Pawhuska. Slowly but surely, we began renovating it, taking things at a pace that suited our busy lives on the ranch with our four kids. Finally, in fall 2016, we opened "The Merc," and what an adventure it's been!

Welcome! Come take a peek inside.

Fun fact: I spent months picking out every single product we sell in the store! Not that I was obsessive or anything.

It was especially rewarding, after all the thinking and planning, to see real folks stopping by and enjoying the wares.

I really like seeing what customers pick out. Some things, I knew they'd be a hit. Other things have been a surprise! (Andy Warhol finger puppets, anyone?)

Every single day is an adventure.

We've also got a restaurant at the Merc.

We aren't known for our tiny portions, that's for sure! Our goal is for everyone to take home leftovers.

The breakfast is Ladd's favorite. (You can see why!)

The Merc has been a dream come true! And a journey, and a learning experience, and a complete and total blast. Also: I need a nap.

I can't wait to see what's in store! (No pun intended.)

THE MERC'S QUESO

MAKES ABOUT 6 CUPS

It's tough to improve on the basic queso recipe, which is so easy anyone can make it blindfolded. But when we were testing recipes for the restaurant at The Mercantile, I knew I wanted the queso to be something special, considering it's its own food group in our household. And oh . . . is it ever special. It's everything that's good about regular ol' queso, but with all these little flecks of flavor that make your soul (and your taste buds) sing.

It's a great thing to make in the slow cooker, but a nonstick pot on the stove works just as well.

6 Anaheim or Hatch chiles

½ pound bacon, cut into small pieces

One 9-ounce package fresh chorizo sausage

1 medium onion, diced

2 garlic cloves, minced

2 pounds Velveeta or other processed melting cheese, cut into cubes

Two 10-ounce cans diced tomatoes and chiles (such as Ro*Tel)

1½ cups whole milk

Tortilla chips, for serving

1. First, roast the fresh chiles, which is really a cinch! If you have a gas burner, lay 2 or 3 at a time right over the flame, using metal tongs to turn them until the skin is totally blackened. (Or you can put them on a baking sheet right under the broiler, turning them until blackened.)

2. Repeat with all the chiles, then place them in a plastic bag. Seal it to let them sweat for 15 to 20 minutes.

4. Set the skillet over medium-high heat and cook, crumbling the sausage with a spoon as you go, for about 5 minutes.

3. While that's happening, put the bacon and chorizo in a large skillet.

5. Add the diced onion and the garlic . . .

The "real" queso at the Merc!

6. And cook, stirring occasionally, for another 3 to 4 minutes . . .

7. Until the onion is starting to soften and the bacon and sausage are totally cooked.

8. Pour the contents of the skillet onto several paper towels to drain off as much grease as possible. (Press some paper towels on top as well. Chorizo is greasy!)

9. By now the chiles are ready: Use a knife to scrape off as much of the skin as possible (it's okay to leave behind some of the black—it's great flavor).

10. Cut the chiles open, scrape out the seeds, and chop the chiles.

11. To assemble the queso, put the cheese into a slow cooker.

12. Add the bacon-sausage mixture and the diced tomatoes and chiles (juices and all).

13. Then add the chopped roasted chiles and milk.

14. Place the lid on the slow cooker and cook on high for 45 minutes, stirring once during that time. Turn the heat to low . . .

15. And let it continue to melt and warm up for another 20 minutes. Then get the chips!

16. Serve the queso piping hot with chips.

Tremendously yummy!

NOTE: *To save time on party day, this queso can be made up to 3 days before serving. Just keep it in a bowl, covered in plastic wrap, in the fridge. To reheat, place in a microwave-safe bowl and heat in 30-second intervals, stirring in between (or reheat in a nonstick saucepan over medium-low heat, stirring occasionally). Or reheat in the slow cooker on high for an hour, stirring occasionally!*

CHANGE THINGS UP!

- *Add 2 minced chipotle peppers in adobo sauce (and extra adobo sauce) with the other chiles for a smoky, spicy kick.*
- *Substitute freshly grated Monterey Jack cheese for ½ pound of the Velveeta.*
- *At the Merc, we stir in ½ cup very finely minced cilantro when the queso is done. It really adds great flavor, and because it's minced fine, you don't have to worry about it turning brown. Try it!*
- *Stir in the juice of 2 limes when the queso is done.*

ZUCCHINI ROLL-UPS

MAKES ABOUT 20 ROLL-UPS

Simple, fuss-free appetizers are my favorite kind of food. And I know I say that every kind of food is my favorite kind of food. But this time I really mean it. More than I meant it the last time I said it (which was five minutes ago).

These veggie roll-ups are all the rage these days, and they're a magical blend of convenience food (store-bought herbed cream cheese) and homemade (grilled zucchini slices). The result is an exceedingly simple snack (or hors d'oeuvre, depending on how fancy you want to act) that you'll want to make again and again. And again. And again!

4 medium zucchini, sliced lengthwise as thinly as possible (about 5 slices per zucchini)

Olive oil, for brushing

Kosher salt and black pepper

¾ cup herbed cream cheese (such as Rondelé or Alouette)

Fresh basil (optional)

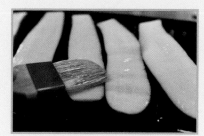

1. Prepare a grill or heat a grill pan over medium heat. Brush both sides of the zucchini slices with olive oil and place them on the grill. Sprinkle them with salt and pepper.

2. Grill them, turning occasionally, until they are very soft but not falling apart, 8 to 10 minutes.

3. Remove them to paper towels to absorb the excess moisture. Let them cool completely.

4. Spread about 2 teaspoons of the herbed cheese onto one of the zucchini slices.

5. Starting at one end, roll the zucchini up . . .

6. Until it's a nice, neat roll. Secure it with a toothpick.

7. Continue with the rest of the zucchini slices and serve them on a platter garnished with small basil leaves, if desired. These can be assembled and chilled up to 3 hours before serving!

CHANGE THINGS UP!

- *Spread softened goat cheese on the zucchini instead. Delicious!*
- *Roll a couple of fresh basil or mint leaves inside the zucchini rolls for delicious flavor.*

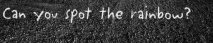

Can you spot the rainbow?

CHEESE LOVER'S CROSTINI

MAKES 18 TO 20 CROSTINI

I could eat things like this every day for the rest of my life and never get bored. Pretty little nibbles with a variety of colors and flavors—preferably enjoyed standing up in the kitchen, definitely accompanied by a glass of cold wine—pretty much give me reason to live.

Clearly, there's no limit to the combinations of crostini toppings you can come up with, but to narrow it down, it's fun to do a mix of cheeses as a base. They will disappear! Cheese has that effect on people.

Make all three of these, make just one, or come up with your own delicious combos! I used what I happened to have in my pantry and fridge, but the possibilities are endless. The crostini world is your oyster.

(Yum . . . oyster crostini! Hmmm . . .)

1 baguette, cut into ½-inch slices

Olive oil, for frying/grilling and drizzling

4 ounces Brie cheese, thinly sliced

3 tablespoons herbed cream cheese (such as Rondelé or Alouette)

¼ cup prepared pesto

2 ounces goat cheese

½ cup grape tomatoes, halved

¼ cup cherry preserves

¼ cup pitted olives (I used pimento-stuffed and kalamata)

4 ounces fresh mozzarella cheese, cut into small cubes

Small basil sprigs

Black pepper

3 tablespoons freshly grated Parmesan cheese

1. Heat a grill pan or griddle over medium-high heat. Drizzle the bread slices with a little olive oil, add as many as will fit in a single layer, and grill on both sides until slightly crisp and browned.

2. Remove from the pan and let them cool. Repeat with the rest of the bread slices.

4. Spread on the herbed cream cheese . . .

3. Then assemble the crostini! Lay on slices of Brie . . .

5. Spoon on the pesto . . .

I can't be trusted with Snapchat.

6. And crumble on the goat cheese.

7. And that's just the beginning of the fun! Lay a couple of tomato halves on the herbed cream cheese version . . .

8. Spoon cherry preserves on the Brie version . . .

9. Press a couple of olives into the goat cheese version . . .

10. And for the pesto version, how about a cube of mozzarella with a little extra pesto on top? Yes, please!

11. A little sprig of fresh basil makes it extra pretty.

12. Back to the herbed cream cheese–tomato version! Just before serving, drizzle on a little olive oil and sprinkle on some pepper . . .

13. And a little Parmesan.

A bodacious bounty!

OTHER CROSTINI TOPPING IDEAS

- *Smashed avocado (add just before serving)*
- *Caramelized onions*
- *Ricotta cheese*
- *Capers*
- *Strips of roasted red pepper*
- *Nutella and strawberries*
- *Chutney (mango is delicious!) or other jams*

Kid-friendly

SLOW COOKER BEEF ENCHILADA DIP

MAKES 18 SERVINGS

When we have our Fourth of July potluck celebration, someone always seems to show up with a slow cooker full of some amazing dip. And by "amazing" I mean "I follow around the owner of the slow cooker all night and pester them until they tell me how to make it." I'm such a gracious, humble hostess!

Enchilada dip is always a crowd-pleaser (and a hostess-pleaser), and unless you call browning ground beef in a skillet difficult, there ain't nothing hard about this recipe.

2 pounds ground beef

1 medium onion, halved and thinly sliced

Two 14-ounce cans red enchilada sauce

One 28-ounce can pinto beans, drained and rinsed

Two 4-ounce cans diced green chiles, undrained

One 8-ounce package cream cheese, at room temperature

2 cups freshly grated Cheddar cheese

1 cup cilantro leaves

Tortilla chips, for serving

1. In a large skillet over medium-high heat, brown the ground beef until fully cooked. Drain off the excess grease . . .

2. And place the beef in the slow cooker.

3. Add the onion . . .

4. The enchilada sauce . . .

5. The beans . . .

6. And the chiles with their liquid.

7. Stir to combine, cover, and cook on low for 4 hours.

8. At that point, use a large spoon to skim off any grease that has collected at the top. (I promise you won't miss it.)

9. Plop in the cream cheese . . .

10. And stir it slowly until you have a creamy masterpiece. (Proving once again that "masterpiece" is a relative term.)

11. Sprinkle the Cheddar evenly over the surface, then cover the slow cooker and let the cheese melt for about 15 minutes.

12. Again: a masterpiece! Sorta.

13. Sprinkle the cilantro leaves all over the top . . .

14. And serve it with chips.

CHANGE THINGS UP!

- *Add 4 cups beef broth with the enchilada sauce and call it soup! Just sprinkle the Cheddar on individual servings instead of melting it on top of the full batch.*

- *Add 4 boneless, skinless chicken breasts to the slow cooker instead of the cooked beef. After the 4 hours of cooking time, shred the chicken with two forks (or remove it to finely chop, then return to the cooker). Then add the cream cheese.*

Ladd clearly likes redheads. Just look at his horse!

$\mathcal{U}$NDER 40

Ladies and gentlemen, start your engines: These delicious dinners can be thrown together in forty minutes or less! (Cut me some slack; don't include the grocery trip in the timing. ☺) We all need an arsenal of super-quick dinnertime options, and this is a great stack of recipes to add to your collection. Ready, set, cook!

Cap'n Crunch Chicken Strips 102

Roasted Red Pepper Soup 104

Mango-Chile Chicken 106

Tex-Mex Butternut Squash Soup 108

Shrimp Mango Lettuce Cups 110

Hamburger Steaks with Mushroom Gravy 113

Fried Shrimp 116

Shrimp Po' Boys 118

Smothered Pork Chops 123

Chicken Piccata 125

Taco Quesadillas 128

CAP'N CRUNCH CHICKEN STRIPS

MAKES 4 SERVINGS

Weirdness makes the world go round! And that is most certainly true with these crispy, slightly sweet chicken strips, which are a version of the famous chicken that originated at Planet Hollywood restaurants years ago. The minute I heard about their chicken strips way back when, I was intrigued. I've been a fan of sugared cereal all my life. Don't tell my children.

The breading for the chicken is—get ready—Cap'n Crunch (see page 2; I clearly love the stuff), and even though it's sweet as all get-out, once you add some salt to balance things, the result is a super-delicious coating that both crisps and caramelizes (because of the sugar) as it fries. Another sprinkling of salt after frying makes everything perfect, and a side of ketchup is absolutely required.

1 cup all-purpose flour

1 teaspoon kosher salt, plus more for sprinkling

½ teaspoon black pepper

2 eggs

2 cups Cap'n Crunch cereal

12 chicken tenders or strips

Vegetable oil, for frying

Ketchup, for serving

1. In a pie plate or shallow dish, mix the flour, salt, and pepper.

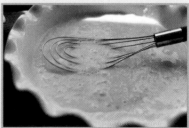

2. In a shallow bowl, lightly whisk the eggs.

3. Finally, pour the cereal into a third dish . . .

4. And crush it (I used the bottom of a metal measuring cup) . . .

5. Until you have fine crumbs plus some larger chunks. This'll make the strips extra crunchy!

6. Dip the chicken first in the flour . . .

7. Then in the egg . . .

8. Then in the cereal.

9. Keep going until all the chicken is breaded!

10. In a large skillet, heat ¼ inch of vegetable oil over medium heat. Add half the chicken strips . . .

11. And cook them until they're golden brown and cooked through, about 3 minutes per side. Watch them so they don't burn!

12. Drain them on paper towels and sprinkle with salt. Finish cooking the rest of the chicken.

13. Serve them with ketchup!

ROASTED RED PEPPER SOUP

MAKES 8 TO 12 SERVINGS

I like roasted red pepper *anything*, but it took me years and years (okay, decades) to realize that using jarred peppers saves loads of time without sacrificing much flavor. So pick up a few jars next time you're in the grocery store! They are amazing!

3 tablespoons olive oil

1 medium onion, finely diced

3 garlic cloves, grated

10 to 12 jarred roasted red peppers, drained, a few thin slices reserved for garnish

8 cups (2 quarts) vegetable broth

Leaves from 3 thyme sprigs, a few reserved for serving

Kosher salt and black pepper

½ cup sour cream, at room temperature

½ cup heavy cream, at room temperature, plus more for serving

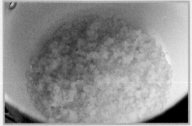

1. In a medium to large Dutch oven, heat the olive oil over medium heat. Add the onion and garlic and cook until just starting to soften, about 3 minutes.

2. Add the roasted red peppers, stirring to heat them up.

3. Add the broth, thyme, and salt and pepper to taste.

4. Bring to a boil, then reduce the heat and simmer the mixture for 20 minutes.

5. Carefully puree with an immersion blender . . .

6. Until perfectly smooth. (Hint: You can also puree the mixture in a blender in batches; just make sure it's cooled to room temperature first, as blending hot soups is "dangerooooooos," as my mom used to say.)

7. Add the sour cream . . .

8. And the heavy cream . . .

9. And stir to blend. Taste and adjust the seasoning.

10. Garnish with a little thyme, a slice of red pepper, and a few drops of extra cream. Delicious!

CHANGE THINGS UP!

- *Substitute sherry for ½ cup of the broth.*
- *Add a teaspoon of red pepper flakes to the soup to give it some heat!*
- *Add grilled chicken slices or shrimp to the top of each bowl of soup when you serve it.*
- *Stir 2 tablespoons pesto into the finished soup before serving.*

Fancy

MANGO-CHILE CHICKEN

MAKES 6 SERVINGS

This dinner could be a beauty pageant winner! The grilled marinated chicken with its gorgeous golden color, the vibrant kale salad with strips of mango and red bell pepper . . . it's a looker for sure.

As an added bonus, it's incredibly easy, too. I love to use jarred mango slices here, because first, they're widely available even when fresh mangoes aren't. Second, they're slightly sweeter than fresh mango, and that's a nice complement to the savory chicken. But most important, you don't have to mess with peeling and slicing a dang mango! (A dango?) I'm sold!

6 boneless, skinless chicken breasts

1 tablespoon chili powder

Zest and juice of 1 lime (reserve a lime wedge for serving)

¼ cup plus 2 tablespoons olive oil

2 teaspoons kosher salt, plus more to taste

½ teaspoon black pepper, plus more to taste

2 tablespoons chopped cilantro

One 20-ounce jar sliced mango, drained and sliced thinner, 2 tablespoons of the liquid reserved

1 bunch curly kale, finely shredded

1 orange or red bell pepper, very thinly sliced

1 jalapeño, thinly sliced

1 bunch green onions, thinly sliced

1. Put the chicken breasts in a plastic zipper bag and add the chili powder, lime zest, 2 tablespoons of the olive oil, and the salt and black pepper.

2. Seal the bag and squish it around to mix all the ingredients and coat the chicken. Refrigerate for at least 30 minutes and up to 4 hours.

3. Heat a grill pan over medium-high heat. Remove the chicken from the bag and let any excess marinade drip off. Place the chicken breasts on the grill pan . . .

4. And cook until they are done, 4 to 5 minutes per side, depending on the thickness of the chicken.

5. While the chicken is cooking, make the dressing: In a medium bowl, whisk together the lime juice, cilantro, reserved 2 tablespoons mango liquid, the remaining ¼ cup olive oil, and salt and black pepper to taste.

6. Whisk it until everything is totally combined.

7. Put the kale into a large bowl and pour three-quarters of the dressing over the top. (You can add the rest later if it needs it!)

8. Give it a toss to make sure the kale is all coated. Kale is a little hardier than lettuce and can sit with the dressing for a while without wilting, so don't worry about tossing it too early.

9. Add the bell pepper, mango slices, and jalapeño on top of the kale.

10. Finally, add the green onions and toss! (This is a gorgeous salad on its own. Wow.)

11. Pile the salad next to the chicken and squeeze some lime juice on top.

This is a great low-carb meal!

TEX-MEX BUTTERNUT SQUASH SOUP

MAKES 8 TO 10 SERVINGS

Imagine everything that's wonderful about butternut squash soup. I'll give you a minute. Go ahead—imagine.

Now imagine all that wonderfulness with the addition of Tex-Mex flavors and sweet little jewels of pomegranate seeds.

Yeah. I know. Too much to even think about. So let's stop thinking and start looking! This one's a winner, folks.

1 tablespoon olive oil

1 medium onion, finely diced

1 large butternut squash, peeled, seeded, and cut into chunks (see page 244)

1 red bell pepper, seeded and finely diced

1 jalapeño, some seeds and membranes removed, finely minced

2 garlic cloves, minced

½ teaspoon ground cumin

½ teaspoon chili powder

½ teaspoon kosher salt

½ teaspoon black pepper

6 cups low-sodium chicken broth

Crumbled Cotija cheese, for serving

Pomegranate seeds, for serving

Mexican crema (or sour cream mixed with a little milk), for serving

Cilantro leaves, for serving

1. In a Dutch oven, heat the olive oil over medium-high heat. Add the onion, and sauté until it begins to soften, about 4 minutes.

2. Add the butternut squash and the red bell pepper. Cook, stirring occasionally, for about 5 minutes, until the squash starts getting brown edges.

3. Add the jalapeño and garlic . . .

4. And stir and cook for another minute or so.

5. Add the cumin, chili powder, salt, and pepper . . .

6. And stir and cook for another minute or so to toast the spices.

7. Add the broth, stir, and bring to a boil.

8. Turn the heat to low and simmer the soup for 15 to 20 minutes, until the squash is very tender.

9. Now it's time to puree the soup! I love an immersion blender for this job, but if you don't have one, a countertop blender works fine! But if you use a countertop blender, let the soup cool and blend it in batches. (Blending hot soup is very dangerous!)

10. Look at the gorgeous color! Butternut squash soup is usually beautiful, but with the chili powder and other ingredients, it's got a real Southwestern vibe going on.

11. Pour it into a bowl . . . and get ready to garnish!

12. Add some crumbled Cotija, sprinkle on some pomegranate seeds, and use a spoon to drizzle the crema in any swirly design you want!

13. You don't have to be ultra-artistic. Just sprinkle on some cilantro leaves and it'll look like a masterpiece.

CHANGE THINGS UP!

- *Garnish with grilled corn kernels. Delicious!*
- *Caramelize some diced red onion for additional garnish.*
- *For a little more spice, use a serrano or habanero pepper in place of the jalapeño.*

SHRIMP MANGO LETTUCE CUPS

MAKES 6 SERVINGS

This is one of those fancy-schmancy, frou-frou–looking recipes that ain't fancy at all! I like to buy already-cooked shrimp (either from the seafood counter of the supermarket or just a bag of the frozen stuff) to make this absolutely delicious salad one of the easiest things to pull off. It's great for a quick weeknight dinner on a hot summer day.

Cool, fresh, and tasty!

Zest and juice of 1 lemon

1 garlic clove, grated

1 cup cilantro, chopped

½ cup olive oil

18 jumbo shrimp, cooked and chilled

2 avocados, pitted, peeled, and cut into large chunks

1 mango

½ red onion, thinly sliced

12 Bibb or butter lettuce cups

Minced fresh chives, for serving

1. In a medium bowl, combine the lemon zest, lemon juice, and garlic.

4. Then whisk until it's all mixed together.

7. Then dice up the mango: Slice off both halves around the pit . . .

2. Add the cilantro . . .

5. Place the shrimp in a plastic zipper bag, pour half the lemon-cilantro mixture in, seal the bag, and place in the fridge to marinate for 20 minutes or up to a couple of hours.

8. Score the flesh inside the skin . . .

3. And the olive oil . . .

6. Add the avocado to the bowl with the rest of the dressing . . .

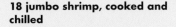

9. And invert the skin to pop out the good stuff . . .

10. Then slice off the mango pieces so they fall into the bowl.

11. Add the red onion and gently mix it all together! (This is a yummy salad in itself.)

12. To serve, arrange 3 shrimp in the center of a lettuce leaf . . .

13. Then spoon the mango-avocado salad on top.

14. Sprinkle chives over the top to make 'em extra pretty!

CHANGE THINGS UP!

- *Make it a more "special" seafood dish by adding cooked lobster and crabmeat with the shrimp.*
- *Use jarred mango for softer, sweeter fruit.*
- *Serve the shrimp and mango-avocado salad over cold noodles for a shrimp pasta salad!*

Caleb and Todd aren't little shrimps anymore!

HAMBURGER STEAKS WITH MUSHROOM GRAVY

MAKES 4 SERVINGS

This is (slightly retro) comfort food at its finest and for some reason, it makes me think of *The Brady Bunch*. Never mind that this recipe didn't appear on any *Brady Bunch* episode that I remember, and I remember them all. But a synapse fired at some point in my life that connected *The Brady Bunch* and hamburger steak, and nothing shall tear the two asunder.

Oh, how I could talk about *The Brady Bunch* for hours! Anyone want to join me?

1½ pounds ground beef

Kosher salt and black pepper

6 tablespoons olive oil

12 ounces white button mushrooms, sliced

2 tablespoons all-purpose flour

½ cup red wine or beef broth

2 cups low-sodium beef broth, plus more if needed

2 thyme sprigs

Several dashes of Worcestershire sauce

1. Form the ground beef into oval patties to resemble "steaks." Sprinkle both sides with salt and pepper.

2. In a large skillet, heat the oil over medium heat. Add the burger patties and cook them on one side for about 3 minutes . . .

3. Then flip them over and cook them until no longer pink, another 2 to 3 minutes.

4. Remove them to paper towels.

5. Increase the heat to medium-high and add the mushrooms. (Don't clean the skillet first! You want all that good stuff.)

6. Stir them around so that they're coated in all the flavor . . .

7. Sprinkle them with the flour . . .

8. And stir them around for about 2 minutes, letting the flour cook and the mushrooms start to brown.

The world is a safer place with Captain Todd around.

9. Pour in the wine . . .

12. Strip the leaves off the thyme sprigs into the sauce.

15. And it's ready!

10. And stir the mixture, letting the wine bubble up and cook down, 1½ to 2 minutes.

13. Reduce the heat to medium and cook the sauce, stirring occasionally, until it's nice and thick, another 3 minutes.

16. Place the hamburger steaks on plates . . .

11. Pour in the beef broth.

14. Stir in the Worcestershire sauce . . .

17. And spoon the sauce all over the top.

This is a good one!

FRIED SHRIMP

MAKES 4 SERVINGS

Ahhh . . . fried shrimp! It's a favorite from my childhood, and even though we don't have it for dinner in our house very often, it's always a hit when we do. And by "a hit," I mean brawls break out over who gets the last one. Family dinnertime is so important for bonding!

Believe it or not, fried shrimp really is a cinch to make, as shrimp is one of those beautiful proteins that takes almost no time at all to cook through. It lends itself well to fast cookin'!

(Be careful frying with hot oil if you have youngsters in the house. Sorry to be bossy. As usual!)

½ cup cornstarch

½ cup all-purpose flour

3 large eggs

1 cup panko breadcrumbs

½ cup seasoned breadcrumbs

Vegetable oil, for shallow-frying

1 cup ketchup

2 tablespoons prepared horseradish

A few dashes of Worcestershire sauce

1½ pounds peeled, deveined jumbo shrimp, tails on

Kosher salt and black pepper

1. In a bowl, combine the cornstarch and flour. In a second bowl, beat the eggs with ½ cup water. In a third bowl, combine the panko and seasoned breadcrumbs.

2. Pour about ½ inch of oil into a nonstick skillet over medium heat. Drop in a couple of breadcrumbs; if they sizzle gently, the oil is ready.

3. Make the cocktail sauce by combining the ketchup, horseradish, and Worcestershire and stirring to combine.

4. Next, butterfly the shrimp by carefully slicing three-quarters of the way through the back side of each shrimp so that they open up into a larger, flatter piece.

5. Bread the shrimp by dipping them first in the flour mixture, shaking off the excess . . .

6. Then dipping quickly in the egg wash . . .

7. Then dipping/coating in the crumbs.

8. Fry the shrimp in batches until golden and crispy, turning halfway through, about 2 minutes per side.

9. Drain them on paper towels and season them with salt and pepper . . .

10. And continue frying until all the shrimp are done! Serve with the cocktail sauce (and Curly Fries, page 290).

(And cold beer!)

(And a hearty appetite!)

SHRIMP PO' BOYS

MAKES 4 GENEROUS SANDWICHES

If you've got the rolls and a few basic ingredients, you can turn a batch of fried shrimp into a platter of po' boys in no time at all! These are so big and generous that they can easily be split in two and shared (though this is obviously not required for those of you who think you can make it through the whole darn thang).

Have a po' boy party! I'd RSVP to that one.

1 cup mayonnaise

1 tablespoon ketchup

2 tablespoons Dijon mustard

¼ cup pickle relish

Juice of 1 lemon

2 garlic cloves, minced

½ teaspoon kosher salt

Hot sauce

Black pepper

4 good French deli rolls, split and toasted (I put them under the broiler for a minute)

Baby arugula

Roma tomatoes, sliced

Fried Shrimp (page 116; skip the cocktail sauce and take the tails off the shrimp first)

1. First, make the delicious sauce! In a bowl, combine the mayonnaise, ketchup, mustard, pickle relish, lemon juice, garlic, and salt. Add hot sauce and pepper to taste . . .

2. And stir until it's all mixed together.

3. Spread some of the sauce on the bottom half of each toasted roll.

4. Pile on arugula and lay slices of tomato on top . . .

5. Lay a few fried shrimp on the tomatoes . . .

6. And (generously!) spoon on more sauce. The sauce makes the sandwich oh so divine!

Be right back . . . I need to grab a cold beer. Or two.

Oh, and one more thing: *How good does this look???*

Oh, Pa-Pa. There's no one on earth like you.

Pa-Pa is Chuck, my father-in-law, and we go way back. Twenty-one years, in fact—longer if you count the time Ladd and I dated! But officially, on paper, according to a priest and a marriage license and God (and a few tax returns, I suppose), I have been Chuck Drummond's daughter-in-law for twenty-one years.

And what a ride it has been.

One of my mother-in-law's many one-liner musings about married life has always made me laugh: "I've been tired since the day I married Chuck." She says this with love, I assure you, and she also means every word. Chuck has an uncanny way of creating work for everyone in his path: He organized huge cutting horse events at their homestead when their three boys were young, and Nan remembers those weeks of cleaning, mowing, cooking, and entertaining as if they were a war she barely survived. "It's a miracle I made it through those cuttings . . ." she remarks, gazing blankly at the ceiling. Again: This has always made me laugh.

If my kids have ever expressed boredom at various times through the years, they were wise enough never to say it within earshot of Pa-Pa. If they did, he'd load them up in the pickup and find some fence for them to fix. Or some gravel for them to move. Or some barns for them to clean out. They'd get home sometime after dark covered in mud and desperation, and they quickly learned that boredom is actually a good thing. And that it's something you never, ever complain about in front of Pa-Pa.

As Ladd and his brother Tim have always said, "Dad creates work." Chuck always has a project going on. He tears down old fence and builds new fence in its place. He cleans out the ponds (or at least supervises the cleaning out of the ponds), and when all the ponds are cleaned out, he digs a new pond. He decides to move all the old cake houses (small shacks that hold cake feed for cattle) on the ranch and won't stop until they're all moved—usually dragging Ladd and Tim along for the ride before it's all said and done.

Through the years, Chuck has organized Drummond family reunions (and boy, are there a lot of Drummonds—talk about mouths to feed!) and has volunteered to have various events at my house, my sister-in-law Missy's house . . . you get the picture. He informs us with an ornery smile that he might have accidentally signed us up for Steak Night . . . or so-and-so's birthday dinner . . . or such-and-such's welcome home party. And we all know there was nothing accidental about it.

So why do we all put up with this? Why do we allow ourselves to be subject to Chuck's many plans, projects, and whims? *Why do we keep hosting his Steak Nights?!?* The answer is simple.

There is nothing—*absolutely nothing*—my father-in-law wouldn't do for us if we asked him. And we do ask him. At a moment's notice, he will run any errand, pick up a kid, arrange for a tractor, a trailer, or a picnic table (or twelve), bring us 200 chicken legs from Walmart, bring us 300 ears of corn from the farmers' market, and I think one summer he actually brought something like 30 watermelons to our Fourth of July party. He simply never runs out of the energy required to get a job done, and if the job is helping someone in his family, it fuels him all the more.

Chuck loves Nan, he loves his sons, he loves Missy and me, and man—does he love his grandchildren. He wanted twelve and he got six, so he loves each of them double. Well, he loves all of us double.

So I'll keep hosting Steak Night whenever he wants me to!

SMOTHERED PORK CHOPS

MAKES 4 SERVINGS

Sometimes you just need a big honkin' plate of pork chops smothered with bell pepper gravy. And by sometimes, I mean once a day. (Once a week is welcome, too!)

1½ cups plus 3 tablespoons all-purpose flour

1 teaspoon seasoned salt

1 teaspoon lemon-pepper seasoning

½ teaspoon ground cumin

¼ teaspoon cayenne pepper

Kosher salt and black pepper

8 thin bone-in breakfast pork chops

7 tablespoons butter

¼ cup olive oil

1 large onion, thickly sliced

1 green bell pepper, seeded and thickly sliced

1 yellow bell pepper, seeded and thickly sliced

1 red bell pepper, seeded and thickly sliced

2 cups chicken broth, plus more if needed

2 tablespoons heavy cream

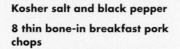

1. In a pie plate or other shallow dish, whisk together 1½ cups of the flour, the seasoned salt, lemon-pepper, cumin, cayenne, a pinch of salt, and black pepper to taste.

3. In a heavy skillet, melt 4 tablespoons of the butter in the olive oil over medium heat. Working in batches, fry the pork chops . . .

5. Add the onion and bell peppers to the same skillet and cook, stirring occasionally . . .

2. Season the pork chops with salt and black pepper, then dredge them in the flour mixture, shaking off the excess.

4. Until well browned, 2 to 3 minutes per side. Remove the chops to a plate as you go and keep warm.

6. Until slightly softened and starting to brown, about 5 minutes. Remove them to a plate and set aside.

7. To the same skillet, add the remaining 3 tablespoons butter and 3 tablespoons flour.

10. Whisk in the stock a bit at a time . . .

13. Return the onions and peppers to the pan . . .

8. Whisk it into a paste . . .

11. And cook until it's thick enough to coat a spoon. If it seems too thick, feel free to splash in a little more broth.

14. And stir to coat them in the gravy.

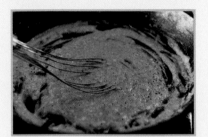

9. And cook, whisking constantly, until the roux turns dark golden.

12. Whisk in the cream, then taste and add salt and black pepper as needed. (This isn't an overly creamy gravy; the cream just adds a little richness and awesomeness.)

15. Serve the pork chops on a plate with the bell pepper gravy spooned over the top.

CHANGE THINGS UP!

- *Add 8 ounces sliced mushrooms to the skillet with the peppers.*
- *Use chicken cutlets, pounded thin, instead of pork chops.*
- *Substitute hamburger steaks (page 113) and beef broth for the pork chops and chicken broth.*

Fancy

CHICKEN PICCATA

MAKES 4 SERVINGS

This is by no means traditional chicken piccata; it's simply my Middle America, shoot-from-the-hip, I-use-whatever-the-heck-I-have-on-hand (which is why this didn't have capers—sorry, man) version . . . and it's absolutely scrumptious! Whether you serve it with pasta, potatoes, salad, or veggies, you'll eat every bite and slurp up the sauce. (And go back for seconds!)

4 boneless, skinless chicken breasts

Kosher salt and black pepper

½ cup all-purpose flour

4 tablespoons (½ stick) butter

4 tablespoons olive oil

1 cup dry white wine or chicken broth

¾ cup low-sodium chicken broth

Juice of 2 lemons

½ cup heavy cream

1 teaspoon chopped parsley, plus more for serving

1 pound angel hair pasta, cooked according to the package directions

1. If the chicken breasts are overly thick, pound until slightly flattened. Season with salt and pepper on both sides, then dredge them in the flour.

4. In a large skillet, heat 2 tablespoons of the butter and 2 tablespoons of the oil over medium-high heat. Fry two of the chicken breasts at a time . . .

7. Pour in the wine, chicken broth, and lemon juice . . .

2. Shake off the excess . . .

5. Until golden brown on both sides and cooked through, 3 to 4 minutes per side.

8. And whisk the sauce, scraping the bottom of the pan to loosen up all the flavorful bits. Let the sauce cook and bubble and thicken until reduced by about half. Sprinkle in a little salt and pepper as it's cooking.

3. And set them aside.

6. Repeat with the remaining butter, oil, and chicken breasts and remove to a plate. Set aside.

9. Turn the heat to low, pour in the cream . . .

10. And whisk the sauce, letting it cook for a couple of minutes to thicken.

11. Stir in the parsley, then taste and adjust the seasonings. Expect the sauce to have a real lemony tang to it. Counter it with a little more broth and cream if it's too strong!

12. Serve the chicken next to a pile of noodles and spoon the creamy sauce over the whole thing.

13. Finish it with a sprinkling of parsley.

CHANGE THINGS UP!

- *Sauté sliced mushrooms in the pan after cooking the chicken and before starting the sauce.*
- *Omit the cream for a more concentrated lemony pan sauce.*
- *Add capers to the sauce if you have 'em!*
- *Serve with mashed or roasted potatoes instead of pasta.*
- *Serve with a salad to keep things a little lighter.*
- *Serve over a bed of wilted spinach. Yum!*

TACO QUESADILLAS

MAKES 4 OR 5 SERVINGS

Quesadillas are one of my favorite things on earth, and I never get tired of them. Lately, even though flour tortillas are the usual choice for quesadillas, I happen to be a sucker for quesadillas made with corn tortillas, because you get that lovely texture and flavor from the corn tortilla and it's a really nice change.

I've been eating quesadillas since I was eighteen, so it's about time I put a spin on things! It would break my heart for something I love so dearly to become run-of-the-mill.

1½ pounds ground beef

2 heaping tablespoons chili powder

1 teaspoon ground cumin

½ teaspoon cayenne pepper

3 tablespoons tomato paste

¾ teaspoon kosher salt, plus more to taste

Butter, for frying

8 corn tortillas

12 ounces Monterey Jack cheese, grated

Shredded lettuce, for serving

Pico de gallo, for serving (page 150)

1. In a large skillet over medium-high heat, brown the ground beef. Drain the excess fat.

2. Add the chili powder, cumin, cayenne, tomato paste, salt . . .

3. And 1 cup water, then stir to combine.

4. Simmer for a few minutes for the flavors to blend.

5. Heat a separate skillet over medium heat and smear butter on the surface. Place a tortilla in the skillet.

6. Top it with a generous amount of the cheese . . .

7. Then cover the surface with beef.

8. Sprinkle on a little more of the cheese . . .

9. Then place another tortilla on top. By now the edges of the bottom tortilla should be sizzling, so flip the quesadilla over with a spatula.

10. Let the second side cook until the cheese is melted and the edges are sizzling.

11. Remove the quesadilla from the pan and repeat with the remaining tortillas. (You can use a larger griddle to fry more than one quesadilla at a time.)

12. Slice the quesadillas in half. Serve two or three halves on a plate . . .

13. And top with lettuce and pico de gallo.

CHANGE THINGS UP!

- *Leave the quesadillas whole, top them with lettuce and pico de gallo, then fold them like a taco and dig in! Your fingers will be messy, but that's part of the fun.*

- *Use flour tortillas instead of corn for traditional quesadillas.*

- *Serve with salsa, guacamole, and/or sour cream as well!*

$\mathscr{U}$NDER 20!

If this cookbook were *Who Wants to Be a Millionaire?*, this chapter would be your lifeline. You won't believe how lickety-split fast these meals are, and I promise you'll return to them again and again. Life is that busy, and we all deserve a fighting chance. I'm gonna warn ya: Between the flavor and the "fast," these recipes will become "favorites" as soon as you try them!

Doctored-Up Ramen 132

Veggie Tortellini Soup 134

Honey-Soy Salmon 136

Turkey Taco Skillet 138

Spaghetti Carbonara 140

Marsala Mushroom and Goat Cheese Flatbreads 144

Steaks with Chimichurri 146

Dinner Nachos 149

Pepperoni Chicken 152

Lamb Chops with Mint Sauce 154

Steaks with Wasabi Cream Sauce 156

Parmesan-Panko Chicken 158

DOCTORED-UP RAMEN

MAKES 1 LARGE SERVING (ENOUGH FOR 2 TO SHARE)

There's no quicker, easier path to "homemade" soup than using a trusty, rusty package of store-bought ramen as a foundation. That sentence is absolutely full of contradictions, I realize. But contradictions are what make life so exciting!

One 3-ounce package chicken-flavor ramen

1 tablespoon sriracha sauce

¼ cup shredded carrots (I used packaged)

1 green onion, thinly sliced

One 4-ounce can straw mushrooms, drained

⅓ cup canned baby corn, drained and sliced in half

Juice of 1 lime

2 cups boiling water

2 tablespoons chopped salted peanuts (optional)

1. In a large, heatproof, single-serving bowl, sprinkle the chicken seasoning from the ramen package.

4. Sprinkle the carrots on top . . .

7. Then add the lime juice and pour on the boiling water. Set the bowl aside for 3 minutes without stirring.

2. Add the sriracha . . .

5. And the green onion.

8. Stir it around with a fork . . .

3. And lay on the dry ramen noodles.

6. Add the mushrooms and the baby corn . . .

9. Then sprinkle with the chopped peanuts, if you like, and serve!

CHANGE THINGS UP!

- *Sprinkle cilantro leaves on top.*
- *Use cashews instead of peanuts.*
- *Add shredded cooked chicken to the bowl before the boiling water.*
- *Add ½ teaspoon grated fresh ginger to the bowl.*

Super-quick · Kid-friendly

VEGGIE TORTELLINI SOUP

MAKES 6 SERVINGS

This is one of those "recipes" (and it's so easy, it's hardly a recipe at all!) that came about on a day when there was absolutely nothing quick to fix for dinner, so I stared at the pantry shelves, then opened both the fridge and freezer doors approximately 900 times until I finally came up with something. And by then, the whole concept of "quick" was way out the window, but at that point it had become a quest.

The fact that the recipe wound up being one of my girls' favorite soups of all time was a hilarious and rewarding development!

8 cups (2 quarts) vegetable or chicken broth

One 6-ounce can tomato paste

One 10-ounce package frozen mixed vegetables

One 9-ounce package fresh cheese tortellini

½ cup heavy cream

½ teaspoon dried parsley flakes

½ teaspoon dried basil

Kosher salt and black pepper

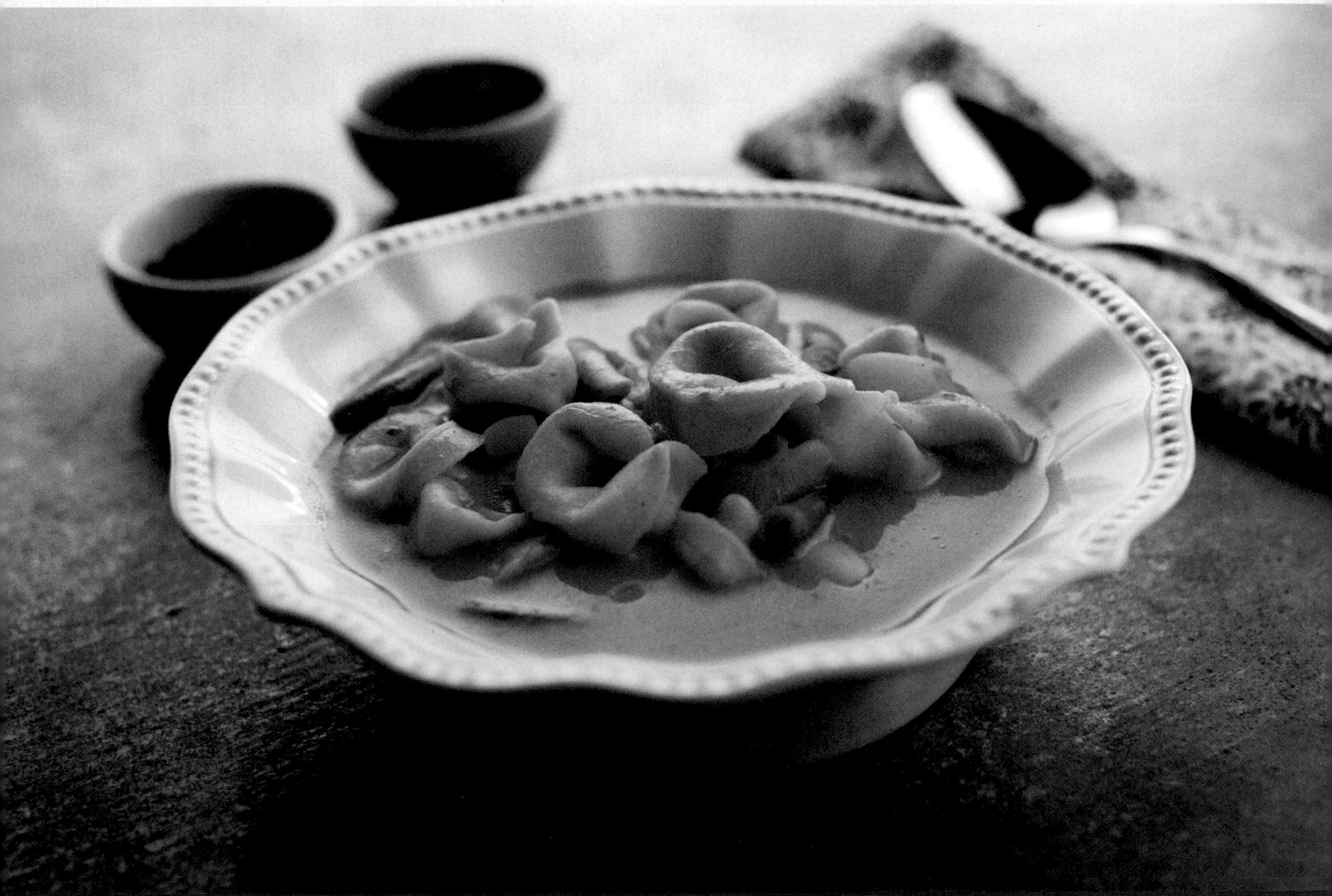

1. In a medium pot, bring the broth to a simmer over medium-high heat.

2. Add the tomato paste and stir until it's well combined; you should have a nice light tomato broth.

3. Add the frozen vegetables and return to a strong simmer.

4. Add the tortellini and cook until just tender, 3 to 5 minutes.

5. Add the heavy cream . . .

6. And stir until everything's nice and creamy.

7. Add the parsley, basil, and salt and pepper to taste and stir to combine. Serve immediately!

CHANGE THINGS UP!

- *Leave out the cream for a more tomatoey broth.*
- *Use fresh herbs instead of dried.*
- *Serve with Parmesan shavings over the top.*
- *Use frozen tortellini (or ravioli) if you prefer; just adjust the time it simmers in the soup according to the package directions.*

Two men and a sunrise.

HONEY-SOY SALMON

MAKES 2 SERVINGS

Guess what? I hated salmon until I was in my forties! Will you ever look at me the same way again? I hope so.

But back to the salmon: I can't explain this late-blooming food thing of mine. I love all food, and it's strange for me to rule something out entirely.

Wait. Scratch that. I hate bananas with every ounce of my being. But I love most other food, and it's strange for me to rule something out entirely.

I also really hate tea.

Oh, never mind! This is getting convoluted and I'm confused. Just make this salmon sometime, okay? It's become a favorite of mine! I wish I'd tried it in my thirties. But I probably wouldn't have liked it. Or maybe it would have turned me around?

As I said above: never mind. Sheesh, Ree!

---

3 limes (2 for zest and juice and 1 for garnish/more juice)

2 cups cooked rice

Two 6-ounce salmon fillets (I like the skin on, but this is optional)

Kosher salt and black pepper

Olive oil

2 tablespoons butter

3 tablespoons honey

3 tablespoons low-sodium soy sauce

Chopped cilantro leaves, for serving

1. Zest 2 of the limes into the rice and stir to incorporate. Set aside.

2. Season the salmon with salt and pepper.

3. In a nonstick skillet, heat a little olive oil over medium-high heat. Place the salmon skin side down (if you left the skin on) in the pan.

7. And add the honey . . .

10. Return the salmon to the skillet and spoon the sauce all over the top.

4. Cook for 5 minutes, being careful not to burn the surface. Carefully flip to the other side and cook for another 2 minutes.

8. The soy sauce and the juice from the 2 zested limes.

11. Pile some of the lime rice onto a dinner plate and add one of the salmon fillets on top.

5. Remove the salmon to a plate while you make the sauce.

9. Cook the sauce over medium heat for a couple of minutes, until it is bubbling and thick. Taste and adjust the flavors, adding more soy sauce or lime juice if it needs it. Cook for another minute or two if the sauce needs thickening.

12. Spoon on some sauce . . .

6. Back in the same skillet, melt the butter . . .

13. Sprinkle with cilantro and serve with a lime wedge.

TURKEY TACO SKILLET

MAKES 4 TO 6 SERVINGS

This one-pan meal is for those days when you've been shuttling kids to and fro, washing mud off the dogs (on a cattle ranch, what's the point, anyway?), working on projects, and just trying to keep your head on straight. I've never, ever made this for dinner and not watched it completely disappear. It's just a big, yummy taco explosion and you don't even have to build tacos to enjoy it!

4 corn tortillas

1½ pounds ground turkey

1 teaspoon chili powder

1 teaspoon ground cumin

Kosher salt and black pepper

One 14.5-ounce can black beans, drained and rinsed

1 cup bottled salsa, plus more for serving

1 canned chipotle pepper in adobo sauce, chopped

1 tablespoon adobo sauce (from the chipotle can)

FIXINS

Sour cream

Diced tomato

Diced avocado

Thinly sliced radishes

Crumbled queso fresco

Fresh cilantro leaves

1. Lightly char the tortillas over an open flame (I used the stovetop burner): Just lay them over medium-low heat for 20 to 25 seconds . . .

2. Then flip them to the other side to char. (If you have an electric stove, just heat a heavy skillet over medium-high heat and lay the tortillas in one at a time, flipping after about 45 seconds.) Let them cool, then tear them into small pieces.

3. Heat a large nonstick skillet over medium-high heat. Add the turkey and season with the chili powder, cumin, and salt and pepper.

4. Cook, breaking up the meat with a spoon, until it's browned, about 5 minutes.

5. Add the beans and stir them in . . .

6. Then add the salsa, chipotle, and adobo sauce and cook, stirring often, until warmed through and slightly thickened, about 5 minutes more. Add a little water if you'd like it to be saucier.

7. Add the tortilla pieces . . .

8. And stir them in.

9. Turn off the heat. Top with sour cream, tomato, avocado, radishes, and queso fresco.

10. Spoon on some extra salsa . . .

11. And finish with cilantro.

CHANGE THINGS UP!

- *Use ground beef instead of turkey.*
- *Sprinkle on shredded Cheddar or Monterey Jack instead of queso fresco.*
- *Add cooked diced zucchini with the turkey to give the skillet a veggie component.*

SPAGHETTI CARBONARA

MAKES 6 SERVINGS

I can't eat, think about, dream about, or even remotely ponder pasta carbonara without thinking of *Heartburn*, the Meryl Streep/Jack Nicholson movie from the eighties that I both love and hate. Love, because it's incredibly written by Nora Ephron and incredibly acted by Meryl and Jack. And because Carly Simon sings the songs. And because Meryl and Jack feast on pasta carbonara on the night of their first date.

Hate, because man, does their relationship get hit by a train. It seriously makes my heart burn. Hence the title.

Fortunately, this spaghetti dish will not make your heart burn. It will make your tummy smile.

1 pound spaghetti

2 tablespoons olive oil, plus more for drizzling

4 ounces pancetta, chopped

4 large eggs

½ cup freshly grated Parmesan cheese, plus more for garnish

Kosher salt and black pepper

3 tablespoons minced parsley

1. Cook the spaghetti according to the package directions while you start the sauce.

2. Heat a large skillet over medium-high heat and add the oil and pancetta. Cook until the pancetta gets browned and crispy, 3 to 4 minutes.

3. Meanwhile, in a bowl, whisk the eggs with the Parmesan and some salt and pepper.

4. Keep whisking until the mixture is thick but still pourable.

5. Drain the excess grease from the pancetta, and when the spaghetti is done, drain it, reserving some of the cooking water. Add the pasta to the hot skillet . . .

6. And toss to coat the pasta with the pancetta flavor.

7. Remove the skillet from the heat and pour the egg mixture on top, tossing the pasta quickly so the eggs don't scramble.

8. As you toss, you'll notice the egg-cheese mixture becoming a beautiful golden sauce that coats the noodles in gorgeous, glossy love.

9. If needed, add some of the hot pasta cooking water to thin out the sauce slightly.

10. Toss in the parsley and serve immediately!

If you don't want to bother with using plates, no worries!

Jack and Meryl didn't either.

CHANGE THINGS UP!

- *Carbonara purists will balk, but adding fresh green peas is yummy!*
- *Caramelized onions are, too. Cook minced onions with the pancetta.*
- *Add a little goat cheese to the sauce. Me oh my!*

Pop Quiz!

WHAT IS LADD DOING IN THESE PHOTOS?

A. Zapping a villain with his superpowers

B. Harnessing the power of the sun

C. Conducting a symphony

D. Trying his hand at tai chi

E. Showing me the area of the ranch and the gates I need to drive through to meet him later

F. It doesn't matter, because look at his arms!

MARSALA MUSHROOM AND GOAT CHEESE FLATBREAD

MAKES TWO 7-INCH FLATBREADS

When I visit restaurants in civilization, I notice more and more flatbread options on the menu. I always thought this was just a newfangled way of saying "pizza," but I decided to go along with it, act like the cool kids, and say "flatbread." But after trying a variety of flatbreads over the past couple of years, I can honestly say that there is, in fact, no difference between flatbread and pizza. I mean, sure . . . we could argue size and thinness and the amount of chew to the crust, but basically, we're talking about bread with stuff on top. And that's pizza, my friends!

With that, here's my flatbread recipe! (I guess I'm still striving to be one of the cool kids!) It makes a great light lunch or dinner (or appetizer!) and uses my very favorite store-bought option for a soft, delicious crust: naan, an Indian flatbread available in most large supermarkets. When I go to the big city, I stockpile and store them in the freezer.

12 ounces mixed mushrooms (I used white button, cremini, and portobello)

1 tablespoon olive oil

1 tablespoon butter

2 garlic cloves, minced

Pinch of kosher salt and black pepper

⅓ cup Marsala wine (or any white or red wine or chicken stock)

1 tablespoon finely minced parsley

½ cup prepared pesto

2 naan flatbreads, or any soft flatbread or baked pizza crust

¾ cup shredded mozzarella cheese

4 ounces goat cheese

8 large fresh basil leaves

1. Heat a grill pan over medium-low heat or preheat the oven to 350°F.

2. Slice the mushrooms.

3. Place a medium skillet over medium-high heat and add the olive oil, butter, mushrooms, garlic, salt, and pepper.

4. Stir and cook for a couple of minutes, then pour in the wine.

5. Keep cooking the mushrooms for several minutes, stirring occasionally, until most of the wine has been absorbed and the mushrooms are nice and dark.

6. Remove the 'shrooms from the heat, add the parsley . . .

7. And stir it in.

8. Spread the pesto on the flatbreads . . .

9. Then sprinkle on the mozzarella.

10. Spoon some mushroom mixture on top of each flatbread . . .

11. Then crumble on the goat cheese.

12. Place the flatbreads on the grill pan and let them sit and warm up until the mozzarella is melted and the breads are very warm, about 5 to 7 minutes. The goat cheese won't get overly melted, but it will be nicely warm. Check the underside to make sure it doesn't burn. If using an oven, bake for about 8 minutes.

13. Tear the basil leaves over each flatbread . . .

14. And serve immediately. Slice them into quarters using a pizza cutter if you'd like smaller pieces. (I just dive in with a knife and fork!)

CHANGE THINGS UP!

- *Substitute caramelized onions for the mushrooms. Wowzers!*
- *Use fig spread or fig preserves instead of the pesto.*
- *Use marinara sauce instead of the pesto.*
- *Other ideas for toppings: chopped sun-dried tomatoes, prosciutto, diced pepperoni.*

STEAKS WITH CHIMICHURRI

MAKES AS MANY STEAKS AS YOU LIKE, WITH ENOUGH SAUCE FOR 8 TO 10 STEAKS

I think steak really is the perfect solution for a quick dinner. First, there's a steak to fit any budget, from pricey filets and rib-eyes (if it's a special dinner) to sirloin and bottom round for a regular weeknight meal (see page xvi). Second, steaks can so easily be changed up with different serving sauces (see page 156!). If you haven't ever tasted the bright-green magic of chimichurri sauce (a South American specialty) spooned over a medium-rare steak . . . oh, boy. You're in for a treat!

I like to pile whole or sliced steaks on a cutting board next to a bowl of chimichurri, then let everyone serve themselves. So fresh and fun.

2 cups packed cilantro leaves

2 cups packed flat-leaf parsley leaves

Small handful mint leaves

2 garlic cloves, grated

2 tablespoons red wine vinegar

1 teaspoon red pepper flakes

Kosher salt and black pepper

¾ cup plus 2 tablespoons olive oil

Any steak of your choice: rib-eye, filet, sirloin, and so on, about 1½ inches thick

2 tablespoons butter

Rib-eye!

1. First, make the chimichurri by placing the herbs and garlic into a food processor (or blender).

2. Add the vinegar . . .

3. And the red pepper flakes and salt and black pepper to taste.

4. Pulse it a few times . . .

5. Then continue pulsing while adding ¾ cup of the olive oil.

6. Keep pulsing until the mixture is pulverized, leaving just a little texture from the herbs. Transfer to a bowl, then cover and refrigerate until you need it (you can make it up to 1 day ahead, though it's best to make it the same day).

7. Season the steak on both sides with salt and pepper.

8. Heat a cast-iron skillet over medium-high heat and add the butter and remaining 2 tablespoons olive oil. When it's melted and starting to brown, add a steak. Fry until medium-rare, 3 to 4 minutes per side. Remove the steak and let it rest for 3 minutes. (If you're frying more steaks, just add a little more butter and oil to the pan as needed.)

9. Slice the steak. Serve it with the chimichurri on the side.

DINNER NACHOS

MAKES 8 SERVINGS

I take nachos very seriously. Very, very, *very* seriously.

No, I'm serious. Don't even joke about it. I'm not even kidding. I'm being serious here, people! *Dead serious.*

Actually, just kidding! Hahahahaha.

See? That right there is the perfect example of why I was always terrible at prank calls. I just never could keep it going. My sister Betsy could keep a prank call going for hours if she ever had the chance. She never cracked. Not once. But me? I'd deliver the first line or two, then I'd either become crippled from laughing or I'd say, "Never mind, just kidding," and hang up. Honestly, my middle name should be Just Kidding. It's the first thing I say whenever I lose my nerve.

All this is to say that we really do love nachos in our house, and they can pass as a super-casual dinner (rather than an appetizer) if you load them up with enough deliciousness.

1 tablespoon olive oil

1 yellow onion, cut into medium dice

2 pounds ground beef

½ teaspoon chili powder

½ teaspoon paprika

½ teaspoon ground cumin

¼ teaspoon red pepper flakes

Kosher salt

½ teaspoon black pepper

One 14.5-ounce can pinto beans or chili beans (rinse them first!)

½ cup hot water

6 Roma tomatoes, finely diced

1 jalapeño, finely diced

Leaves from ½ bunch cilantro, chopped

Juice of 1 lime

Tortilla chips

1½ cups grated Cheddar cheese

1½ cups grated Monterey Jack cheese

1 avocado, pitted, peeled, and cut into medium dice

1. In a large skillet over medium-high heat, combine the olive oil and half the onion. Cook until the onion starts to soften, then add the ground beef.

2. Cook the meat until it's totally browned, then drain the fat.

3. Add the chili powder, paprika, cumin, red pepper flakes, ½ teaspoon salt, and the black pepper and stir to combine.

4. Add the beans . . .

5. And the hot water and stir. Turn the heat to low and simmer while you prepare the other ingredients.

6. To make the pico de gallo, combine the other half of the onion with the tomatoes, jalapeño, cilantro, lime juice, and ½ teaspoon salt. Stir together and set aside.

7. To build the nachos, place a layer of tortilla chips on a large platter or plate. Top with about half of the beef-bean mixture . . .

8. Then all but ¼ cup of the Cheddar cheese.

9. Add another layer of chips . . .

10. Most of the remaining beef-bean mixture . . .

11. And the Monterey Jack cheese.

12. Add a final small layer of chips, then the remaining beef-bean mixture, then a final sprinkling of Cheddar.

13. Microwave the nachos in 45-second increments until the cheese is melted and bubbling. (You may also place the platter into a 325°F oven if it's heatproof. Just leave it in until the cheese has melted.)

14. Immediately sprinkle on the avocado . . .

15. And plenty of the pico de gallo!

16. Dig in immediately! Use plates if you want to split up the nachos . . . or, if you're a close family like we are (ha ha), just let everyone go for it.

CHANGE THINGS UP!

- *Use finely diced chicken instead of ground beef.*
- *Swap in blue corn tortilla chips for a richer color.*
- *Top with guacamole and sour cream.*

"You want some nachos, Walter?"

PEPPERONI CHICKEN

MAKES 2 SERVINGS

Here's what this recipe isn't: fussy, complicated, complex, difficult, elaborate, laborious, burdensome, or tricky.

Here's what this recipe is: fast, simple, easy, versatile, satisfying, and speedy.

Oh, and one other thing: *delicious!*

1 boneless, skinless chicken breast

Kosher salt and black pepper

2 tablespoons butter

2 tablespoons olive oil

3 cups good-quality marinara sauce

One 3.5-ounce package sliced pepperoni

2 deli slices mozzarella cheese

Minced parsley, for garnish

Cooked pasta, for serving

1. Use a sharp knife to slice the chicken breast in half through the middle, so that you wind up with two thinner chicken cutlets. Season them with salt and pepper.

2. In a heavy skillet, melt the butter in the olive oil over medium heat. Add the chicken . . .

3. And cook until it has nice color on the outside and is cooked through, about 2½ minutes per side.

4. Remove the chicken to a plate.

5. Pour the marinara sauce into the pan and stir to heat it through.

6. Nestle the chicken cutlets in the sauce . . .

7. Then arrange the pepperoni slices on top . . .

8. Followed by the mozzarella. Cover the skillet and cook for 2 to 3 minutes . . .

9. Until the cheese has melted.

10. Sprinkle with parsley!

11. Spoon plenty of the sauce over the pasta, then lay a chicken breast on top.

CHANGE THINGS UP!

- *Turn this into a pepperoni chicken sandwich! Serve the chicken cutlet inside a toasted ciabatta bun.*

- *Serve it with a simple side salad (instead of pasta) to keep things a little lighter.*

- *Or . . . you could serve the chicken with mashed potatoes.* ☺

Ree and Ladd, sittin' in a tree . . .

LAMB CHOPS WITH MINT SAUCE

MAKES 2 SERVINGS

I have all these strange confessions relating to disliking certain foods well into my forties (see page 136, and also see every moment anyone has ever offered me a banana), and I'm about to put forth another one: I was about 44½ years old before I learned to love lamb chops. I don't know what the holdup was; it could be that I was a vegetarian before meeting my cowboy husband in my twenties and moving to his cattle ranch?

I'm always exploring the "whys" in my life. It's the reason I can never remember to pay my phone bill.

Anyway, if you don't have a lot of experience with lamb, this is a great way to initiate yourself. Lamb chops are so elegant, but you'd never know it when you find out how easy they are to make!

Baked Sweet Potato
(page 271)

SPICE RUB AND LAMB

2 teaspoons kosher salt

1 teaspoon black pepper

½ teaspoon ground coriander

¼ teaspoon cayenne pepper

Zest of 1 lemon

Four 4-ounce lamb rib chops

MINT SAUCE

1 bunch mint leaves

¼ cup parsley leaves

2 anchovy fillets (optional)

1 garlic clove

Pinch of red pepper flakes

½ cup olive oil

Kosher salt

Vegetable oil, for grilling

1. First, make the rub: In a small bowl, combine the salt, black pepper, coriander, and cayenne.

2. Add the lemon zest and stir until it's all mixed.

3. Season the lamb chops on both sides with the spice rub. Let them sit at room temperature while you make the mint sauce.

4. Make the mint sauce: In a food processor, combine the mint, parsley, anchovies (if using), garlic, and red pepper flakes. (Pssst. The anchovy flavor isn't strong at all! They just add a little marvelous mystery.)

5. Process the mixture, adding the olive oil as you go until the sauce is just loose enough to drizzle. Taste and add salt if needed.

6. Prepare a grill or heat a grill pan over medium-high heat. Oil the grill and pat the chops dry. Place the lamb chops on the grill . . .

7. And cook the chops for about 2 minutes per side for medium-rare (my favorite way to enjoy lamb!).

8. Serve the chops with the mint sauce spooned over the top. (Delicious with a baked sweet potato on the side!)

STEAKS WITH WASABI CREAM SAUCE

MAKES AS MANY STEAKS AS YOU LIKE, WITH ENOUGH SAUCE FOR ABOUT 8 STEAKS

Vail, Colorado, is my happy place. Funny, isn't it? I have to escape the stressful prairie by running to the mountains. Clearly I have issues.

My list of loves in Vail is very, very long, and high on the list is a steakhouse called Flame, which serves a variety of six sauces with every steak that's ordered. Let's just say I could pretty much leave the steak and eat the sauces with a spoon, and possibly my favorite is a cream-based sauce with the blessed hot mustard flavor of wasabi.

It makes live worth living! And it's a nice, easy way to change up a regular weeknight steak.

¾ cup sour cream

½ cup mayonnaise

2 tablespoons chopped cilantro

2 tablespoons heavy cream

2 tablespoons prepared wasabi paste

1 garlic clove, grated

Kosher salt and black pepper

Thick (2-inch) beef filet steaks or sirloin steaks, set out at room temperature for 20 minutes

Olive oil, for drizzling

1. Up to a day ahead of time, make the wasabi cream sauce: In a medium bowl, combine the sour cream, mayonnaise, cilantro, and heavy cream.

2. Add the wasabi paste, garlic, and salt and pepper to taste. Stir until it's nice and smooth. (Cover and refrigerate if you make it ahead of time.)

3. For the steaks: Preheat the oven to 425°F. Heat a cast-iron skillet over high heat until hot. Drizzle the steaks with olive oil and season them with salt and pepper.

The ranch is just like Vail, Colorado . . . but without the mountains.

4. Add the steaks to the skillet and sear them quickly . . .

5. About 1 minute per side. Transfer the skillet to the oven and roast for 5 minutes.

6. Serve the steaks with a simple green salad and the wasabi cream on the side.

You can dip it, or you can douse it like I do! (The sauce is so good, dipping is kinda hard.)

PARMESAN-PANKO CHICKEN

MAKES 4 SERVINGS

You can't beat a thin, crispy piece of chicken when it comes to an easy weeknight dinner. You can serve it on its own with a gorgeous salad on the side, or it can be a foundation for dishes like chicken Parmesan. (Or you can top it with arugula and lemon juice and call it chicken Milanese!) Good ol' seasoned breadcrumbs are a safe bet for something like this, but I think the combination of ultracrispy panko breadcrumbs mixed with Parmesan makes a winner of a chicken dinner!

The chicken breasts are nice and thin, too, so they hardly take any time to cook!

2 boneless, skinless chicken breasts

½ cup all-purpose flour

1 teaspoon kosher salt

½ teaspoon black pepper

2 large eggs

¼ cup whole milk

1 cup panko breadcrumbs

½ cup finely grated Parmesan cheese, plus more for serving

2 tablespoons butter

2 tablespoons olive oil

Citrus Salad with Vinaigrette (page 236)

1. Carefully slice the chicken breasts in half horizontally, to wind up with 4 thinner cutlets.

2. Place the cutlets between two sheets of plastic wrap and use a mallet (or rolling pin) to gently pound them to a uniform thickness, about ¼ inch.

3. In a pie plate, combine the flour, salt, and pepper. In a second pie plate, whisk together the eggs and the milk. In a third, stir together the panko and Parmesan. The assembly line is ready!

4. Lightly dredge each cutlet in the flour mixture . . .

5. Then quickly coat both sides with the egg mixture . . .

6. And finally coat both sides in the crumbs, pressing to get them to stick. Remove to a plate.

7. In a large skillet, melt 1 tablespoon of the butter in 1 tablespoon of the oil over medium heat. When melted and hot, add 2 of the chicken cutlets . . .

8. And cook, flipping once, until the breading is golden and the chicken is cooked through, 2 to 3 minutes per side.

9. Remove them to a plate lined with paper towels. Add the remaining 1 tablespoon each butter and oil to the pan and repeat with the remaining cutlets.

10. Sprinkle with a little extra Parmesan before serving! (I serve it here with Citrus Salad.)

CHANGE THINGS UP!

- *Use chicken tenders instead of cutlets for Parmesan-panko chicken strips!*

- *Turn a cutlet into a fried chicken sandwich by putting it on a pretzel bun with honey mustard and slaw!*

- *Top with marinara sauce and melted mozzarella; serve with spaghetti. Yum.*

$\mathcal{T}$AKE YOUR TIME

Lightning-fast recipes are great and all, but hopefully you have those days here and there when you can slow down and spend a little more time in the kitchen. From casseroles to slow cooker sensations to delicious soups, here are some of my current favorites. They take time, but boy are they a cinch.

Slow Cooker Glazed Ribs...162

Slow Cooker "Pot" of Beans...164

Slow Cooker BBQ Chicken..167

Slow Cooker Spaghetti Sauce...169

Slow Cooker Mexican Chicken Soup...174

Slow Cooker Broccoli Cheese Soup..176

Bean with Bacon Soup..179

Meatball Tortilla Soup...181

Pan-Roasted Chicken Thighs...185

Stuffed Bell Peppers..189

Mini Turkey Meatloaves...193

King Ranch Chicken...196

Cincinnati Chili..199

Meat Pies..202

Lobster Mac and Cheese...207

Kid-friendly

SLOW COOKER GLAZED RIBS

MAKES 8 SERVINGS

You will never, ever experience more tender baby back ribs than the ones you make in a slow cooker. Some kind of crazy magic happens under that lid, I tell you!

A "mistake" (which you really can hardly call a mistake because they taste great no matter what) that can happen when making ribs in a slow cooker is cooking the sauce along with the ribs for the entire time. The problem with this is that the ribs give off so much liquid as they cook that the sauce will wind up watery and won't stick to the ribs. You'll see my solution for this on the next page!

If you're a fan of ribs that fall smooth off the bone . . . you're in for a heavenly experience right here.

Two 2½- to 3-pound packages pork loin back ribs or "baby back ribs"

1 large onion, thinly sliced

12 garlic cloves

1 teaspoon kosher salt

½ teaspoon black pepper

1 cup plum preserves

½ cup ketchup

½ cup barbecue sauce

Several dashes of hot sauce

1. Cut the racks of ribs in half . . .

2. And place them in the slow cooker.

3. Add the onion, garlic, salt, and pepper.

6. Next, make the sauce. In a medium bowl, combine the preserves, ketchup, barbecue sauce, and hot sauce . . .

9. And use tongs to move the ribs around in the sauce as much as you can. Note that the ribs will be falling apart by this stage, so don't be too rough with them. Place the lid back on the slow cooker, set it to high, and cook for 15 minutes.

4. Place the lid on the cooker and cook on low for 8 hours, making sure not to lift the lid or otherwise disturb the ribs.

7. And stir it until it's all combined.

10. Remove the ribs to a cutting board to separate them into portions, which won't be difficult at all. I mean . . . look at how easily the bone comes out! How good are these going to be?

5. This is what they look like after that time. Totally weird, but they're about to get super delicious. Start by straining off all the cooking liquid, making sure not to lose any of the garlic or onions.

8. Pour the sauce over the ribs . . .

11. Serve 'em on a plate, if they can travel that far without falling to pieces. Succulent and delicious!

SLOW COOKER "POT" OF BEANS

MAKES 12 TO 16 SERVINGS

A big ol' pot of cooked pinto beans will take you far in life. They're great for chili, for tacos, or just served in a bowl with onion and cheese sprinkled over the top. It's one of the best no-brainer recipes you can make for your family: They're so good for you—full of fiber and important nutrients—and if you cook 'em in the slow cooker, it's like you didn't even lift a finger to make them!

1½ pounds dried pinto beans

2 teaspoons chili powder

1 teaspoon ground cumin

½ teaspoon paprika

¼ teaspoon cayenne pepper

3 slices thick-cut bacon, cut into thirds

3 garlic cloves

2 bay leaves

1 medium onion, cut into medium dice (reserve a bit for serving)

1 red bell pepper, seeded and cut into small dice

2 teaspoons kosher salt

1 teaspoon black pepper

Grated Cheddar, for serving

1. Pour the beans into a slow cooker.

4. Lay the bacon on top, along with the garlic, the bay leaves . . .

2. Add water to the beans to cover them by 1 inch . . .

5. The onion, bell pepper, salt, and black pepper . . .

7. Serve the beans with dishes of grated Cheddar and diced onion alongside.

3. And add the chili powder, cumin, paprika, and cayenne.

6. And stir together. Put the lid on the slow cooker and cook the beans on high for 5 hours or on low for 8 hours. When the beans are tender and the liquid is thick and luscious, the beans are ready! Be sure to taste them and add more salt and/or black pepper if they need it.

OTHER FIXIN IDEAS

- *Diced avocado*
- *Pico de gallo (page 150)*
- *Salsa*
- *Crumbled cornbread*
- *Warm flour tortillas (served on the side)*

SLOW COOKER BBQ CHICKEN

MAKES 12 TO 15 SERVINGS

Oh, is this a scrumptious crowd-pleaser!

Now, about slow cooker BBQ chicken: With such a name, one might expect that it would involve nothing more than adding chicken to the slow cooker, pouring barbecue sauce on top, and cooking it for several hours. And you can definitely do that! But (as with the ribs on page 162) I've found that barbecue sauce can often lose its thickness (or, if you wanna hear a more technical term: viscosity) when it simmers in the slow cooker forever, and sometimes you can wind up with a soupier pulled chicken than you set out to make.

Try the method below! It's not much more complicated, and the extra step or two will wind up making you smile. Big time.

8 boneless, skinless chicken breasts

2 tablespoons chili powder

1 teaspoon kosher salt

1 teaspoon black pepper

1 large onion, thinly sliced

8 to 10 garlic cloves

One 40-ounce bottle barbecue sauce

Soft hamburger buns, for serving

Chips, for serving

1. Lay the chicken breasts in the slow cooker . . .

2. And generously sprinkle with the chili powder, salt, and pepper.

3. Add the onion and garlic . . .

4. And pour on 1 cup of the sauce. (You'll use the rest of the bottle later!)

5. Pour in 1 cup water. Place the lid on the slow cooker and cook on high for 4 hours, stirring once in the middle of the cooking time.

6. When the time is up . . . the chicken doesn't look like much. But just you wait, 'Enry 'Iggins!

7. Remove it to a cutting board and let it cool for a few minutes.

8. Meanwhile, pour the cooking liquid out of the slow cooker into a fine-mesh strainer set over a bowl in order to capture the onions and garlic. Save the onions and garlic, as well as 1 cup of the strained cooking liquid.

9. Use two forks to shred the chicken completely!

10. You can shred it fine like this, or you can leave it in larger chunks—whatever makes your skirt fly up.

11. Return the chicken to the slow cooker and pour in the rest of the barbecue sauce.

12. Next—yum!—add the onion, garlic, and reserved cooking liquid . . .

13. And stir to combine. Set the cooker to low to keep warm until you need it!

14. Serve the chicken on soft buns with a side of chips.

CHANGE THINGS UP!

- *Double the amount of onions if you really like onions.*
- *Add several dashes of hot sauce to give the chicken a nice kick.*
- *Add a cup of pickled jalapeño slices at the beginning with the other ingredients.*
- *On the sandwiches, top the pulled chicken with coleslaw for a nice cool crunch.*

SLOW COOKER SPAGHETTI SAUCE

MAKES A TON (ABOUT 24 SERVINGS!)

This spaghetti sauce is good, my friends! It's rich, meaty, straightforward to make (hello, slow cooker!), and, aside from being absolutely perfect served over the pasta of your choice, it's also great layered in lasagna or spooned on top of garlic bread (Italian sloppy joes?) or ricotta-stuffed pasta shells. Or pretty much over anything you want!

4½ pounds ground beef

1 large onion, roughly chopped

5 garlic cloves, minced

8 cups canned crushed tomatoes
(two 28-ounce cans plus one
8-ounce can)

½ cup tomato paste

One 24-ounce jar good-quality
marinara sauce

2 teaspoons kosher salt

1 teaspoon black pepper

2 tablespoons sugar

1 teaspoon ground oregano

1 teaspoon ground thyme

1 tablespoon dried parsley flakes

1 tablespoon dried basil

4 bay leaves

½ teaspoon red pepper flakes

1 cup white wine (or chicken or
beef broth)

Olive oil

Cooked spaghetti, for serving

Minced fresh parsley, for serving

1. In a large skillet or Dutch oven, combine the ground beef, onion, and garlic.

2. Cook the meat over medium-high heat until it's totally browned, then drain off the excess grease.

3. In a 6-quart slow cooker, combine the cooked beef, crushed tomatoes . . .

4. The tomato paste . . .

5. The marinara sauce (trust me!) . . .

6. And the salt, black pepper, sugar, oregano, thyme, dried parsley, basil, bay leaves, and red pepper flakes.

7. Next comes the wine!

11. Serve the sauce over the pasta . . .

12. And sprinkle the fresh parsley on top.

8. Stir everything together, place the lid on the slow cooker, and cook on high for 4 hours or on low for 8 hours.

CHANGE THINGS UP!

- *Substitute Italian sausage for 1½ pounds of the ground beef.*
- *Use red wine instead of white wine for a richer flavor and color.*
- *Serve the sauce over rigatoni, penne, or any pasta!*
- *Top with freshly grated Parmesan cheese.*
- *Melt thick slices of mozzarella cheese on top.*

9. *Mmmm.* Look at how rich and gorgeous! Be sure to taste the sauce and add more salt if it needs it. If there is excess grease on top, skim it off before stirring.

"Me likey spaghetti."

10. Drizzle a little olive oil over the spaghetti and toss it to coat.

The Reluctant Cowboy

I try never to go too far down the path of predicting what any of my children will do when they grow up, because I've learned firsthand that life can change on a dime and it very often turns out completely different than originally planned. And I haven't even grown up yet myself, so who am I to even think about such things? Of all my children, though, I would say that (God willing and the creek don't rise) my older son, Bryce, is the one who seems most destined to be a rancher. Since he was young, he has sprung out of bed when it's time to saddle the horses, and the cowboy way of life just comes naturally to him.

Now, my youngest, Todd, on the other hand? Well . . . I'm not sure! While he started working on the ranch at the same age (birth) as his older brother, he's never exactly inhaled and embraced his ranching duties in the same way. Oh, he shows up and he does the job, all right. He's Todd Drummond, after all, and he's a great kid! It's just that he doesn't lie awake at night thinking about the herd he'll have one day.

But that's the cool thing about Todd. There's a whole world going on under the surface, and as he's saddling and riding his horse, I can see that thirteen-year-old mind a-churning. He might be thinking about the next Marvel movie that's on its way to theaters. He might be remembering the suit of armor he saved scrap metal to build when he was young. He might be imagining what position he'll play in football (his favorite sport) next year. Or he might be noodling on the long conversation he had with one of the older congregants at our Presbyterian church last Sunday. He's got a rich bank of memories and perspectives swimming around in that noggin of his. And this is only something a mama would say: I love to watch the kid think.

What will Todd be when he grows up? There's no way of knowing. He might be an illustrator for a comic book series, the host of a radio sports show, an accountant, a doctor, a salesman, a diplomat, minister, missionary, or coach.

Although . . . I do know a certain cattle rancher around these parts who was reportedly exactly like Todd when he was a boy. His head was somewhere else when he was on his horse, and ranching wouldn't have been described as his favorite line of work. This gentleman loved Spider-Man and football, and he never lay awake at night thinking about the herd he'd have one day. Then, when he grew up, his love for ranching set in. He realized he loved Osage County, raising cattle, and living on the land. And he made the choice to do the thing he never thought he'd wind up doing. And he's never regretted it for a single day!

(I know the gentleman. I'm married to him.)

It'll be fun to watch Todd's future unfold.

SLOW COOKER MEXICAN CHICKEN SOUP

MAKES 8 TO 10 SERVINGS

I start to lose interest in slow cooker recipes that require much more work than just chucking in a bunch of ingredients and turning it on, because let's face it: That's the dang beauty of slow-cooker cooking! This incredibly flavorful, crowd-pleasing soup pretty much fits that bill, but for a couple of minutes you need to spend shredding the chicken at the end. A small price to pay for a super-tasty dinner!

3 boneless, skinless chicken breasts

1 teaspoon chili powder

1 teaspoon ground cumin

1 teaspoon kosher salt

1 teaspoon black pepper

One 28-ounce can whole or diced tomatoes, with juice

One 10-ounce can diced tomatoes and green chiles (such as Ro*Tel)

3 cups low-sodium chicken broth (more if you like the soup more liquid)

One 15-ounce can black beans, drained and rinsed

2 heaping tablespoons tomato paste

1 medium onion, chopped

1 canned chipotle pepper in adobo sauce (or 2 or 3, if you like things spicier)

1 red bell pepper, seeded and chopped

1 yellow bell pepper, seeded and chopped

Juice of 1 lime

Fixins: lime wedges, avocado, sour cream, grated cheese, crushed tortilla chips, and fresh cilantro leaves

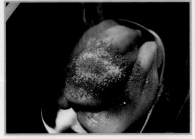

1. Place the chicken in a slow cooker. Sprinkle on the chili powder, cumin, salt, and black pepper.

4. The chipotle pepper and bell peppers . . .

7. Remove the chicken to a plate and use two forks to break it into chunks (or shred it finely).

2. Add the plain tomatoes with their juices, diced tomatoes and chiles, chicken broth . . .

5. And stir. Place the lid on the slow cooker and cook on high for 5 hours or on low for 8 hours.

8. Return the chicken to the soup, stir in the lime juice, then taste and add more seasoning if necessary.

3. The black beans, tomato paste, and onion . . .

6. Great things happen during that time!

9. Serve piping hot in a bowl with all the fixins!

CHANGE THINGS UP!

- *Tear up a few corn tortillas and stir them into the soup toward the end.*
- *Stir in 6 ounces processed American cheese (Velveeta!) toward the end for a cheesy soup.*
- *Stir in ½ cup tequila with ½ hour left in the cooking process.*

SLOW COOKER BROCCOLI CHEESE SOUP

MAKES 10 TO 12 SERVINGS

Broccoli cheese soup is a favorite of my firstborn son, Bryce, who is now taller than me by at least four inches even though he still looks like the sweet, blond, cherubic little pookie head he was fifteen years ago. Sniff sniff. *Wahhh!*

And I'm here to show you the easiest slow cooker version of B-Man's most beloved soup ever. It uses frozen broccoli, which ups the easy factor without sacrificing nutrients, and except for a little pureeing and cheese grating toward the end, it's pretty durn effortless.

1 pound frozen broccoli florets

5 cups low-sodium chicken broth

1 medium onion, diced

2 carrots, finely diced

Two 10.5-ounce cans cream of celery soup

¼ teaspoon seasoned salt

¼ teaspoon kosher salt

½ teaspoon black pepper

⅛ teaspoon cayenne pepper

1½ pounds processed melting cheese (such as Velveeta)

2 cups grated sharp Cheddar cheese, plus more for serving

Crumbled saltine crackers, for serving

1. Place the frozen broccoli right in the slow cooker . . .

2. And add the chicken broth . . .

3. The onion and carrots . . .

4. The cream of celery soup, seasoned salt, kosher salt, black pepper, and cayenne . . .

5. And stir it all together. Place the lid on the slow cooker and cook on high for 4 hours.

6. The veggies will be soft and the flavors will be marvelous!

7. Use an immersion blender (or potato masher) to puree the soup about three-quarters of the way . . .

8. In order to leave some chunks for delicious texture. (You can also use a regular blender. Just be sure to blend only 1 cup at a time and use extreme caution. Then return it to the slow cooker.)

9. Add the processed cheese . . .

10. And the Cheddar, and stir them in.

11. Then cover, set the cooker to low, and cook for 15 minutes.

12. Utterly creamy and delicious! Here's where you want to taste the soup and add more of what you'd like: a little more salt, a little more cayenne, and so on.

13. Serve it warm with a sprinkling of Cheddar and some crumbled saltines.

CHANGE THINGS UP!

- *Substitute frozen cauliflower for half the frozen broccoli.*
- *Add 6 cooked, crumbled slices of bacon with the cheese.*
- *Add two drained 4-ounce cans green chiles with the cheese.*
- *Use Monterey Jack or pepper Jack instead of the Cheddar.*

Unbelievably delicious!

BEAN WITH BACON SOUP

MAKES 8 TO 10 SERVINGS

Canned soups are not widely accepted as the best option out there, but as with all blanket opinions about food, there are some exceptions. Canned chicken and rice soup, for example. It's not terrible! Canned tomato soup? Add a little cream and basil and the heavens open up!

And good ol' canned bean with bacon soup? Well, it's a taste of my childhood, and I don't care who knows it. When I first made it from scratch, I was bowled over by how much it tasted like the original. Absolutely delicious.

Are you laughing at the fact that I'm about to teach you how to make a homemade soup that tastes almost as good as the canned stuff?

Because I am.

1 pound dried great northern beans

4 cups (1 quart) low-sodium chicken broth, plus more as needed

1 pound thick-cut bacon, cut into 1-inch pieces

1 onion, finely diced

2 large carrots, finely diced

2 celery stalks, finely diced

Kosher salt and black pepper

4 garlic cloves, minced

2 tablespoons tomato paste

2 bay leaves

3 Roma tomatoes, chopped

Minced parsley

1. Pick through the beans and give them a rinse. Put them in a bowl and cover them with water by 2 inches. Let them soak overnight.

3. Add the chicken broth and 4 cups water. Bring to a boil, then reduce the heat to a simmer.

5. Remove to paper towels to drain, then add two-thirds of the bacon to the beans. (Reserve the rest for garnish.)

2. Drain the beans and place them in a large pot.

4. Meanwhile, in a large skillet, cook the bacon over medium heat until crisp.

6. Pour the bacon grease out of the pan . . .

7. And add the onion, carrots, and celery. Season them lightly with salt and pepper and cook until they just begin to soften, 3 to 4 minutes.

8. Add the garlic and stir . . .

9. Then add the tomato paste . . .

10. And cook for another minute or two to release all of 'dem flavors!

11. Add the vegetables to the beans . . .

12. Along with the bay leaves.

13. And give it a good stir. Cover and cook over low heat until the beans are tender, about 1½ hours. Add a cup or two of broth if the liquid level gets too low.

14. And this is what it looks like! Taste it and add more salt and pepper if needed.

15. Finally, turn off the heat, add the tomatoes . . .

16. And stir them in.

17. Serve it up, sprinkled with the bacon and some minced parsley.

You will go berserk over this! So incredibly delicious.

MEATBALL TORTILLA SOUP

MAKES 8 SERVINGS

To describe this delicious soup as merely a "delicious soup" is the understatement of the year! First of all, it's so far beyond delicious. Flavorful, fabulous, and fantastic is more like it. And it's really much more of a stew than a soup. A stew full of wonderful texture and color, with an added bonus of yummy meatballs in every bowlful. You'll love every bite! (And as an extra thrill: It freezes beautifully!)

MEATBALLS

1 pound ground beef

½ cup grated pepper Jack cheese

2 tablespoons minced parsley

1 large egg, lightly beaten

2 garlic cloves, minced

½ teaspoon kosher salt

¼ teaspoon black pepper

¼ teaspoon ground cumin

¼ teaspoon chili powder

¼ cup seasoned breadcrumbs

Juice of 1 lime

SOUP

4 tablespoons (½ stick) butter

½ large onion, diced

3 garlic cloves, minced

2 ears of sweet corn, kernels sliced off (or 1½ cups frozen corn kernels)

1 red bell pepper, seeded and finely diced

6 cups low-sodium beef broth

One 10-ounce can diced tomatoes and chiles (such as Ro*Tel)

2 heaping tablespoons tomato paste

½ teaspoon kosher salt

¼ teaspoon chili powder

¼ teaspoon ground cumin

One 14.5-ounce can black beans, drained and rinsed

6 corn tortillas, cut into strips

FIXINS

Sour cream

Sliced avocado

Grated pepper Jack cheese

Cilantro leaves

1. Combine all the meatball ingredients in a large bowl . . .

2. And mix well.

3. Shape the meat mixture into small balls (about 24 total) and refrigerate for 30 minutes.

4. Make the soup: In a heavy pot, heat 2 tablespoons of the butter over medium heat. Add one-third of the meatballs and lightly brown on all sides (they won't be cooked through) . . .

5. Then remove them to a plate.

6. Repeat with the remaining meatballs!

7. Add the remaining 2 tablespoons butter to the pan and let it melt.

8. Add the onion, garlic, corn, and bell pepper and cook, stirring, until softened, 2 to 3 minutes.

9. Add the broth . . .

10. The diced tomatoes and chiles . . .

11. And the tomato paste, salt, chili powder, and cumin . . .

12. And stir in. Bring it to a boil, then add the beans.

13. Return the meatballs to the pot, cover, and simmer until the meatballs are cooked all the way through, 15 to 20 minutes.

Delicious!

14. Just before serving, stir in the tortilla strips.

15. Serve the soup with a dollop of sour cream, a slice of avocado, a little grated cheese, and a few cilantro leaves.

King Duke! He's large and in charge.

PAN-ROASTED CHICKEN THIGHS

MAKES 6 SERVINGS

Chicken thighs are my life. Absolutely, positively my life. If I had to choose a cut of chicken to chow down on for the rest of my days, I would choose thighs every day of the week, and nine hundred times on Sunday. I always wonder why breasts get all the dang attention in this world. Thighs are the way to go, baby!

(Sorry. There's just no dignified way to talk about breasts and thighs.)

(I'm snickering.)

6 tablespoons olive oil, more as needed

6 bone-in, skin-on chicken thighs

Kosher salt and black pepper

1 cup all-purpose flour

1 medium onion, finely diced

5 garlic cloves, minced

½ cup white wine or chicken broth

1 cup chicken broth

1 lemon, zested and halved

Cooked rice, for serving

1. Preheat the oven to 350°F.

2. In an ovenproof skillet, heat the olive oil over medium heat.

3. Season the chicken thighs with salt and pepper . . .

4. Then dredge both sides in the flour.

5. Place them in the hot pan, skin side down, and cook until the skin is golden, 3 to 4 minutes. (Move them around in the pan a bit if needed to brown the skin evenly.)

6. Turn them to the other side and cook for another couple of minutes . . .

7. Then remove them to a plate (they won't be cooked through). Pour off all but about ¼ cup of grease from the skillet.

8. Add the onion and garlic to the pan and sauté until softened, about 3 minutes.

11. Along with half the zest and the juice from 1 lemon half. Sprinkle in a little salt and pepper and cook for 2 minutes, stirring constantly.

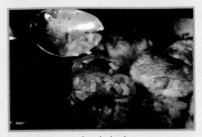

14. Remove the lid, then spoon some of the sauce over each chicken thigh.

9. Pour in the wine, stir, and let it reduce for 1 to 2 minutes.

12. Nestle the chicken thighs back in the pan, skin side up. (They should not be submerged; the liquid should come about one-third of the way up the sides of the chicken.)

15. Roast the chicken, uncovered, for 15 minutes, making sure it doesn't get too brown.

10. Add the broth . . .

13. Place the lid on the skillet (if you're using an iron skillet without a lid, you can invert a second skillet on top), transfer to the oven, and roast for 15 minutes.

16. Stir the rest of the lemon zest and a little salt into the cooked rice.

17. Serve a piece of chicken with some of the rice and spoon the sauce over both.

Tasty, juicy, and tender!

CHANGE THINGS UP!

- *Use dry sherry or Marsala wine instead of the white wine for a different flavor.*

- *Add 2 tablespoons capers to the liquid as it simmers in step 11.*

Caught in the rain!

STUFFED BELL PEPPERS

MAKES 6 STUFFED PEPPERS

My mom used to make stuffed green peppers growing up, and I'm ashamed to say that I took them for granted for all those years. I guess it says a lot about my mom that her cooking was so yummy that it almost became commonplace!

Not that your cooking was ever commonplace, Mom! I just meant that it was such an everyday thing that your dinners were delicious that I didn't know a good thing when I saw it.

I mean I just . . . I just . . . I think I'm digging myself a deeper hole.

While these peppers might not be as good as my mama's (did you hear that, Mom?), they sure do run a close second. And they can be assembled ahead of time (even the day before!), so all you have to do is pop 'em in the oven when your family starts bangin' their forks on the table.

6 bell peppers, any color

4 tablespoons olive oil, plus more for drizzling

1½ pounds lean ground beef

Kosher salt and black pepper

1 onion, finely diced

1 garlic clove, minced

1 medium zucchini, finely diced

4 Roma tomatoes, seeded and finely diced

Red pepper flakes

1 cup cooked long-grain rice

1½ cups grated pepper Jack cheese

1. Preheat the oven to 350°F.

2. Cut the tops off the peppers. Remove the stems and chop up the pepper tops.

4. Place the peppers upright in a baking dish and set them aside.

3. Remove and discard the stems, seeds, and membranes.

5. In a large skillet, heat 2 tablespoons of the olive oil over medium-high heat. Add the beef, season with salt and black pepper, and cook until the beef is browned.

6. Place the meat on a plate and set it aside.

7. Add the remaining 2 tablespoons olive oil to the skillet. Add the onion and chopped pepper tops and cook until they begin to soften, 3 to 4 minutes.

8. Add the garlic and zucchini and cook for another minute.

9. Add the tomatoes and season with salt and a pinch or two of red pepper flakes.

10. Cook until everything is heated through, about 2 minutes.

11. Add the beef . . .

12. And the rice . . .

13. And stir it together.

14. Stir in 1 cup of the cheese. Taste and adjust the seasoning.

15. Fill the peppers with the rice-beef mixture . . .

16. And top the peppers with the remaining cheese.

17. Pour a small amount of water into the bottom of the baking dish, then cover the pan with foil and bake the peppers for 30 minutes.

18. Uncover and bake until the peppers are soft and the cheese is melted and lightly browned, another 15 to 20 minutes.

19. Serve up 1 to 2 peppers, depending on each person's appetite. (I'll give you one guess as to how many I had!)

HELPFUL HINTS

- *Make the rice-beef mixture, assemble the peppers, cover the pan, and refrigerate, for up to 24 hours before baking.*

- *Turn this into a meal kit! Store the hollowed-out peppers, the rice-beef mixture, and the cheese in separate containers up to 2 or 3 days ahead of time. Assemble the peppers and bake them as you need them—all together, or one at a time!*

Contemplative cattleman.

Broccolini with Garlic and
Lemon (page 282)

MINI TURKEY MEATLOAVES

MAKES 18 MEATLOAVES

I make no bones about how much I love meatloaf. I have a great recipe for a full-size loaf that I still get love letters about, over ten years after first sharing it online. And okay, they aren't love letters. They're emails. And the love is actually directed toward the meatloaf, not toward me. Or if it's directed toward me, it's only indirectly directed. Or something like that. Point is, I may not be a professionally trained culinary genius . . . but meatloaf? I got this one!

Sometimes it's fun, rather than making a big whopper of a meatloaf (which can take upward of 90 minutes to cook all the way through, by the way), to make smaller loaves using a plain ol' muffin pan. And to prove that I have no official business relationship with the beef industry (well, other than the fact that my beloved is a cattle rancher), I sometimes like to take a walk on the wild side and substitute ground turkey for the beef. Of course, I compensate for the loss of fat in a dastardly way that you'll see in the recipe, proving, I suppose, that I'm shameless.

These are wonderful, guys!

Cooking spray

6 slices white bread

1 cup whole milk

2½ pounds ground turkey

4 slices bacon, cut into very small bits

1 cup ketchup, plus more if needed

½ teaspoon seasoned salt (such as Lawry's)

½ teaspoon black pepper

½ teaspoon red pepper flakes

3 tablespoons finely minced parsley, plus more for serving

Life is too short for matching socks! (Right, Alex?)

1. Preheat the oven to 350°F. Generously coat 18 muffin cups with cooking spray.

2. Place the bread in a small bowl and slowly pour the milk over it. Toss and let the bread sit for a few minutes.

3. In a separate large bowl, place the turkey and bacon.

4. Add the bread and any extra milk in the bowl . . .

5. Along with ¼ cup of the ketchup and the seasoned salt, black pepper, red pepper flakes, and parsley . . .

6. And use your hands to mix it all together, stopping when you still have some nice chunks of bread visible. It will look completely bizarre and a little grody at this point, but don't you worry!

7. Place a ¼-cup scoop of the mixture in each muffin cup . . .

8. Then squirt about ½ teaspoon of the ketchup on the top of each meatloaf.

9. Use a spoon to smear the ketchup evenly over the top, then use it to nudge the edges of the meatloaf away from the pan a bit. (This just neatens them up a little.)

10. Bake the meatloaves for 25 minutes, then carefully squirt another ½ teaspoon of ketchup on top of each one, spreading it carefully with a spoon to cover as much of the surface as possible. Continue to bake for another 30 minutes . . .

11. Until completely cooked through and sizzling around the edges. If there are any large areas without ketchup, go ahead and squirt/spread as needed.

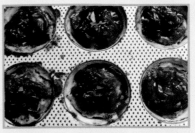

12. Sprinkle the meatloaves with parsley, then let them sit in the pan for 5 to 7 minutes before serving. This will be difficult because they smell *soooooo* good, but letting them sit allows them to firm up a bit and come out of the pan more easily. Run a sharp knife around the edges of the loaves to loosen them if they stick.

13. Serve them warm with a veggie on the side.

Yum yum yum! These are so tasty. The chunks of bread inside are heaven.

If only she would mow.

HELPFUL HINT: Let the meatloaves cool, flash freeze them, then pop them into plastic zipper bags. Reheat them in the microwave!

CHANGE THINGS UP!

• *Substitute ground beef for the ground turkey. Halve the amount of bacon.*

• *Dice and caramelize half an onion and add it to the meat mixture.*

• *Substitute any kind of bread—whole wheat, ciabatta, French, and so on.*

"Eat mor turkee."

Make-ahead · Freezes well

KING RANCH CHICKEN

MAKES 8 TO 12 SERVINGS (DEPENDING ON HOW HUNGRY THEY ARE!)

This is a very popular casserole round these parts, and it's named for the famous King Ranch in south Texas. It's definitely under the "brown . . . hot . . . and plenty of it" category of recipes, and while it might not win any beauty contests anytime soon, it just might be one of the finalists for "Most Tasty"!

A plus: You can assemble this yummy casserole ahead of time and bake it when you're ready. It's very forgiving! (Most popular casseroles are.)

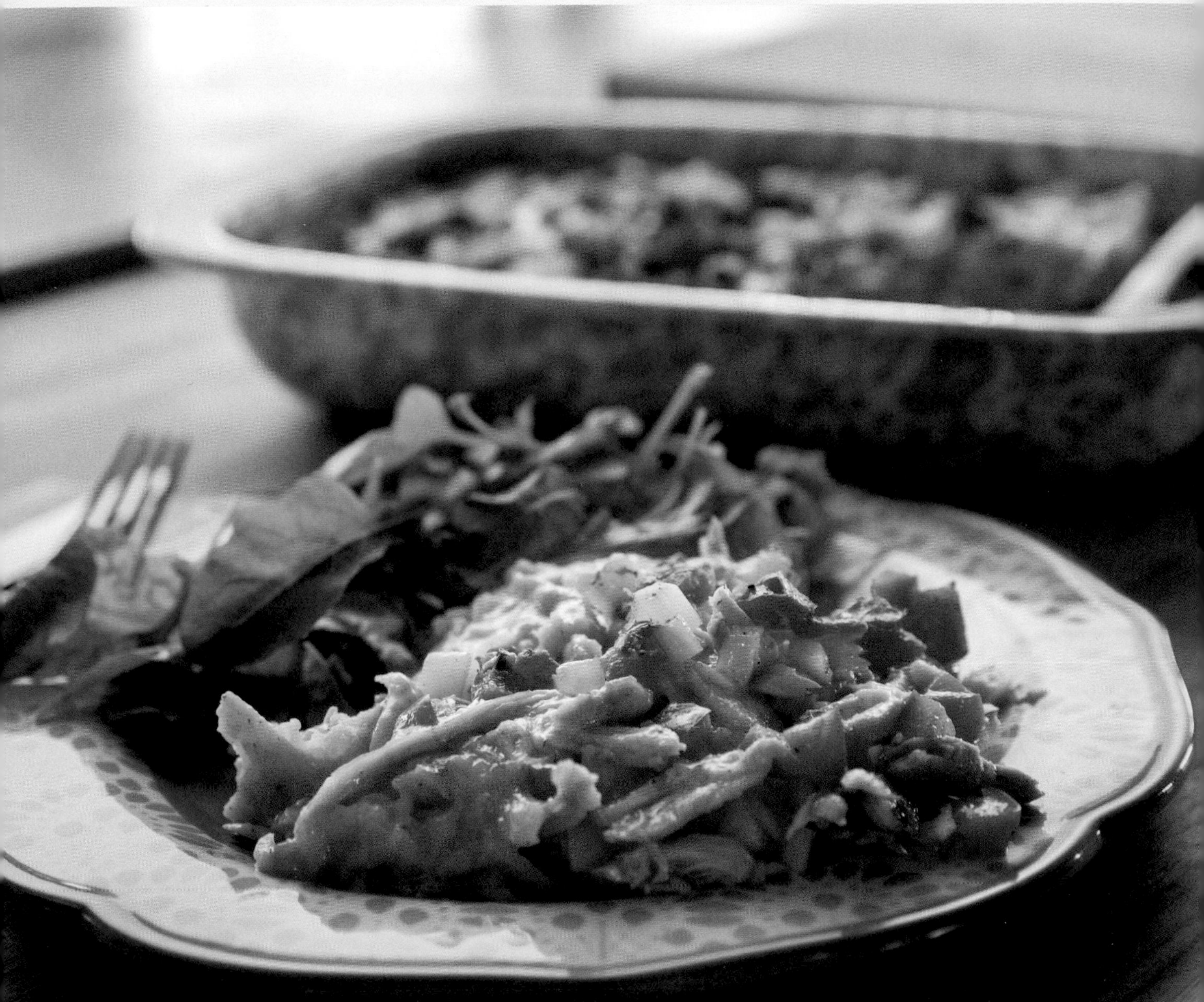

Butter, for greasing

1 large white or yellow onion, finely diced

1 red bell pepper, seeded and finely diced

1 yellow bell pepper, seeded and finely diced

1 jalapeño, finely diced

1 whole chicken, roasted and cooled (rotisserie chicken works great!)

One 10.5-ounce can cream of chicken soup

One 10.5-ounce can cream of mushroom soup

One 10-ounce can diced tomatoes and chiles (such as Ro*Tel)

2 tablespoons chili powder

1 teaspoon ground cumin

¼ teaspoon cayenne pepper

½ teaspoon kosher salt

½ teaspoon black pepper

2 cups chicken broth

16 corn tortillas, torn into pieces

1½ cups grated sharp Cheddar cheese

1½ cups grated Monterey Jack cheese

1. Preheat the oven to 350°F. Butter a 9 x 13-inch baking dish.

2. Prep all the veggies and tear the cooked (and cooled!) chicken into chunks.

3. Next, make the soup-tomato mixture, which is very bizarre and might scare you off. But please: Be brave and stick with me through this challenging time. You won't be sorry! In a large bowl, combine the soups and diced tomatoes and chiles.

4. Add the chili powder, cumin, cayenne, salt, black pepper, and chicken broth . . .

5. Then—this is the time to be strong—stir it all together. Trust me!

6. Line the bottom of the baking dish with half the torn tortillas. Layer on half the chicken . . .

7. And half the onion, bell peppers, and jalapeño.

8. Sprinkle on half the cheeses . . .

9. And pour on half the wacky soup mixture.

10. Then repeat the layers, beginning with the rest of the tortillas . . .

11. And ending with the rest of the *you-know-what.*

12. Cover with foil and bake for 45 minutes, then uncover and bake until bubbling, another 15 minutes.

13. Look at that! Serve it with a salad and a dang hearty appetite.

CHANGE THINGS UP!

- *Turn the casserole into well-behaved enchiladas: Put the vegetables and chicken into corn tortillas, roll them up, pour the sauce over them, and top with cheese.*

- *Turn it into lasagna! Use layers of cooked lasagna noodles instead of corn tortillas.*

Me and Paige, Paige and me, we're always together as you can see. (Shout out to Shel Silverstein!)

CINCINNATI CHILI

MAKES 10 TO 12 SERVINGS

Over my years of blogging I've made a few friends from Cincinnati, and since I usually wind up talking about food with my friends (no matter where they're from!), I've learned all about the fine art of Cincinnati chili. And as I'll explain in a minute, the restaurants that serve it have the most interesting ordering system as a way to keep the variations separate. It takes the fun of chili to a whole new level (and you'll love the interesting mix of spices, too!).

2 tablespoons vegetable oil

1 large onion, finely chopped, plus more for serving

5 garlic cloves, minced

2 pounds ground beef

One 15-ounce can tomato sauce

2 cups beef broth

2 tablespoons white vinegar

2 tablespoons tomato paste

3 tablespoons chili powder

2 teaspoons ground cumin

1 teaspoon ground cinnamon

¼ teaspoon ground cloves

¼ teaspoon ground allspice

2 bay leaves

1 tablespoon Worcestershire sauce

1 pound spaghetti, cooked, for serving

Finely grated sharp Cheddar cheese, for serving

Drained canned kidney beans, for serving

1. In a large Dutch oven, heat the oil over medium-high heat. Add the onion and garlic and cook for a couple of minutes, until they start to soften. Add the beef . . .

4. The tomato paste . . .

7. And stir together. Reduce the heat to low and cook the chili for 1 hour, stirring occasionally.

2. And cook until it's totally browned. Drain off the excess fat; you don't need that stuff!

5. The chili powder, cumin and other spices, and bay leaves . . .

8. It's all ready . . . and it smells amazing!

3. Add the tomato sauce, beef broth, and vinegar . . .

6. And the Worcestershire . . .

9. Now, serving it up is the fun part! There's 2-Way, which is chili served over spaghetti.

10. There's 3-Way, which is chili served over spaghetti and topped with cheese . . .

11. But wait! There's more! 4-Way is the aforementioned, plus chopped onion.

12. And—crazytown!—5-Way, which includes beans on top! My goodness.

So many choices. And I'll make the time!

There's a bright golden haze on the meadow. Big time.

MEAT PIES

MAKES 36 HAND PIES

Meat pies are big around here. It's a popular specialty in the Native American community in and around Osage County, and you can often find meat pie artisans selling their creations at sidewalk stands and in parking lots. They are delicious, and I never met a meat pie I didn't like.

My way of making meat pies involves using frozen dinner rolls, which is perhaps one of my top five favorite convenience ingredients of all time. They take all the hassle out of making dough from scratch, which means you can spend more time enjoying every bite of your pie. (Or pies, in my case!)

36 frozen unbaked dinner rolls (I use Rhodes)

1 tablespoon vegetable oil

2 poblano peppers (or green bell peppers), seeded and roughly chopped

1 onion, cut into medium dice

½ teaspoon red pepper flakes

4 garlic cloves, minced

1½ pounds lean ground beef

1 tablespoon chili powder

1 teaspoon ground cumin

Kosher salt

2 heaping tablespoons tomato paste

1 cup grated pepper Jack cheese

⅓ cup chopped parsley

Black pepper

Flour, for rolling

Egg wash: 2 eggs whisked with 2 tablespoons water

1. To start the crust, put the frozen rolls on a baking sheet. Cover with a tea towel and let thaw and rise for 2 to 3 hours.

4. Add the red pepper flakes and garlic and cook for another couple of minutes. Transfer to a bowl or plate and set aside.

7. Add the tomato paste and ¼ cup water and stir until combined.

2. For the filling: In a large skillet, heat the oil over medium heat. Add the poblano peppers and onion . . .

5. Put the same skillet over medium-high heat, add the beef, and start to cook, breaking up the lumps with a spoon.

8. Return the cooked vegetables to the pan and stir them in.

3. And cook until softened, about 4 minutes.

6. Add the chili powder, cumin, and ¾ teaspoon salt and cook until the meat is no longer pink, 5 to 7 minutes. Pour off the excess grease.

9. Transfer the meat mixture to a bowl and set aside to cool.

10. When the meat is completely cool, add the pepper Jack and parsley. Season with salt and black pepper to taste . . .

11. And stir to combine.

12. Preheat the oven to 400°F. Line a baking sheet with parchment paper. On a lightly floured surface, roll out each dinner roll into a 4-inch round about ¼ inch thick.

13. Put 1½ tablespoons of the meat filling in the center of each round.

14. Fold over the dough . . .

15. To form half-moon shapes and lightly press the edges together.

16. Crimp the edges with a fork . . .

17. And transfer the pies to the prepared baking sheet.

18. Brush the tops with the egg wash.

19. Bake the pies until they're golden brown, 10 to 12 minutes.

Presley has perfected the art of the canine head tilt!

They're absolutely amazing.

HELPFUL HINTS

- *Freeze the meat pies after baking. Heat them in the microwave for 3 to 4 minutes, then let them stand for 1 minute before serving. (Or you can heat them in a 300°F oven for 10 minutes!)*

- *If you want to bake them fresh, flash freeze the meat pies after you brush on the egg wash, then transfer to a plastic zipper bag. Let them thaw for 30 minutes outside the bag, then bake as per the recipe.*

"I don't know anything about meat pies, but I can show you a COW pie if you'd like."

Make-ahead · Fancy

LOBSTER MAC AND CHEESE

MAKES 6 TO 8 SERVINGS

Lobster mac and cheese is an extravagance, no question! But that doesn't mean it's complicated—*au contraire*. If you can watch for sales on lobster tails, you can pull this off without breaking the bank. So make it for that special birthday dinner . . . or heck, that regular Tuesday-night dinner. What's stoppin' ya?

3 raw lobster tails

6 tablespoons (¾ stick) butter, plus more for buttering the baking dish

¼ cup all-purpose flour

2 cups whole milk

½ cup half-and-half

1 teaspoon kosher salt

Black pepper

1 cup shelf-stable grated Parmesan cheese (such as Kraft)

¾ cup grated sharp Cheddar cheese

¾ cup grated Fontina cheese

4 ounces goat cheese

8 ounces cavatappi (or any macaroni-style pasta), cooked a little less than al dente

1 tablespoon finely minced parsley

1. Preheat the oven to 350°F. Butter a 2-quart baking dish.

2. First, remove the lobster meat from the tails, which really is simple! Use kitchen shears to snip the soft part of the shell (the underside) down both sides.

3. Grab one end of the underside and gently peel it away from the meat . . .

Took me about a minute and a half! I could have kept going, but the mac and cheese was getting more expensive with each tail, so I decided to stop here.

4. Then pull the meat away from the hard shell.

5. In a large skillet, melt 2 tablespoons of the butter over medium-high heat. Add the lobster tails and cook them for about 1 minute on one side . . .

6. Then turn over and cook for another minute. Remove to a plate. It won't be fully cooked yet, but don't worry—it's going in the oven.

7. Add the remaining 4 tablespoons butter to the skillet. Sprinkle in the flour . . .

8. And whisk to combine, cooking it for a couple of minutes. This is the roux!

9. Pour in the milk, whisking constantly, then cook the white sauce until thick and bubbling, 3 to 5 minutes.

10. Add the half-and-half, salt, and plenty of pepper and stir to keep cooking.

11. Add the Parmesan (holding back some for the topping) . . .

12. Along with the Cheddar and Fontina . . .

13. And, finally, the goat cheese (which is the cat's meow).

14. Chop the lobster into large chunks . . .

15. And mix it into the sauce.

16. Add the pasta and stir it in . . .

17. Then pour the mixture into the prepared baking dish.

18. Top with the reserved Parmesan . . .

19. And bake until bubbling and a slight crust forms on top, 20 to 25 minutes. Garnish with the parsley when it comes out of the oven.

Lobster mac and cheese is Alex's favorite!

And wow. Look at the results.

CHANGE THINGS UP!

- *Use 1 pound jumbo deveined shrimp in place of the lobster for a lower-cost dish. Or skip the seafood altogether!*
- *Add caramelized onion for even more amazing flavor.*
- *Add ½ cup sherry to the roux and cook for 1 minute, then add the milk.*

It's a winner!

SHEET PAN SUPPERS

There's nothing more indispensable than a simple rimmed sheet pan, and while they might resemble your favorite flat cookie sheet . . . they're definitely not just for cookies! The magic of these dinners is that they're all made in (and on) one pan, making prep and cleanup an absolute pleasure. Sheet pan suppers are sweeping the nation, and I'm definitely their number one fan.

Roasted Shrimp with Cherry Tomato..212

Chicken (Legs) and 40 Cloves of Garlic..214

Teriyaki Salmon and Kale..216

Veggietastic...219

Tuscan Chicken..222

Sausage and Root Vegetables...224

Chicken Fennel Bake..226

Spanish Salmon..230

Steak and Bell Pepper..232

ROASTED SHRIMP WITH CHERRY TOMATO SHEET PAN SUPPER

MAKES 4 SERVINGS

This is a lovely pan of shrimp and tomatoes, roasted in the oven until the tomatoes just start to burst, and it can be served with bread, pasta, or a simple salad.

(Or if you want to get sassy, pile it onto a hoagie bun with some spicy mayo and call it a sandwich!)

1 pound peeled, deveined shrimp, tails on

2 cups cherry tomatoes

8 garlic cloves, thinly sliced

Olive oil, for drizzling

Kosher salt and black pepper

1 lemon, halved

1. Preheat the oven to 400°F.

2. Place the shrimp and cherry tomatoes on a rimmed sheet pan. . .

3. Then add the garlic and drizzle everything with olive oil.

4. Sprinkle the whole thing with salt and pepper and toss so everything's coated.

5. Roast until the shrimp are opaque and the tomatoes begin to burst, 10 to 12 minutes.

6. Squeeze half the lemon over the top! (Cut the other half of the lemon into wedges.)

7. Serve it with salad and a wedge of lemon.

So light and lovely!

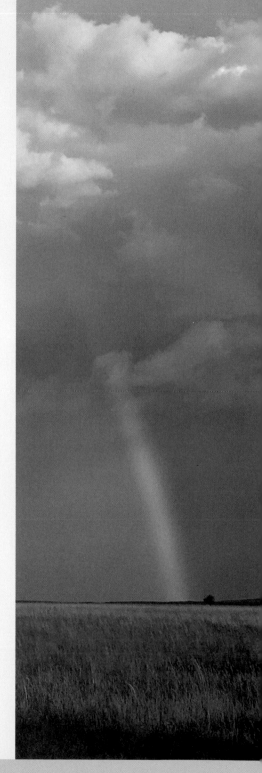

Every rainbow is a gift! I love them.

CHICKEN (LEGS) AND 40 CLOVES OF GARLIC SHEET PAN SUPPER

MAKES 6 SERVINGS

Whether it's carrying groceries in from my car or emptying the dishwasher, there are just some things I've gotten lazy about in my forties. Roasting whole chickens is one of those things. Oh, I love a roasted chicken just as much as anyone, but it's the cutting up and messing with the chicken after roasting that has wound up on my list of Nearly Banned Activities in the Kitchen.

My fix is to use chicken pieces and just throw them on a sheet pan. Sometimes I do a whole cut-up chicken, sometimes I do a mix of white and dark pieces, but my family's content forever if I roast a whole pan of legs. They're fun to eat, and let's face it . . . dark meat is sheer heaven.

12 chicken legs
40 garlic cloves
Kosher salt and black pepper
Olive oil, for drizzling
2 lemons
Crusty French bread, for serving

1. Preheat the oven to 400°F.

2. Arrange the chicken and garlic on a sheet pan.

3. Sprinkle with salt and pepper and drizzle with olive oil.

4. Squeeze on the juice of 1 lemon . . .

5. Then cut the other lemon into slices and arrange them on the pan.

6. Roast the chicken until cooked through, 40 to 45 minutes, carefully shaking the pan once or twice during the cooking process to keep the garlic from burning.

7. Serve with crusty French bread and spread the roasted garlic cloves on. Yum.

NOTE: *This chicken is just as good the next day, cold out of the fridge.*

Absolute angel. (Him, not me.)

TERIYAKI SALMON AND KALE SHEET PAN SUPPER

MAKES 4 SERVINGS

This is definitely one of the easiest recipes in this here cookbook. When I made it for the first time, I had it in the oven 4 minutes after starting the process, and I sort of looked around my kitchen, startled, thinking, *What just happened?* If anything could logically be described as "impossibly easy," this would be it.

If you've never experienced crispy kale, you are in for a serious treat. It's a great snack on its own, but *sooooo* perfect with the tender salmon. This dinner is a keeper, man!

1 large bunch kale	Four 6- to 8-ounce salmon fillets	½ cup teriyaki sauce (look for the thick kind)
1 tablespoon olive oil	Kosher salt and black pepper	

1. Preheat the oven to 425°F.

2. Strip the stems and center ribs out of the kale leaves and place the leaves on a baking sheet. Discard the ribs and stems.

3. Tear the leaves into smaller chunks.

4. Drizzle the kale with olive oil and toss, making sure the oil lightly coats all the pieces.

5. Nestle the salmon among the kale leaves, skin side down (if your fillets have skin) . . .

6. And sprinkle them with salt and pepper.

7. Drizzle a couple of teaspoons of teriyaki sauce over each fillet . . .

8. And brush it to lightly coat the surface.

9. Bake for about 10 minutes, shaking the pan once to make sure the kale doesn't burn. (It should brown a little around the edges.)

10. Warm the remaining teriyaki sauce in the microwave for about 15 seconds and pour it over each piece of salmon . . .

11. Letting it sit for a couple of minutes before serving.

(I can't even wait for a plate!)

CHANGE THINGS UP!

- *Use hoisin or any sticky sauce (even BBQ sauce!) instead of the teriyaki.*

- *Use a combo of honey and soy sauce for a slightly different flavor.*

- *Sprinkle the salmon with a little chili powder along with the salt and pepper to give it a bit of spice.*

VEGGIETASTIC SHEET PAN SUPPER

MAKES 4 SERVINGS

Warning: This recipe contains tofu. I realize this will make some of you run for the hills. I hope you'll stick around and consider trying this super-easy throw-together meatless meal, but I guess I'm saying that I understand if the word "tofu" makes you feel uneasy. Even scared. I want this to be a safe place for you, so I'm not going to push it.

Just know this: I am married to a cattle rancher and love a medium-rare rib-eye more than life itself. And I'll still eat tofu any time I get a chance. If it's prepared well, it can be downright delightful, and it's so good for you.

1 head cauliflower, broken into small florets

2 cups Brussels sprouts

1 large red bell pepper, seeded and cut into 1-inch chunks

One 14-ounce package extra-firm tofu

Olive oil, for drizzling

Kosher salt and black pepper, for sprinkling

¼ cup soy sauce

1. Preheat the oven to 375°F.

2. Let me show you the beauty of a sheet pan. If you have a cutting board that's thicker/higher than the rim of the pan, you can just prep the veggies . . .

4. Prep the Brussels sprouts: Cut off the stem ends, pulling off the outer leaves in the process . . .

6. And add them to the pan with the cauliflower.

3. And slide them right over. Doesn't get any easier than that!

5. Then cut the sprouts in half . . .

7. Next comes the tofu! Do not be afraid. I will be on this journey with you.

8. Remove the block of tofu from the package and press paper towels onto the surface to remove as much excess moisture as possible.

10. Cut the slices in half diagonally . . .

12. Drizzle the tofu and veggies with olive oil (probably ¼ to ⅓ cup total) and gently toss everything so it has a nice light coating. Use tongs or your fingers to turn the tofu slices to coat.

9. Slice the block vertically into rectangular slices, then pat the slices to remove even more moisture.

11. Then arrange them on the baking sheet with the vegetables.

13. Add a sprinkling of salt and pepper. Be generous with the salt, as the tofu needs a little help!

"Can someone show me how to dribble?"

14. Then add a little drop of soy sauce to the top of each triangle of tofu.

15. Use a brush or your fingers to spread everything out, then pop the pan in the oven to roast for 25 minutes . . .

16. Removing the pan and flipping the tofu halfway through.

17. When the tofu and veggies are browned around the edges, they're ready!

If you're looking for a nice, light meal . . . well, make yourself at home. No need to look any further! It's lovely with a glass of wine.

And a juicy rib-eye. Haha.

CHANGE THINGS UP!

- *Use other veggies: sliced zucchini, halved mushrooms, chunks of red onion, different colors of bell pepper.*
- *Omit the tofu and do an all-vegetable version; just do a little sprinkling of soy sauce with the olive oil and toss it all together.*
- *Serve the tofu-veggie mixture over cooked rice or noodles, with extra soy sauce on the side.*

TUSCAN CHICKEN SHEET PAN SUPPER

MAKES 4 SERVINGS

Don't tell anyone, but I do actually have a handful of recipes in this book that I can say are my favorites. Of course, I love every recipe in this book or else they would have been rejected, terminated, fired, and nixed long ago. But there are just a few that I love a *teeeeeny* bit more than the others, much like I always loved Charlie a *teeeeeny* bit more than the other dogs. I can't believe I just put that down on paper. I've hardly ever said it out loud. But I'm getting up there in years, and more and more I'm finding that I have things I need to say, and by golly, I'm going to say them!

(I can hear you, along with my parents, saying, "Um . . . I don't think you've had any problem expressing yourself up to this point." You think I don't hear you, but I do.)

(Also, please don't be mad at me for saying that I loved one of my dogs above the others. At least I wasn't talking about my children! And if you'd ever met Charlie, you would understand. I miss the malodorous ol' fella [see page 366].)

Anyway, this blessedly easy sheet pan meal is way up there for me. It couldn't be simpler, but it's always something I devour!

1 cup olive oil

⅓ cup balsamic vinegar

5 garlic cloves, minced

1 teaspoon dried parsley flakes

1 teaspoon dried basil

1 teaspoon kosher salt

1 teaspoon black pepper

4 boneless, skinless chicken breasts

5 or 6 large Roma tomatoes

1 pound green beans

2 tablespoons finely minced fresh parsley

1. In a bowl or pitcher, combine the olive oil, balsamic, and garlic . . .

2. Along with the parsley flakes, basil, salt, and pepper. Whisk until the marinade is emulsified.

3. Place the chicken in a large plastic zipper bag and pour in half the marinade. Seal the bag and set it aside.

4. Halve the tomatoes lengthwise . . .

5. And trim the ends off the green beans.

6. Place the veggies in a large zipper bag . . .

7. And pour in the rest of the marinade. Seal the bag and marinate both bags in the fridge for up to 2 hours (or make it right away).

8. Preheat the oven to 425°F. Arrange the chicken and veggies on a sheet pan (discard any marinade left in the bags).

9. Roast for 25 minutes, gently shaking the pan once during that time. The chicken should be cooked through and the vegetables starting to brown nicely.

10. Sprinkle on the fresh parsley and serve!

CHANGE THINGS UP!

- *A few minutes before the chicken is done, lay slices of fresh mozzarella on each breast. Return the pan to the oven until melted.*

- *Sprinkle ½ cup grated Parmesan all over the pan as soon as you remove it from the oven. Let it sit a few minutes before serving.*

- *Serve with crumbled feta cheese all over the top (my favorite way to enjoy this!).*

SAUSAGE AND ROOT VEGETABLES SHEET PAN SUPPER

MAKES 4 GENEROUS SERVINGS

To me, a girl who grew up in the center of the country, sausage comes in the form of a patty. It is served with breakfast and it's packaged with names like Jimmy Dean and J.C. Potter. But over the years of working on my cooking show with a largely British television crew, I have learned that sausage is a whole food group unto itself. Those guys take sausage seriously, and it often takes the prime spot as the main protein of a weeknight dinner.

Personally, I think this is weird, but sometimes weird things can be delicious! Sausages are great for sheet pan suppers because their flavors can't help but make their way onto the veggies you use, and golly, by the time dinner is over, you feel like a proper Englishman! (Or Englishwoman, in my case.)

You'll love this easy, throw-together supper. The veggies take a few minutes to prep, but that's pretty much all there is to it!

½ pound Brussels sprouts, trimmed and halved

2 parsnips, peeled and cut into wedges

2 sweet potatoes, peeled and cut into wedges

2 medium red onions, quartered

3 tablespoons olive oil

½ teaspoon dried sage

2 teaspoons kosher salt

1 teaspoon black pepper

8 Italian sausages

1. Preheat the oven to 375°F.

2. Scatter the Brussels sprouts, parsnips, sweet potatoes, and onions onto a sheet pan.

3. Drizzle with the olive oil and sprinkle with the sage, salt, and pepper. Toss everything with your hands.

4. Lay the sausages right on top of the vegetables . . .

5. And roast until the sausages are cooked through and the vegetables are tender, 40 to 45 minutes.

6. Serve a couple of sausages on a plate with the delicious veggies!

CHANGE THINGS UP!

* *Serve with a small dish of spicy mustard on the side for dipping.*
* *Use a combination of onions and sliced bell peppers instead of the Brussels sprouts and root veggies for a sausage-and-pepper sheet of wonder!*

"Hahahaha! You just slay me!"

CHICKEN FENNEL BAKE

MAKES 6 SERVINGS

I don't use fennel very much at all, but it is so special and tasty that anytime I *do* use it, I always feel really clever. I also feel really *dumb*, because if it's so tasty, why don't I use it more?

Is life supposed to be this hard?

I think I was scared about fennel because of my fear that it would taste like black licorice, which is right up there with bananas on my short list of foods that I loathe, but it doesn't taste like licorice at all, especially when it's slow-roasted alongside lemony chicken thighs. That was an extremely long sentence.

I repeat: Is life supposed to be this hard?

2 fennel bulbs

Kosher salt and black pepper

5 lemons

¼ cup olive oil

1 pound baby potatoes

1 cup baby carrots or 3-inch peeled carrot chunks

6 bone-in, skin-on chicken thighs

1. Preheat the oven to 375°F. Line a sheet pan with foil.

2. Trim the fennel bulbs, quarter them, and cut out the hard cores. Cut the fennel quarters into thick slices.

3. Arrange them on the center of the baking sheet and sprinkle them with salt and pepper.

4. Zest 2 of the lemons and set the zest aside, then juice these lemons into a medium bowl. Whisk the olive oil into the lemon juice and season with salt and pepper.

5. Halve the remaining 3 lemons and add them to the bowl, along with the potatoes . . .

6. And the carrots. Toss to coat the vegetables.

7. Spread the potatoes and lemons on either side of the fennel on the baking sheet.

8. Put the chicken in the same bowl, along with the lemon zest and more salt and pepper. Toss to coat . . .

9. And lay the chicken on top of the fennel, skin side up.

10. Bake, stirring the potatoes and carrots halfway through, until the chicken is cooked through and the vegetables are tender, 50 minutes to 1 hour.

11. Serve the chicken with the vegetables and roasted lemon halves.

CHANGE IT UP!

- *Add 3 sliced celery stalks to the bowl with the vegetables.*
- *Add 1 teaspoon paprika and ½ teaspoon ground cumin to the bowl with the chicken thighs to give it a different flavor.*
- *Add chunks of peeled sweet potato instead of carrots.*

Cattle Ranch Communications

When Ladd and I were married in 1996, cell phones certainly existed, but they had not become handheld and portable in any widespread way. And they certainly hadn't infiltrated communications on a cattle ranch: All the vehicles, whether personal pickups or feed trucks, were fitted with CB radios (yes, the "Breaker 1-9, this is CB Savage" kind), and that was the method of communication between cowboys.

And cowboys' wives. I remember riding with Ladd in his feed truck late one afternoon when a female voice sung through the radio: "Roy?" she asked. "What time are you going to be home for dinner?" When no one answered, she repeated her question with a little more gusto. "Roy!!! Roy??? What time will you be home for dinner?!?"

Roy was a cowboy from a neighboring ranch, and since the radio channel the cowboys used was often shared by many different people in the area, his wife Darla's inquiry was likely heard by up to fifty (or more) rough-and-tumble agricultural types. I remember glancing over at Ladd somewhere in the middle of Darla's second attempt. While he didn't say a word, he had the most uncomfortable look on his face, and I swear he almost imperceptibly shook his head as if to say, "Aw, c'mon . . . don't do that to old Roy." I vowed to myself that day that I would never in my life get on the CB radio, period, let alone to ask Ladd what time he'd be home for dinner. I think that's why I taught myself to make roasts and other slow-cooked dinners—so timing wouldn't be an issue and I wouldn't care what time he'd be home for dinner. I didn't want to run the risk of being tempted to use that blasted radio.

Through the years, CB radios dropped out of sight. The old vehicles with CBs installed started being replaced by radio-less trucks, and today, there's not a cowboy (or cowgirl) without a cell phone in his (or her) pocket. This really comes in handy, even more so than CBs did, because communication can take place between cowboys on horses as well as cowboys in trucks. It's incredibly efficient, and I'm not sure how Drummond Ranch ever got by without them!

(A bonus: Paige can post selfies and text her friends from her horse. Cowgirl social media is a real thing, you know!)

SPANISH SALMON SHEET PAN SUPPER

MAKES 6 SERVINGS

As I vociferously state on page 136, I positively hated salmon from age zero to age approximately forty-five. Well, let me clarify that: I started loving *smoked* salmon when I was about thirty-nine. Cooked salmon fillets were what I had monumental problems with. But I am so happy I made it to forty-five so I could discover the glory! Salmon is incredibly versatile, and particularly wonderful in the sense that it cooks really, really quickly.

And that'll make ya smile.

3 red onions, cut into wedges

3 red bell peppers, seeded and cut into 6 slices each

¾ cup pitted green olives

1 small round sourdough bread loaf, cut into 1-inch cubes

1 teaspoon smoked paprika

Kosher salt and black pepper

5 tablespoons olive oil

Six 6-ounce skinless salmon fillets

2 tablespoons chopped parsley

1. Preheat the oven to 375°F.

2. Drop the onions and peppers onto a sheet pan . . .

3. Along with the olives.

4. Arrange the bread cubes all over the veggies . . .

5. Then sprinkle on the paprika and salt and black pepper to taste.

6. Drizzle 3 tablespoons of the olive oil over the bread and veggies and toss them with your hands. Bake for 15 minutes.

7. Rub the salmon with the remaining 2 tablespoons olive oil and sprinkle it with salt and black pepper. Arrange the salmon among the vegetables and croutons on the baking sheet.

8. Bake until the salmon is just barely cooked through, 10 to 12 minutes. Sprinkle the whole pan with the parsley . . .

9. And divide the salmon and veggies among six plates.

Delicious, light (well, except for the whole bread thing, but we'll think about that tomorrow!), and lovely.

CHANGE IT UP!
- *Use a mix of olives—a variety of colors and sizes are great!*
- *Substitute any boneless fish for the salmon.*

Smile, and the world smiles with you!

STEAK AND BELL PEPPER SHEET PAN SUPPER

MAKES 2 SERVINGS

I go years—I'm not exaggerating!—between cooking steaks under my broiler. I don't know why; I'm just not programmed that way. I'm a skillet kinda girl. Please love me anyway.

I think my hesitation to use the broiler for steaks has to do with my fear of gray meat. You all know what I'm talking about: that awful color when the surface isn't cooked with adequate heat. Blech. Gray meat is the stuff of nightmares! Right up there with elevators with no buttons! And rats!

But then I make something like this and realize just how wonderful a tool the ol' oven broiler is. And if your steak is thick enough, you needn't worry about overcooking it before the surface gets brown. This is my current favorite sheet pan supper in the Western hemisphere!

2 red bell peppers, seeded and cut into thick rounds

2 yellow bell peppers, seeded and cut into thick rounds

1 large onion, cut into thick rounds

2 boneless rib-eye steaks, about 1½ inches thick

4 tablespoons (½ stick) butter

Montreal (or other) steak seasoning, for sprinkling

1. Position one rack in the center of the oven and another one on the highest level in the oven. Preheat the broiler to high.

2. Arrange the peppers and onion on a sheet pan . . .

3. And lay the steaks right on top.

4. Place 1 tablespoon of the butter on each steak and sprinkle the top with seasoning.

5. Place the pan on the center oven rack and broil for 3 to 4 minutes, until the surface of the steak begins to brown.

6. Using metal tongs, carefully turn the steaks over. Sprinkle this side with seasoning and lay the remaining butter on top.

7. Broil until the top is starting to really brown, 3 to 4 more minutes. Take a peek a minute or two into this stage; if it doesn't seem like the broiler is browning the steaks adequately, place the pan on the highest rack and give it another minute or two!

Look at that steak!

Perfectly medium-rare.

Winner winner, steak dinner!

MEATLESS MARVELS

You can't imagine the struggle I endured while trying to decide if I, the wife of a cattle rancher, could possibly include a meatless section in this cookbook and still live with myself in the morning. Finally, I decided that yes! Yes, I could! As a former vegetarian, I know as much as anyone that I can adore meat *and* meatless at the same time. There's good stuff in here, friends!

Citrus Salad with Vinaigrette...236

Pantry Pasta...238

Broccoli Cheese Potatoes...240

Roasted Vegetable Panzanella...243

Festive Pasta Salad..246

Cauliflower Crust Pizza...251

Shortcut Ravioli..254

Greek Grilled Eggplant Steaks...258

Quinoa and Roasted Veggie Salad...260

True Pasta Primavera..263

CITRUS SALAD WITH VINAIGRETTE

MAKES 8 TO 10 SERVINGS

I've always believed—even when I was a little girl—that Heaven must smell like citrus. I don't know where this (admittedly theologically questionable) notion ever came from, but I suspect its roots exist in the fact that I have never taken a big, deep whiff of a citrus fruit without closing my eyes and feeling like I was in paradise.

Any combination of citrus fruit can be used, so just play with whatever combination you can get your hands on. (I even got a little daring and included some limes, mostly for color . . . but they wound up being a nice tart touch!)

3 oranges

2 blood oranges

2 limes

1 medium grapefruit

½ cup olive oil

2 tablespoons white wine vinegar

1 tablespoon fresh thyme leaves

Kosher salt and black pepper

2 heads butter lettuce, leaves separated

1 head romaine lettuce, chopped

1 medium red onion, sliced into thin rounds

½ cup pecans, roughly chopped

1 cup feta cheese crumbles

Sliced fresh chives

Blood oranges = gorgeous!

1. Carefully slice the peel off all the citrus, then cut off the top and bottom. (Reserve half an orange for the juice.)

2. Cut each piece of peeled fruit into neat slices . . .

3. And keep going until all the fruit is sliced.

4. In a medium bowl, whisk together the olive oil, vinegar, juice from the reserved half orange, thyme, and salt and pepper to taste.

5. Arrange the greens on a large platter.

6. Lay slices of citrus all over the greens . . .

7. Overlapping all the citrusy goodness.

8. Add the onion slices (separated into rings) . . .

9. Drizzle on the dressing . . .

10. And sprinkle on the pecans, feta, and chives.

If you love citrus . . . this is pretty much the best day of your life.

PANTRY PASTA

MAKES 8 SERVINGS

It may not look it, but this is one of the most popular quick recipes I've ever made on my teevee show. This fact is hilarious when you consider that *almost* every single ingredient comes from the pantry. It's one of those dinners you make when your fridge is empty, your freezer is pitiful, and it's still a couple of days away from your big shopping trip of the month/quarter/year.

And it's delicious!

2 tablespoons olive oil

½ red onion, diced

⅓ cup vegetable broth or white wine

One 14.5-ounce can diced tomatoes, with juice

⅓ cup assorted olives, pitted and roughly chopped

One 15-ounce can artichoke hearts, drained and halved

2 garlic cloves, minced

Kosher salt and black pepper

8 ounces corkscrew pasta (rotini), cooked according to the package directions

2 tablespoons prepared pesto

½ cup fork-chunked feta cheese

1. In a skillet, heat the olive oil over medium heat. Add the onion . . .

2. And stir and cook for a few minutes, until it softens and starts to turn brown.

3. Pour in the broth and tomatoes with their juices . . .

4. Then add the olives . . .

5. The artichokes . . .

6. The garlic, and salt and pepper to taste.

7. Stir to combine, reduce the heat to low, and simmer, stirring occasionally, for about 15 minutes.

8. Add the cooked pasta to the skillet and stir to combine with the sauce.

9. Add the pesto and stir it in . . .

10. Then add the feta chunks and serve!

CHANGE THINGS UP!

- *Add jarred roasted red peppers, cut into strips.*
- *Add drained capers.*
- *Add minced anchovies.*
- *Add 2 tablespoons toasted pine nuts.*

Kid-friendly

BROCCOLI CHEESE POTATOES

MAKES 6 SERVINGS

A good ol' baked potato is such an awesome foundation for a good ol' weeknight meal. In the Drummond house, we've been known to top baked potatoes with chili, bacon, and Cheddar; beef stew; even leftover spaghetti sauce! (We like to eat.) But a favorite of my blond-headed boy, Bryce, and mine is this tasty broccoli-cheese version. It's a cross between a tater and broccoli cheese soup, and it's pretty much a dream.

6 russet potatoes

Vegetable oil, for frying

1 medium onion, thinly sliced

2 heads broccoli, cut into small florets

4 tablespoons (½ stick) butter

¼ cup all-purpose flour

1½ cups whole milk

2 cups shredded Cheddar cheese

2 cups shredded pepper Jack cheese

1. Preheat the oven to 350°F. Poke a few holes in the potatoes with a fork. Set them on a rimmed baking sheet and bake until tender, 50 to 60 minutes. (Or, if you're in a hurry, cook the potatoes in the microwave!)

2. Fry up some onions for the top of the potatoes: In a skillet over medium-low heat, add ¼ inch of vegetable oil. Add the onion and fry . . .

3. Until browned and crisp, 15 to 20 minutes. Drain on paper towels and keep warm.

4. Meanwhile, bring a pot of water to a boil and fill a bowl with ice water. Blanch the broccoli by throwing the florets into the boiling water for about 1½ minutes.

5. Immediately drain the broccoli and plunge it into the bowl of ice water to stop the cooking process. Drain the broccoli and set it aside.

6. To make the cheesy sauce, in a medium saucepan, melt the butter over medium heat. Sprinkle in the flour . . .

7. And cook for a minute or so, being careful not to let it get too brown.

8. Whisk in the milk and cook until it thickens, about 4 minutes.

9. Reduce the heat to low, stir in the Cheddar and pepper Jack, and let them melt.

10. Add the broccoli . . .

11. And stir it in, letting the broccoli warm through.

12. Make a slit down the length of each potato using a fork. Push in the ends to open up the potatoes and break up some of the potato inside. Pour a big, luscious ladle of the cheese sauce over each potato.

And if this isn't delicious enough . . .

13. Sprinkle on the crispy fried onions.

HELPFUL HINT: *Use frozen broccoli to eliminate the blanching step. Simply thaw it under hot running water, pat dry, and add to the cheese sauce.*

CHANGE THINGS UP!

- Substitute cauliflower florets for half the broccoli.
- Use canned French fried onions for a quick shortcut!

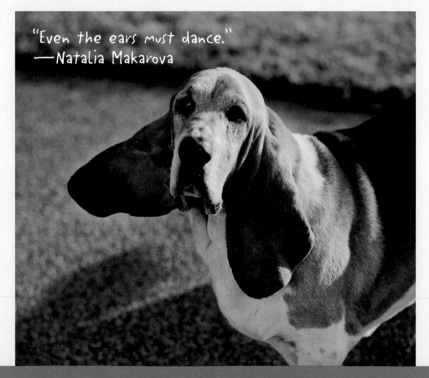

"Even the ears must dance."
—Natalia Makarova

Make-ahead · Fancy

ROASTED VEGETABLE PANZANELLA

MAKES 6 TO 8 SERVINGS

Panzanella is just a fancy name for bread salad! It usually involves tomatoes and cucumbers, tossed with chunks of day-old bread and a zesty vinaigrette . . . but I like to have some fun with my panzanella and use roasted veggies instead. It takes a little extra time, but it isn't complicated at all . . . and since it needs to sit for an hour or two after you make it, it's a great make-ahead dinner for company (or just for family!).

1 small butternut squash

3 carrots, peeled and cut into 2-inch chunks

3 parsnips, peeled and cut into 2-inch chunks

1 medium red onion, cut into 1-inch chunks

1 medium yellow squash, cut into 1-inch chunks

1 medium zucchini, cut into 1-inch chunks

Kosher salt and black pepper

¼ cup olive oil, plus more for drizzling

1½ tablespoons red wine vinegar

Ciabatta or other crusty loaf, cut into 2-inch cubes (see Note)

12 ounces fresh mozzarella cheese, cut into 1-inch cubes

8 basil leaves

1. Preheat the oven to 400°F.

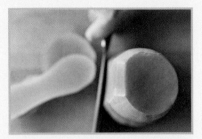

2. First, a quick butternut squash moment: I use a sharp knife to carefully slice off the peel. You can use a vegetable peeler, but it can be a little slow going; that skin is tough!

3. From there you can cut the peeled squash into 2-inch cubes.

4. Put the butternut squash on a rimmed baking sheet with the carrots and parsnips . . .

5. And put the onion, yellow squash, and zucchini on a separate rimmed baking sheet.

6. Season both pans with salt and pepper and drizzle on a little olive oil.

7. Roast the vegetables for 40 to 45 minutes for the butternut squash pan and 25 to 30 minutes for the zucchini pan.

8. Set the pans aside to cool.

9. Next, make the dressing: In a small jar, shake together the olive oil, vinegar, and salt and pepper to taste.

10. Put the ciabatta in a large bowl . . .

11. And add all the roasted veggies.

12. The mozzarella chunks come next . . .

13. Followed by the dressing. I usually add two-thirds to three-quarters of the dressing (then I add more after I toss it, just to make sure I don't add too much).

14. Toss everything together . . .

15. Then tear in the basil leaves! Dang, this looks so good. But here's the hard part! After it's all tossed and ready, you need to lightly cover the bowl with a clean kitchen towel and let it sit for about 1 hour (if you have the time!).

The result will be the best dang bread salad you've ever tasted! Serve with a glass of chilled white wine.

NOTE: *It's best if the bread cubes have been set out at room temperature for several hours to get slightly dry; but if you don't have time, fresh bread is fine!*

HELPFUL HINT: *You can roast the veggies, cube the bread, cube the cheese, and make the dressing well in advance. Then just toss it all together an hour before you want to serve it!*

CHANGE THINGS UP!

- *Use cubes of dried cornbread instead of ciabatta for a totally different experience.*
- *Roast chunks of different colors of tomatoes instead of the other vegetables.*
- *Toss in 4 cups baby arugula or baby spinach.*

Do you have a map? I just got lost in your smile.

FESTIVE PASTA SALAD

MAKES 6 SERVINGS

I made this colorful, crunchy, carb-filled salad one day when my mom was visiting. She had just made a batch of her ultra-healthy muffins (page 24) and I said, "Since you're making your healthy muffins, I'm going to make us a salad for lunch!"

"Oh, sounds perfect!" my mom exclaimed.

"And I'm going to put noodles and cheese in it," I said. "Because we're worth it."

I got no argument from my mom, so I moved forward with this fun, really tasty salad that I had actually started thinking about during the sermon at church the day before. It has crunchy lettuce and colorful tomatoes and the carby wonderfulness of pasta . . . with a delicious pesto flavor throughout. Not that the sermon had anything to do with lettuce, tomatoes, pasta, or pesto. And I promise I did listen to the message of the sermon. It's just that I listened while also fantasizing about what I was going to eat later.

Happens every single Sunday.

8 ounces short fusilli or rotini (corkscrew) pasta

4 tablespoons prepared pesto

½ cup grated Parmesan cheese, plus more for serving

½ cup mayonnaise

½ cup sour cream

¼ cup milk, plus more as needed

½ teaspoon kosher salt

½ teaspoon black pepper

1 large head romaine lettuce, sliced into 1-inch pieces

1 cup grape tomatoes, halved

½ cup pitted black olives, halved

4 ounces mozzarella cheese, cut into cubes

1. Cook the pasta according to the package directions, then drain it and rinse in cold water.

2. Let the pasta dry slightly, then toss it in a bowl with 3 tablespoons of the pesto.

3. Add the Parmesan and toss. Refrigerate until chilled.

4. To make the dressing, in a medium bowl, whisk the mayonnaise, sour cream, milk, salt, pepper, and remaining 1 tablespoon pesto.

5. Now, you can throw everything in a big bowl and mix it all together, but I like to assemble the salads in individual bowls because I'm weird. For each serving, make a bed of lettuce in a large bowl, then add a generous layer of pesto-coated pasta.

6. Add the tomatoes, olives . . .

7. And chunks of cheese.

8. Spoon a good amount of the dressing all over the top; it should be thin enough to seep down into the salad, not so thick it will stay on top of everything. Whisk in a little more milk as needed.

9. Sprinkle the salads with extra Parmesan and serve!

CHANGE THINGS UP!

- *As I mentioned in the steps, toss the ingredients with the dressing in a big bowl for a more traditional pasta salad. It stays good in the fridge for up to 3 days.*

- *Use fresh mozzarella instead of regular.*

- *Use kalamata olives for a more Mediterranean feel!*

Silly Alex

I'm not going to prattle on about how much I miss Alex being home all the time, how the house just isn't the same when she's away at college, how I wish she'd just let me homeschool her for college so we could stay in our jammies and never have to go anywhere, and then everything would always stay the same, which would mean life isn't moving as fast as it feels like it's moving and my little pookie sunshine would always be by my side, lighting up the room with happiness, fun, and joy.

And weirdness. Alex, please wash that bowl before you make the salad, okay?

CAULIFLOWER CRUST PIZZA

MAKES ONE 12-INCH PIZZA

Let me just acknowledge that when I first started hearing about cauliflower crust, I thought, *Okay. That's a little bit of a stretch*, kinda with the same inner voice as the Pace Picante Sauce cowboys sitting around the campfire. ("NEW York CITY?!?" "Git a rope.")

And then I tried it. And it. Is. Absolutely wonderful. And not in a "this is pretty good for a meatless dish" way. I mean, it's beautiful and different and a little bit nutty, and while it's definitely not a substitute for bready pizza crust, I might argue that it's a whole delight in itself.

But the best part? The very, very best part? No yeast! No proofing! No kneading! No rising! It's probably the fastest, easiest homemade pizza crust you can make.

1 medium head cauliflower, broken into florets

¼ cup grated Parmesan cheese, plus more for sprinkling

1 teaspoon Italian seasoning

¼ teaspoon kosher salt

1 large egg

2 cups grated fresh mozzarella cheese

¼ cup marinara sauce

Basil leaves, for garnish

1. Preheat the oven to 425°F. Line a rimmed baking sheet with parchment paper.

2. Place the cauliflower florets in a food processor . . .

3. And pulse them to a fine snowy powder; you should have 2½ to 3 cups.

4. Transfer the processed cauliflower to a microwave-safe bowl and cover it with plastic wrap. Microwave until it's soft, about 5 minutes . . .

5. Then pour it onto a clean, dry kitchen towel and let cool slightly.

6. When it's cool enough to handle, wrap the cauliflower tightly in the towel . . .

7. And wring out as much moisture as possible, twisting and squeezing like crazy.

8. By the time you're done, you should have a pretty dry clump! And don't worry—it shouldn't look like much at this point.

9. In a large bowl, combine the cauliflower and Parmesan . . .

10. And add the Italian seasoning, salt, egg, and 1 cup of the mozzarella.

11. Stir/smush it together until well combined.

12. Form it into a ball and place it on the baking sheet . . .

13. Then use your hands to flatten it . . .

14. Into a large, flat round. Keep in mind that it won't move/rise like regular crust, so whatever shape it's in when you put it in the oven, that's the same shape/size it'll be when you pull it out! (It's super easy to work with! You'll love it.)

15. Bake the crust until it's golden, about 12 minutes.

16. Top with the marinara . . .

17. And the remaining 1 cup mozzarella and bake until the cheese is melted and bubbling, 10 minutes more.

18. As soon as it comes out of the oven, sprinkle on some Parmesan . . .

19. Then cut it into wedges. Sprinkle on basil leaves just before serving.

Don't expect a crispy/chewy crust like regular pizza . . . but do expect an amazingly delicious dinner!

Amber waves.

SHORTCUT RAVIOLI

MAKES 30 RAVIOLI (TO SERVE 6 TO 8)

First, a little background: Any time I visit a restaurant with any sort of Italian/fresh pasta theme—which, okay, is probably once in a blue moon—I can almost guarantee that I will go for the ravioli. I just think homemade ravioli is a triumph, and I don't care what filling is inside. I just love it when that fork breaks open the little pasta package . . . it's enough to make a food-loving gal like me want to live another three hundred years just so I can keep eating ravioli.

I don't know who the blessed person was who first discovered that store-bought wonton wrappers could be used to make "homemade" ravioli, but I do know that I want to marry that person. I've been making wonton ravioli ever since, and once you give this a try, you'll be sold! And because no chopping or hard stuff is required, the assembly is a fun activity for kids to help with! The ravioli might not be perfectly formed, but they're supposed to be a little rustic anyway.

You can fill the ravioli with any number of variations—sautéed mushrooms, chopped cooked lobster, and so on—but my favorite is a creamy herby cheesy filling. Simple is often best!

1½ cups whole-milk ricotta cheese

½ cup grated Parmesan cheese, plus more to shave for serving

2 large eggs

1 tablespoon minced parsley, plus more for serving

1 tablespoon minced basil, plus more for serving

1 garlic clove

One 16-ounce package wonton wrappers

Olive oil, for serving

Kosher salt and black pepper

1. In a large bowl, combine the ricotta, Parmesan, and one of the eggs.

4. Stir until it's all combined.

7. Working with one wrapper at a time, place a dollop of the cheese mixture in the center.

2. Sprinkle in the parsley and basil . . .

5. Unwrap the wonton wrappers and keep the stack between two slightly damp paper towels to keep them from drying out.

8. Use your finger to "paint" a perimeter of the egg wash around the edges of the wrapper.

3. And grate in the garlic.

6. Place the remaining egg in a small dish and whisk in 2 tablespoons water with a fork. This egg wash will act as the "glue" for the ravioli.

9. Place a second wrapper on top and seal the two pieces together, carefully forcing out air as you go (the air can cause the ravioli to burst open during cooking). It'll take a couple of tries to get the hang of it, but it really does get easy.

10. Keep going until you have all the ravioli your heart desires, keeping them covered in plastic wrap as you build them.

13. Remove them with the spoon, let the excess water drip off . . .

16. And shave on some Parmesan.

11. When you're ready to eat, bring a large pot of lightly salted water to a boil. Use a large slotted spoon to carefully lower 3 or 4 ravioli at a time into the pot.

14. And set them straight on the serving plate. Drizzle on a little olive oil . . .

17. Some extra herbs would be great, too!

HELPFUL HINT: *Ravioli can be assembled up to 3 hours before cooking. Just keep them covered in plastic wrap until you cook them.*

CHANGE THINGS UP!

- *Heat jarred marinara sauce with a little cream and serve the ravioli with the tomato cream sauce spooned over the top.*

- *Use a fluted cookie cutter to cut a decorative edge after sealing the ravioli.*

12. The ravioli will sink to the bottom, then slowly rise to the surface. Cook them for 1½ to 2 minutes, using the spoon to turn them over once during cooking.

15. Season with salt and pepper . . .

Howdy, Rowdy!

GREEK GRILLED EGGPLANT STEAKS

MAKES 6 SERVINGS

I always laugh when gals such as myself cut a vegetable into a big, thick piece, throw it on the grill, and call it a steak. Talk about the power of positive thinking! Hahahaha.

And how about when that gal also happens to be married to a beef rancher? Well, *ha ha ho ho hee hee har*. Even funnier.

But all guffawing aside . . . these eggplant "steaks" are actually superbly scrumptious! I'm a lifelong fan of eggplant, and this is a clever way to get a nice big piece in yer belly fast. Or, if you have any vegetarian friends headed over for dinner anytime soon, this is something they're sure to love!

4 Roma tomatoes, diced

1 cucumber, seeded and diced

¼ cup parsley, chopped

8 ounces feta cheese, crumbled

2 tablespoons olive oil, plus more for drizzling

Juice of 1 lemon

2 medium to large eggplants

Kosher salt and black pepper

Chili powder

1. Heat a grill pan over medium heat.

2. Make the salad by combining the tomatoes, cucumber, parsley, feta, olive oil, and lemon juice.

3. Stir until it's all combined and set aside.

4. Cut the tops off the eggplants . . .

5. And slice each eggplant lengthwise into 3 thick steaks (slice the exterior skin off the outer two pieces to expose the flesh).

6. Drizzle the steaks with some olive oil and sprinkle with salt, pepper, and chili powder to taste.

7. Heat a grill pan over medium heat and grill the eggplant steaks until they're tender (but not falling apart) and nicely marked, 4 to 5 minutes per side.

8. Transfer the eggplant steaks to individual plates and top with a generous pile of salad!

CHANGE THINGS UP!

- *Top the steaks with a salad of cherry tomatoes, fresh mozzarella, and basil.*

- *Top the steaks with marinara, mozzarella, and other pizza toppings. Put in a 400°F oven for 5 minutes to melt the cheese.*

- *Place a steak on a hoagie roll and turn the whole mess into a sandwich!*

The show must go on, even if it starts raining. Good job, Todd and Rowdy!

QUINOA AND ROASTED VEGGIE SALAD

MAKES 8 SERVINGS

I have never been able to decide, during the course of the four thousand times I've made this dish, whether it is a salad . . . or a side dish . . . or a meatless meal.

Oh, wait . . . I know! It just occurred to me.

It's a masterpiece! A gosh darn dadgum masterpiece. Great for company (especially of the vegetarian persuasion) or just a nice, lovely weeknight family dinner. Save time by roasting the veggies and making the dressing beforehand!

1 cup uncooked quinoa

8 tablespoons (1 stick) butter

¼ cup olive oil

3 garlic cloves, minced

2 large carrots, peeled, halved lengthwise, and cut into 1-inch chunks

2 large parsnips, peeled, halved lengthwise, and cut into 1-inch chunks

½ red onion, cut into large chunks

½ butternut squash, peeled, seeded, and cut into 2-inch chunks

Kosher salt and black pepper

Juice of 1 lemon

8 ounces baby arugula

1 cup shaved Parmesan cheese

¼ cup pine nuts

1. Preheat the oven to 400°F.

2. Cook the quinoa according to the package directions (times vary depending on the brand). Use a fork to fluff it up and set it aside to cool. (Or totally go rogue and add butter, sugar, and cream and eat it for a snack!)

(I love going rogue.)

3. In a small skillet, melt the butter with the olive oil and garlic over medium-low heat. Remove from the heat and let it sit for 5 minutes.

4. Arrange the carrots, parsnips, onion, and squash on a large rimmed baking sheet. Pour half of the garlic butter–oil mixture on top, season with salt and pepper, and toss to coat.

5. Roast the vegetables, tossing occasionally, until they're nice and deep golden brown, 35 to 40 minutes. Set them aside to cool.

6. Pour the remaining half of the garlic butter–oil mixture into a bowl. Add the lemon juice and salt and pepper to taste and whisk it together. Now it's a dressing! And it's *gooooood*.

7. To assemble the salad: Place the arugula on a large platter or bowl, followed by the Parmesan shavings, quinoa, pine nuts, and roasted vegetables. If you're serving this to guests, it's fun to bring it to the table all separated and neato like this.

8. Drizzle on the dressing . . .

9. Toss it all together, and serve immediately.

(A glass of chilled white wine is required!)

CHANGE THINGS UP!

- *Toss in grilled shrimp or strips of grilled chicken (or arrange them on top after tossing).*
- *Substitute baby spinach for the baby arugula (or do a mix of both).*
- *Add herb leaves such as basil, mint, and oregano.*
- *Add bocconcini (mozzarella balls) for some nice cheesiness.*

TRUE PASTA PRIMAVERA

MAKES 6 TO 8 SERVINGS

For years, I cooked a form of pasta primavera that wasn't really pasta primavera at all. Instead of boasting all the glory and gorgeousness of spring veggies, it had everything from zucchini to yellow onions to summer squash! I mean . . . I didn't even have the decency to avoid adding a vegetable with the word "summer" in its name. Is nothing sacred anymore?

Well, I'll answer that: Yes. And you'll see it right here on these pages. This pasta primavera is so wonderful (the vegetables so true to spring) that you can actually hear little birds chirping with every bite.

This dish takes a little time, but you can sub in a few shortcuts if you're in a hurry—see the list following the recipe!

2 tablespoons pine nuts

2½ cups fresh peas

2 cups basil leaves, plus more for garnish

1 cup mint leaves, plus more for garnish

3 garlic cloves, chopped

¾ cup plus 2 tablespoons olive oil

¼ teaspoon kosher salt

¼ teaspoon black pepper

¾ cup freshly grated Parmesan cheese

3 tablespoons butter

2 shallots (or ½ medium onion), thinly sliced

1 bunch asparagus, tough ends removed, cut into 2-inch pieces

½ cup vegetable broth

½ cup dry white wine or more vegetable broth

1 cup heavy cream

1 cup half-and-half

1 pound short pasta, such as campanelle, cooked according to the package instructions

2 tablespoons chopped fresh chives (or 1 green onion, finely sliced)

1. In a small skillet over low heat, lightly toast the pine nuts until golden, stirring often and watching constantly. Set aside.

3. Add ½ cup of the peas to a food processor . . .

2. In a medium pot of boiling water, blanch the peas until bright green and just tender, about a minute. Shock them in ice water, then drain.

4. Along with the basil, mint, one-third of the garlic, and the pine nuts.

5. Pulse to blend it, then . . .

6. With the machine running, slowly drizzle in ¾ cup of the olive oil.

7. Stop when it's all blended and add the salt, pepper, and ¼ cup of the Parmesan.

8. Mix again until the pesto is all combined. Gorgeous texture!

9. In a large saucepan, melt 2 tablespoons of the butter in the remaining 2 tablespoons olive oil over medium-high heat. Add the shallots . . .

10. And sauté until they start to soften, about 2 minutes.

11. Add the asparagus . . .

12. The rest of the peas . . .

13. And the rest of the garlic.

14. Stir the veggies and cook them for just a couple of minutes, until they're starting to get tender but still have a nice bite to them.

15. Remove them to a plate and set them aside.

16. Into the same skillet, pour the broth and wine and stir, letting the liquid cook for a minute or so.

17. Add the cream and half-and-half . . .

21. Stir until it's luscious and perfect. Wow!

18. And the remaining ½ cup Parmesan . . .

22. Turn off the heat, add the pasta and veggies . . .

24. Serve it up with extra herbs and the chives as a garnish!

19. And stir until it's bubbling and thick.

23. And stir to combine.

HELPFUL HINTS

- *Use store-bought pesto to save the step of making it. Most store-bought pestos don't contain mint or peas, but you can add chopped mint to the sauce if you'd like to have that flavor!*

- *Use frozen peas to skip blanching fresh ones.*

20. Add ½ cup to ¾ cup of the pesto, to your taste (reserve the rest in the fridge for another use).

SENSATIONAL SIDES

Sides are the glue the holds it all together, folks. Whether you're in the mood for lemony vegetables or cheesy potatoes (or, in my case, both), you'll love the recipes you're about to behold. Is it possible to put together a legitimate dinner of only side dishes? It is? Well, great! Because I do it all the time. When Ladd is gone.

Citrus Snap Peas 268

Baked Sweet Potato with Sour Cream and Mint 271

Edna Mae's Escalloped Cabbage 272

Curried Rice 276

Mango-Avocado Salad 278

Hasselback Potatoes 280

Broccolini with Garlic and Lemon 282

Hominy Casserole 286

Spaghetti Squash and Kale 288

Curly Fries 290

Spicy Blue Cheese Green Beans 293

Funeral Potatoes 295

Super-quick · Kid-friendly · Fancy

CITRUS SNAP PEAS

MAKES 8 TO 10 SERVINGS

Sugar snap peas are gloriously green and crazily crisp, and when they're tossed in a tangy citrus coating, they hit a whole new level!

You'll have these on the table in less than 10 minutes if you play your cards right. They're perfect with pasta, chicken, fish, or stir-fry.

(They're also pretty darn great as a snack.)

2 pounds sugar snap peas, ends trimmed

2 tablespoons vegetable oil

1 garlic clove, grated

1 tablespoon rice vinegar

1 tablespoon each grated lemon, lime, and orange zest

½ teaspoon kosher salt, or more to taste

¼ teaspoon black pepper

1. Blanch the sugar snaps by dropping them into boiling water for 1 minute . . .

4. Remove the pan from the heat and add the vinegar, citrus zests, salt, and pepper.

6. Then add it to the peas and toss them until they're all coated.

2. Then shock them in ice water to stop the cooking. Drain and set aside in a bowl.

5. Stir it all around to combine . . .

7. Pretty, gorgeous . . . and pretty gorgeous!

3. In a small skillet over medium heat, heat the oil. Add the garlic and cook for 30 seconds, being careful not to burn it.

"Can I have a ride?"

BAKED SWEET POTATO WITH SOUR CREAM AND MINT

MAKES 1 SERVING

Sweet potatoes are so often seen around Thanksgiving, when they're baked and mashed in a casserole with brown sugar, marshmallows, and other crazy-delicious things. But I've really grown to appreciate the beauty of sweet potatoes as a simple side dish, adorned with a little butter or (my current favorite) a plop of sour cream and a sprig of mint. They have an entirely different texture from russets, and a flavor you'll love more and more each time you enjoy one.

Cooking sweet potatoes in the microwave isn't just the quick way to go; I think it also makes them extra soft, tender, and lovely.

1 sweet potato, scrubbed clean

2 tablespoons sour cream

3 or 4 mint leaves, torn

1. Pierce the sweet potato several times with a fork and microwave until tender—anywhere from 6 to 10 minutes.

3. Then push the ends together to force the potato open. (You can also use a fork to loosen the good stuff so it's easier to eat!)

4. Add the sour cream and the mint and serve piping hot!

2. Slice the potato lengthwise . . .

Moooooooving along.

EDNA MAE'S ESCALLOPED CABBAGE

MAKES 6 GENEROUS SERVINGS

This is a version of a recipe from my husband's beloved grandmother Edna Mae. And that means just one thing: It's going to be splendidly delicious! All things from Edna Mae generally are. It's a cheesy, satisfying cabbage casserole that's perfect as a side dish with things like beef brisket or roasted chicken, and it's also great served with a salad and a chunk of bread.

Warning: There's an ingredient in this casserole that might be slightly offensive to some. But others will be fine with it, so it all evens out in the end! Ha.

But seriously . . . this is a good one! You will love every bite.

2 tablespoons butter, plus more for the pan

Kosher salt

1 head green cabbage, uncored, cut into 6 wedges

2 tablespoons all-purpose flour

1½ cups whole milk

One 15-ounce jar Cheez Whiz

Black pepper

1 cup grated pepper Jack cheese

Paprika, for sprinkling

1 jalapeño, sliced into thin rounds, seeds removed

1. Preheat the oven to 350°F. Butter a 9 x 13-inch baking dish.

2. Bring a large pot of lightly salted water to a boil. Place the cabbage wedges in an insert, lower it into the water, and parboil for 2 minutes.

3. Remove the insert from the water and drain the cabbage well.

4. Slice off the harder cores . . .

5. Then arrange the wedges in the prepared baking dish. Let sit while you make the highly gourmet cheese sauce!

6. In a nonstick skillet, melt the butter over medium heat. Sprinkle in the flour . . .

7. Then whisk and cook for a minute or two.

8. Whisk in the milk and cook until it begins to thicken, about 2 minutes.

9. Add the Cheez Whiz. This is how Edna Mae makes it and she has never, ever steered me wrong!

10. Whisk until it's smooth, sprinkle in a small amount of salt and a generous amount of pepper . . .

11. Then add the pepper Jack . . .

12. And stir until it's luscious.

13. Pour the cheese sauce all over the cabbage . . .

14. Sprinkle a little paprika on top . . .

15. And dot with the jalapeño slices.

16. Bake until bubbling hot, about 20 minutes.

Serve it with salad, steak, chicken . . . or anything you'd like!

Tim, you have never looked slicker! (Get it?)

CURRIED RICE

MAKES 8 SERVINGS

Oh, how I love a good rice dish. And ohhhhhh, how I love curry. This lovely side is nice and mild—not over-powering at all—and once you taste it the first time, you'll be hooked and make it again and again. It's like a good pair of jeans: It goes with everything!

2 tablespoons vegetable oil

½ medium onion, very finely diced

2 garlic cloves, grated

1 cup long-grain white rice

1 teaspoon kosher salt

1 tablespoon curry powder

2 cups vegetable or chicken broth

¾ cup golden raisins (optional)

Spanish Salmon (page 230)

1. In a medium skillet (with a lid), heat the oil over medium heat. Add the onion and garlic and sauté until the onion is softened, a couple of minutes.

2. Add the rice, salt, and curry powder . . .

3. And stir, letting everything cook for 1 minute . . .

4. Then add the broth and stir to combine.

5. Bring it to a gentle boil, then reduce the heat to low, cover the skillet, and let it cook for 15 to 18 minutes . . .

6. Until all the liquid has been absorbed.

7. Add the raisins (unless you hate raisins, but even if you do, I still think you should add them!) . . .

8. And use a fork to fluff the rice. Yum!

9. Serve it with chicken, fish, or steak.

MANGO-AVOCADO SALAD

MAKES 6 SERVINGS

This is one of those salads I whip out when it's blahsville and dreary outside, because the combination of colors is so over-the-top stunning, it totally wakes up my world, brightens my mood, and turns on my taste buds.

And if it's already sunny and gorgeous outside? Well, this salad will make you want to dance a serious jig. For the next ten years.

Food has that effect on me!

1 teaspoon hot sauce, or more to taste

1 teaspoon sugar

½ teaspoon kosher salt

¼ teaspoon ground cumin

Juice of 2 limes

2 garlic cloves, finely chopped

½ cup olive oil

4 mangoes, thinly sliced (or use jarred mango slices!)

4 Roma tomatoes, halved lengthwise, then cut crosswise into half-moons

1 small jicama, peeled and cut into julienne

1 red onion, thinly sliced

¼ cup cilantro leaves

8 basil leaves, torn

2 avocados, pitted, peeled, and thinly sliced

1. In a small bowl or pitcher, whisk together the hot sauce, sugar, salt, cumin, lime juice, and garlic. Whisk in the olive oil.

4. The onion . . .

7. And toss to coat.

2. In a large bowl, combine the mangoes, tomatoes . . .

5. And the cilantro and basil.

8. Stir in the avocado after it's all mixed together (to keep it from getting too mushy!) and serve up this loveliness.

SERVING IDEAS

- *As is, with crusty French bread*
- *Alongside grilled chicken or fish*
- *As a garnish for chicken tacos (oh, yum!)*

3. The jicama . . .

6. Pour the dressing on top . . .

Kid-friendly · Fancy

HASSELBACK POTATOES

MAKES 6 POTATOES

The most difficult part of making Hasselback potatoes is slicing them super thin while not cutting through the bottom of the potato. When I made these for the first time, I mangled the first couple of potatoes and started crying with frustration. And okay, I didn't really cry, but I wanted to. And okay, I didn't really want to cry, but I know I definitely never wanted to see a Hasselback potato again as long as I lived. But then I decided to get obstinate and try it one more time.

I'm so glad I did! Once you master the slicing (and it really isn't that hard, for goodness' sake), you can make these all the time. They're crisp and golden and tender and flavorful, and they'll become your favorite potato side dish, whether you're serving them with filet mignon or burgers!

8 tablespoons (1 stick) butter, softened

½ cup olive oil

⅓ cup finely chopped fresh chives

1 teaspoon kosher salt

½ teaspoon black pepper

6 medium russet potatoes, scrubbed clean and dried

1. Preheat the oven to 450°F.

2. In a small bowl, combine the butter, olive oil, chives, salt, and pepper.

3. Stir until it's smooth and combined. (Use a whisk if necessary.)

4. Now it's time to slice the potatoes, and here's a great trick I learned: One at a time, place the potatoes between the handles of two identical wooden spoons or two chopsticks.

5. Carefully cut the potatoes into thin slices, leaving them connected at the bottom; the spoon handles will keep you from slicing the potato all the way through!

6. Put the potatoes on a baking sheet and brush on the butter mixture, making sure to get it in between all the slices.

7. Keep going until all the potatoes are coated.

8. Bake the potatoes until they're tender and the skin is crisp, 55 to 60 minutes. Serve them on a platter!

CHANGE THINGS UP!

- *Add ½ cup shredded Parmesan cheese to the butter mixture. The potatoes will have little crisp pieces of cheese.*

- *Use sweet potatoes instead! How yummy would that be?*

Walter could easily pose for sculptors. He never moves.

BROCCOLINI WITH GARLIC AND LEMON

MAKES 6 SERVINGS

Now that it's becoming more available in Oklahoma supermarkets, Broccolini is starting to creep into my cooking more and more, and I'll just say it: I'm completely fascinated with this lovely little veggie. At first glance, you just assume it's an immature form of broccoli, which, you may be shocked to hear, it isn't at all! The flavors are actually closer to kale, but with differing textures throughout—and beautiful "trees" at the end that trap whatever flavors you cook it with.

I dare you not to fall in love!

3 small bunches fresh Broccolini (about 1½ pounds total)

5 garlic cloves, thinly sliced

2 tablespoons olive oil

Kosher salt and black pepper

Juice of ½ lemon

1. Preheat the oven to 400°F.

2. Cut ½ to 1 inch off the ends of the stems . . .

3. And strip off (and discard) the leaves.

4. Lay the Broccolini stems on a baking sheet . . .

5. Then add the garlic and drizzle on the olive oil.

6. Sprinkle on salt and pepper to taste . . .

7. And toss it all to coat.

8. Roast the Broccolini until the very ends start to crisp and turn brown, 5 to 6 minutes. Use tongs to turn it over . . .

9. And roast for another 3 to 4 minutes, watching to make sure it doesn't burn. Squeeze the lemon all over the Broccolini and toss lightly.

10. Yum! The garlic is nutty and soft, and the Broccolini is just tender, with a little bit of bite in the stems. Delicious!

CHANGE THINGS UP!

- *After you turn the Broccolini in step 8, sprinkle on ⅓ cup shredded Parmesan cheese, then return it to the oven to finish roasting.*
- *Add 1 teaspoon red pepper flakes (or to taste) for a little kick.*

Guns a-Blazin'

Ladd and the kids were shipping cattle one morning when a big thunderstorm moved in. Sometimes, if it's just a standard morning of working cattle, they can stop and take a break as they wait for the rain to stop. But because the road was lined with cattle trucks, the show had to go on . . . so they just worked through the rain and were drenched from head to toe all morning.

I know this is a family-friendly cookbook and everything, but if there's ever such a thing as a cowboy calendar, I'd like to enter my husband for the months of January through December. I love the smile on his face, even more so because he was soaked, had a big morning of work ahead, and on this day of all days, had every reason not to be smiling.

But his smile is definitely *not* the first thing I'm looking at in these photos.

(Nice guns,
Honey!)

HOMINY CASSEROLE

MAKES 8 TO 10 SERVINGS

My mother-in-law, Nan, and her sister Diane have always rocked hominy casseroles. This is a version of a version of a version they've made before, which is exactly the essence of hominy casseroles! The star of the show is beautiful hominy with its unmistakable mild corn flavor . . . and it really is one of the best-kept secrets in canned goods. One bite of this dish and you'll agree with me!

The casserole can be assembled up to 48 hours in advance and baked straight out of the fridge. And it can be considered a side dish or, with a salad on the side, a meal in itself.

Butter, for greasing the dish

8 slices bacon

1 onion, chopped

1 red bell pepper, seeded and chopped

One 29-ounce can hominy, drained and rinsed

¾ cup half-and-half

Hot sauce

½ cup grated Cheddar cheese

½ cup grated Monterey Jack cheese

Kosher salt and black pepper

½ cup plain breadcrumbs

Seriously epic!

1. Preheat the oven to 375°F. Butter a 2-quart baking dish.

2. In a large skillet, fry the bacon over medium-high heat until crispy, 5 to 7 minutes. Drain the bacon on paper towels, then chop it into bite-size pieces. Pour the excess grease out of the skillet, but don't wash it! If you do, you'll regret it every day for the rest of your life!

3. In the same skillet, combine the onion and bell pepper . . .

4. And cook them until they're just starting to brown, about 5 minutes.

5. Add the hominy . . .

6. And the half-and-half and hot sauce to taste and stir until everything is heated.

7. Remove from the heat and stir in the bacon and three-quarters each of the Cheddar and Monterey Jack, reserving the rest for the top.

8. Taste and add salt, black pepper, and/or hot sauce if needed.

9. Pour the mixture into the prepared baking dish . . .

10. Then top with the remaining cheeses and the breadcrumbs.

11. Bake until the top is golden brown and the casserole is bubbling, about 20 minutes. Let rest for 15 minutes before serving.

Bada *bing*! This is absolutely amazing.

SPAGHETTI SQUASH AND KALE

MAKES 8 SERVINGS

Spaghetti squash is such a wonderfully bizarre vegetable. And there's no end to the ways you can prepare it. You can treat it as the vegetable that it is, or you can treat it as a substitute for noodles; my friend Hyacinth tops it with marinara sauce for her kids just as she would regular spaghetti.

This uses just half a large squash, but the leftovers keep really well in the fridge for a few days. Makes a great snack!

1 spaghetti squash

Olive oil

Kosher salt

½ onion, diced

1 large bunch kale, stems removed, leaves torn into pieces

Black pepper

½ teaspoon chili powder

1. Preheat the oven to 350°F.

2. The hardest part of this recipe is cutting the squash in half. With a sharp knife, *very carefully* pierce the center . . .

3. And cut the spaghetti squash in half lengthwise, holding on to the top of the squash with your other hand. (Again—be careful and take this slow.)

4. Scoop out the seeds and pulp in the center and discard them.

5. Place the squash cut side up on a large baking sheet. Rub a little olive oil over the cut surfaces, sprinkle with some salt, and roast until fork-tender, about 1 hour.

6. When the squash is close to done, in a large skillet, heat 1 tablespoon olive oil over medium-high heat. Add the onion and sauté it for 3 to 4 minutes . . .

7. Or until it starts to turn color.

8. Throw in the kale, sprinkle in some salt and pepper, and stir to cook . . .

9. Until the onions are golden and the kale is wilted, 3 to 4 minutes. Set it aside.

10. When the squash is cooked, use a fork to scrape the stringy squash out of the shell.

11. Keep going until all the good stuff is loosened up! Yum—I could eat this whole thing as a snack. Discard the shell.

12. In a large bowl, combine the squash, 1 tablespoon olive oil, the chili powder, and salt and pepper to taste.

13. Layer the squash and kale together in individual bowls and serve!

CHANGE IT UP!

- *Serve the squash with warm marinara over the top and pretend it's pasta!*

- *Toss the squash with maple syrup, salt, and pepper for a sweeter side dish or snack.*

- *Bake the squash in a small baking dish with a little butter, cream, salt, pepper, and Parmesan. Yum!*

It's not a bowl!
It's the squash shell!

CURLY FRIES

MAKES 4 SERVINGS

Curly fries are always a winner, and these have an easy, light batter that gives them fantastic flavor. I like to prep them early in the day if I know I want to make a batch for dinner; they can sit in the batter for several hours, so it's a great thing to get ready ahead of time.

Who wants curly fries?

(*Raising hand!*)

2 large russet potatoes, peeled

Vegetable oil, for deep-frying

BATTER

½ cup all-purpose flour

2 teaspoons paprika

1 teaspoon seasoned salt

½ teaspoon cayenne pepper

1 teaspoon kosher salt, plus more for sprinkling

1 teaspoon black pepper

1. Prepare the potatoes: Use a spiralizer to slice the potatoes, then soak them in cold water for 1 hour in the fridge. Drain on paper towels.

2. In a pitcher, combine all the batter ingredients and 1 cup water . . .

3. And whisk to combine.

4. Put the potatoes in a large plastic zipper bag, pour in the batter, and smush it around to coat. Set aside for 30 minutes (or place in the fridge for up to 12 hours) so the fries can absorb all the flavors.

5. Pour 3 inches of oil into a heavy pot and heat over medium heat until a deep-frying thermometer registers 365°F.* Grab a large handful of fries, let the excess batter drip off, and fry until golden and crisp, 2 to 3 minutes per batch.

*To be safe, put the pot of oil on the back burner of your stove. Use caution!

6. Use metal tongs to carefully move the fries around in the oil so they fry evenly.

7. Drain them on a paper towel, sprinkle with salt, and dig right in!

B-man is growing up!

SPICY BLUE CHEESE GREEN BEANS

MAKES 4 SERVINGS

Fresh green beans are always a great choice for a quick-and-yummy side dish because they don't take long to cook in a hot skillet (and in fact, they're best when they're still slightly crisp) and can be doctored up with all sorts of different ingredients to make them extra tasty. My current favorite way to go is this super-savory/tangy version with chunks of blue cheese. Green beans have never been so, like, totally awesome!

1 tablespoon butter	1 tablespoon Worcestershire sauce	Fresh lemon juice
1 tablespoon vegetable oil	1 tablespoon sriracha or other hot sauce	2 ounces crumbled blue cheese
½ pound green beans, trimmed		

1. In a large skillet, melt the butter in the oil over medium-high heat.

3. When the beans are just beginning to color, stir them around . . .

5. And cook until the beans are crisp-tender and starting to brown, a few more minutes.

2. Add the green beans in a single layer so that they're all touching the bottom of the pan.

4. Then add the Worcestershire, sriracha, and lemon juice to taste . . .

6. Transfer them to a plate, sprinkle over the blue cheese, and serve!

FUNERAL POTATOES

MAKES 12 SERVINGS

Funeral potatoes come from the Mormon community, and once you taste them you'll understand why they've stood the test of time. They're everything that's wonderful about potato casseroles, and are unapologetic in their potato-cheesiness. (And the topping? Well . . . it could be a snack in itself.)

I make the white sauce from scratch, but have also subbed in a couple of cans of cream of mushroom soup (which the original recipe uses; it's good!)—see page 296 for details.

8 tablespoons (1 stick) butter

One 28- to 32-ounce bag frozen hash browns

1 medium onion, finely diced

¼ cup all-purpose flour

1 cup whole milk

2 cups low-sodium chicken broth

1 teaspoon kosher salt

½ teaspoon black pepper, or more to taste

1½ cups grated Monterey Jack cheese

½ cup grated sharp Cheddar cheese

1 cup sour cream, at room temperature

2 cups kettle-cooked potato chips

¼ cup grated Parmesan cheese

1. Preheat the oven to 350°F. Grease a 9 x 13-inch baking dish with 1 tablespoon of the butter. Take the potatoes out of the freezer while you are preparing the rest of the ingredients.

2. Heat a large, deep skillet over medium-high heat, then melt 6 tablespoons of the butter. Add the onion and cook, stirring occasionally, until it starts to soften, 3 to 4 minutes.

3. Reduce the heat to medium, sprinkle the flour over the onion . . .

4. And stir to incorporate. Cook for a minute or two, stirring constantly, but do not let it brown too much. Sorry to be bossy.

5. Whisk in the milk, making sure to get out all the lumps.

6. Add the broth and whisk again if there are still lumps. Bring the mixture to a simmer and let it thicken as you whisk, about 3 minutes.

7. Season with the salt and pepper.

8. Remove from the heat and add the Monterey Jack, Cheddar, and sour cream.

9. Add the hash browns . . .

10. And fold everything together. It's a gigantic mess of carbs and cheese, and that's why it's so durn good.

11. Transfer the mixture to the prepared baking dish and set it aside.

12. Melt the remaining 1 tablespoon butter. Put the potato chips and Parmesan in a bowl . . .

13. And crush the potato chips using a wooden spoon or your fist. Ha. Pour in the melted butter and toss the crumbs to coat.

14. Sprinkle the crumb mixture over the potatoes and cover the baking dish with foil. Bake for 20 minutes, then remove the foil and bake until golden brown on top and bubbling around the edges, about 15 minutes more.

15. Let it rest for 15 minutes before serving.

CHANGE IT UP!

- *Omit the cooked white sauce and mix the cheese, broth, and sour cream with 2 cans cream of mushroom, cream of chicken, or cream of celery soup.*
- *Use cornflakes or panko breadcrumbs instead of potato chips for the topping*
- *Add 1 seeded, diced fresh jalapeño to the casserole for a little spice.*

Tim directing a cattle truck. (He looks like he's striking a
John Travolta/Saturday Night Fever pose if you look closely.)

BREAD, BABY!

Oh, carbs. Where would I be without you? And why do so many people want you to go away? You don't have to worry about that with me: I'll love you (and gobble you up) for the rest of my life. From simple dinner rolls to luscious zucchini bread, here's where you can get your bread fix for any occasion. (They're all super easy, too!)

Roasted Garlic Pull-Apart Cheese Bread 300

Zucchini Bread 303

Shortcut Olive Focaccia 306

Checkerboard Rolls 308

Confetti Cornbread 311

Quick-and-Easy Garlic Rolls 314

ROASTED GARLIC PULL-APART CHEESE BREAD

MAKES 4 TO 6 SERVINGS

Pull-apart bread is the very definition of fun. Just plop it down in front of a table of people and watch it disappear within 2.4 seconds. It really is that good, and can pass as an appetizer or accompaniment to a pot of soup.

And here's the best-kept secret in Pull-Apart Breadland: You can throw the whole mess together up to a day before you need to bake it. Simply pull it out of the fridge and pop it in the oven when you're ready. In 25 minutes, your world is gonna look a lot brighter!

(And cheesier.)

8 garlic cloves

2 tablespoons olive oil

Kosher salt and black pepper

4 ounces mozzarella cheese, grated

4 ounces Fontina cheese, grated

4 ounces Parmesan cheese, grated

4 ounces Pecorino Romano cheese, grated

2 teaspoons chopped fresh chives

2 teaspoons red pepper flakes

1 round artisan or sourdough loaf

8 tablespoons (1 stick) butter, melted

1. Preheat the oven to 375°F.

2. Place the garlic cloves on a square of heavy foil, drizzle the olive oil over them, and sprinkle with salt and pepper.

3. Wrap it up into a parcel and roast for 1 hour . . .

4. Or until the garlic is golden, nutty, and soft. Set it aside to cool and reduce the oven temperature to 350°F. (You can roast the garlic up to a couple of days ahead of time and keep it in a small jar of oil in the fridge. Roast a bunch of cloves! You never know when you'll need 'em.)

5. In a bowl, combine the cheeses, roasted garlic, chives, red pepper flakes, and some black pepper.

6. Stir to mix everything together, smushing the garlic cloves so that little bits are distributed throughout the cheese. (You can get in there and use your fingers if you'd rather!)

7. Cut the bread in 1½-inch-wide strips in one direction, taking care not to cut all the way through the loaf.

8. Rotate the bread 90 degrees and cut the bread crosswise again. Move slowly and use caution! A serrated knife helps immensely.

9. Ta-da!

10. Set the bread on a large piece of foil and stuff the cheese mixture in between the rows . . .

11. And keep going until that bread is so stuffed with cheese, it can't see straight!

12. Drizzle the melted butter evenly all over the surface of the bread. Wrap the bread in foil and bake for 25 minutes. Open up the foil and bake it for another 10 minutes.

14. And dig right in!

CHANGE THINGS UP!

- *Make a pizza version: Add chopped pepperoni, diced green bell pepper, and spoonfuls of marinara sauce.*

- *How about a French onion version? Diced caramelized onions, Gruyère cheese, and chopped chives. Drizzle on beef broth instead of butter. Yum!*

- *My friend Meseidy has made a Buffalo chicken version: Add mozzarella and a bunch of shredded chicken simmered in Louisiana hot sauce. Barbecue chicken would also be dreamy.*

13. Carefully unwrap the bread . . .

ZUCCHINI BREAD

MAKES 2 LOAVES

Zucchini bread is my best friend, because it's actually cake with the word "bread" in the title instead. And any recipe that allows me to pretend like I'm not being naughty is okay by me. And hey! It's got vegetables in it! So it's actually a health food.

This blessedly delicious bread is pleasantly sweet, so it can pass for a snack or dessert but is just as at home served alongside dinner. And it makes two neat loaves, which is supposed to encourage sharing! Just wrap the cooled loaf in plastic wrap and tie a little bow around it.

Now that's my kind of gift.

Baking spray

1 cup granulated sugar

1 cup packed brown sugar

3 large eggs

1 cup vegetable oil

1 tablespoon vanilla extract

2 cups grated zucchini (from about 2 medium zucchini)

3 cups all-purpose flour

1 teaspoon kosher salt

1½ teaspoons baking powder

1 teaspoon baking soda

¾ teaspoon ground cinnamon

Softened butter and honey, for serving

1. Preheat the oven to 325°F. Spray two 8½ x 4½-inch loaf pans with baking spray.

2. In a medium bowl, combine the granulated sugar, brown sugar, eggs, and oil . . .

3. And stir vigorously until the mixture is very smooth.

4. Add the vanilla and stir.

5. Place the zucchini in a couple of paper towels, then form a ball and squeeze out some of the excess water.

6. Add it to the bowl . . .

7. And stir it in.

8. In a large bowl, combine the flour, salt, baking powder, baking soda, and cinnamon and stir to combine.

9. Pour in the zucchini mixture . . .

10. And slowly fold until the mixture just comes together.

11. Divide the batter between the two prepared loaf pans and place them in the center of the oven. Bake for 50 minutes, or until the tops are set and firm.

12. Mmmm. Magical! Let the bread cool in the pans for 5 minutes . . .

13. Then remove it carefully.

14. Wrap a tea towel around the bottom half; it's hot!

15. Then slice away and marvel at the beautiful golden color and the bright green flecks of zucchini.

16. Serve with a pat of butter and a little honey.

SHORTCUT OLIVE FOCACCIA

MAKES 8 SERVINGS

I make a totally-from-scratch olive focaccia that is yummy and all, but it takes approximately one million years to make. First you have to proof the yeast. Then you have to make the dough. Then you have to let the dough rise. Then you have to add a little more flour and mix it in. Then you have to let the dough rise some more. And by that time you really don't even want olive focaccia anymore, but you've already invested approximately one million years into it so you just keep going. You'll enjoy that totally-from-scratch olive focaccia right around your seventy-fifth high school reunion.

So lately I've been having fun making focaccia with a loaf of store-bought frozen bread dough! Sure, it takes time to thaw and rise, but that's about as complicated as it gets. I love this stuff!

1 loaf frozen bread dough, thawed and risen according to the package directions (it usually takes about 4 hours at room temperature)

2 cups assorted pitted olives (I used Castelvetrano and kalamata), chopped

2 tablespoons olive oil

1 teaspoon kosher salt

1. When the dough is ready, smush it slightly flat, then lay two-thirds of the olives on top.

2. Fold up one side of the dough to cover the olives, then continue folding the dough over on itself three or four more times to "swallow up" the olives.

3. Flatten the dough slightly and lay the remaining olives on top.

4. Fold it over itself another couple of times to cover the olives . . .

5. Then use a rolling pin to roll it out into a larger oval. Some of the olives will slide out the sides here and there; just place them on top and press them into the dough. If the dough seems overly wet, pat it dry with paper towels before rolling.

6. Place the dough on an ungreased baking sheet . . .

7. Then cover it with a light kitchen towel and let it rise for 45 minutes.

8. When it's nice and puffy, preheat the oven to 400°F.

9. Flatten the dough with your hands, then use your fingertips to create dimples in the dough.

10. Drizzle the olive oil over the surface, smearing it with your fingers, then sprinkle with the salt.

11. Bake until golden, about 25 minutes. Let cool slightly, then cut or tear it into large pieces for serving.

CHANGE THINGS UP!

- *Add 1 tablespoon finely chopped fresh rosemary with the olives.*
- *Sprinkle the top with grated Parmesan before baking.*
- *Substitute ¾ cup caramelized onions for the olives.*

CHECKERBOARD ROLLS

MAKES 24 ROLLS

I saw this recipe floating around the homeschool mom world a while back, and it always looked a little . . . shall we say, ambitious? Cute, yes. Different, sure. Fun, you bet. But not exactly the rolls you want to try to whip up on a Wednesday night.

But now that I've made them a handful of times, I've found that they really aren't difficult at all to make; they just require a *leeeeetle* bit of planning.

½ pound (2 sticks) butter, melted and slightly cooled, plus more butter for greasing the pan

20 frozen dinner rolls, unbaked

¼ cup poppy seeds

¼ cup sesame seeds

¼ cup yellow cornmeal

¼ cup grated Parmesan cheese

1. Generously butter a 9 x 13-inch baking pan and place the frozen rolls in the pan, evenly spaced.

2. Cover the pan with plastic wrap and let the rolls rise for 2 hours at room temperature, until almost doubled. You can start this in the morning, then place them in the fridge and let them rise at a slower pace all day!

3. When the rolls have almost doubled in size, preheat the oven to 400°F.

4. In one bowl, mix together the poppy seeds and sesame seeds.

5. In a separate bowl, mix together the cornmeal and Parmesan.

6. Start by brushing butter on every other roll in the pan.

7. Sprinkle the poppy seed–sesame seed mixture all over the top of those rolls, making sure they adhere to the surface (if a few fall off into the pan, that's fine).

8. Keep going until half the rolls are coated.

9. Brush the remaining rolls with butter . . .

10. And coat them in the cornmeal mixture!

How cool are these?

11. Now cover the pan again (you can use the same plastic wrap) and let them rise for another 45 minutes to 1 hour. Just time this so that it works with your life! They'll be ready when you come back.

These are so delicious warm out of the oven and slathered with softened butter! (Understatement of the century.)

12. They should be risen to the point of almost touching by now, so you can bake them for 20 to 25 minutes.

13. And here they are!

Alex still comes home for the summer and helps. Giddy-up, Alex!

CONFETTI CORNBREAD

MAKES 9 THICK SQUARES OR 18 THINNER PIECES

This cornbread contains creamed corn, and you know what? I don't even know what *creamed corn* is. I only know that it comes in a can, it's very weird looking, and it makes for a really delicious cornbread if you dump it in the batter.

But what *is* creamed corn anyway?

Never mind. Don't answer that.

2 tablespoons butter, melted, plus more for the pan and softened butter for serving

1 cup fine-grind or coarse cornmeal

1½ cups all-purpose flour

2 tablespoons sugar

1 tablespoon baking powder

1 teaspoon kosher salt

½ cup buttermilk (or use a little less than ½ cup milk with 1 tablespoon white vinegar—instant buttermilk!)

2 large eggs

One 14-ounce can cream-style corn

One 14-ounce can fiesta corn, drained

1. Preheat the oven to 425°F. Grease a 9-inch square pan with butter. (If you want a thinner cornbread, use a 9 x 13-inch pan and bake for about 20 minutes.)

2. In a large bowl, combine the cornmeal, flour, sugar, baking powder, and salt. Stir it together.

3. In a large bowl or measuring pitcher, lightly whisk the buttermilk and eggs.

4. Add the creamed corn . . .

5. And the fiesta corn . . .

6. And stir it together.

His ears double as LEDs. (Labrador Evasion Devices)

7. Slowly pour the corn mixture into the dry ingredients . . .

10. And fold until it's mixed together.

13. Cut the cornbread into squares . . .

8. Folding as you go.

11. Pour the batter into the pan . . .

9. Pour in the melted butter . . .

12. And bake until golden on top and set in the middle, 23 to 25 minutes.

It doesn't always work.

14. And serve it warm with softened butter!

QUICK-AND-EASY GARLIC ROLLS

MAKES 12 ROLLS

Carbs are my life. And when the carbs take the form of a crispy, golden garlic roll, their influence is even greater. And when said rolls can be ready within about 15 minutes and don't require any yeast or kneading or angst? Well . . . stick a fork in me. I'm done.

Serve these babies with pasta, salad, soup, or pretty much any meal you can think of!

½ **pound (2 sticks) butter**

3 **garlic cloves, grated**

1 **teaspoon dried parsley flakes**

1 **teaspoon dried basil**

½ **teaspoon dried oregano**

¼ **teaspoon kosher salt**

¼ **teaspoon black pepper**

6 **good, crusty dinner rolls, halved horizontally**

1. Preheat the oven to 400°F.

2. In a small skillet, melt the butter over medium-high heat until hot and almost sizzling. Remove from the heat and add the garlic . . .

3. Then add the parsley, basil, oregano, salt, and pepper . . .

4. And stir to combine.

5. Lay the rolls cut side up on a rimmed baking sheet. Generously brush the butter mixture on each of the rolls.

6. Bake the rolls for 8 to 10 minutes . . .

7. Until the edges are golden and beautiful.

CHANGE THINGS UP!

- *Stir ⅓ cup grated Parmesan cheese into the butter mixture before brushing.*
- *Use the butter mixture on two halves of French bread for traditional garlic bread.*

SWEETS, GLORIOUS SWEETS

Should I be embarrassed that this chapter contains the most recipes in this cookbook? Because I'm not! A little nibble of something sweet is a reward at the end of a long day, and none of these treasures is complicated to pull together. I hate to be cliché, but *yum*!

Marvelous Mille-Feuille 319

Milk Chocolate Mousse 322

Dump Cakes 324

Ice Cream Pie 326

Chocolate Cake in a Mug 328

Caramel Apple Sundaes...332

Nutella Krispie Treats 334

Glazed Apple Dumplings..337

Peach Dumplings...339

Baked Alaska 342

Potato Chip Cookies 345

Mocha Lava Cakes 348

No-Bake White Chocolate Raspberry Cheesecake 353

Skillet Apple Crisp 355

Lemon Bars 358

Blueberry Cake Milkshake 362

Itty-Bitty Cakes 364

MARVELOUS MILLE-FEUILLE

MAKES 6 SERVINGS

The British crew that hauls over from London to film my cooking show are the ones who introduced me to mille-feuille, and I had the most hilarious time trying to pronounce it.

Mi-few?

Milla-fee-yoo-lay?

Mew-few?

It gave them even more reason to ridicule me for my accent.

For the record, the pronunciation of this super-easy dessert is *meel-foy*, but it doesn't really matter how you pronounce it. All that matters is that you give it a try the next time you have a special dinner or birthday celebration! It looks like it's way more difficult to make than it actually is (and those are my favorite kinds of desserts to make).

1 sheet frozen puff pastry, thawed according to the package directions

2 tablespoons powdered sugar, plus more for dusting

8 ounces mascarpone cheese

1 cup heavy cream

2 vanilla beans

2 tablespoons raspberry liqueur (or nonalcoholic raspberry syrup, the type sold for coffee)

Zest of 1 lemon

4 cups fresh raspberries

Mint sprig, for garnish

1. Preheat the oven to 425°F. Line a baking sheet with parchment paper or a baking mat.

2. Unfold the pastry and gently roll it to a large rectangle.

3. Cut the sheet into three rectangles and transfer them to the prepared baking sheet. Prick the pastry all over with a fork to keep it from puffing too much in the oven.

4. Dust the pastry with powdered sugar (this will give the pastry a slightly caramelized surface as it bakes).

5. Bake until golden brown and risen, about 15 minutes. Set aside to cool for about 15 minutes.

6. In the bowl of a mixer fitted with a whisk attachment, combine the powdered sugar, mascarpone, and cream.

7. With a small paring knife, split each vanilla pod lengthwise down the middle . . .

8. Then open the pod and use the back of the knife to scrape out the vanilla seeds . . .

9. And add them to the bowl.

10. Add the raspberry liqueur and lemon zest . . .

11. And whip the mixture until smooth.

14. Arrange half the fresh raspberries on top of the cream in rows, making sure they are lining the edge so they'll be visible between the layers.

17. Lay the last piece of pastry glaze side up and generously dust it with powdered sugar.

12. Place a dab of the whipped mixture on a serving platter to anchor the dessert. Place one piece of pastry onto the plate glaze side down and spoon on half the mascarpone cream . . .

15. Top it with another sheet of pastry, glaze side down.

13. Then spread it all over the surface.

16. Top the second sheet of pastry with the remaining cream and raspberries.

18. Add a raspberry and mint sprig and impress your friends and family!

NOTE: *The dessert slices very easily with a sharp serrated knife. Just start on one end and carefully cut into six equal slices. Take your time and everything will stay together very well!*

CHANGE THINGS UP!
- *Use blackberries instead of raspberries!*
- *Use different berries on the two layers—one with raspberries, one with blackberries.*
- *Use diced kiwi for a totally fun burst of color.*

MILK CHOCOLATE MOUSSE

MAKES 4 TO 6 SERVINGS

Chocolate mousse is one of those things that sounds (but is not) fancy or fussy. The result is a dessert that's *sooooooo* chocolatey and smooth and creamy. It's a glorified chocolate pudding, is what it is, and it really is easy to make!

Darker chocolates are usually used, but Bryce and Todd go nutso for this milk chocolate version. Bryce and Todd's mom goes nutso for it, too! (I have this on good authority. I know the chick.)

8 ounces milk chocolate, broken into pieces, plus more for grating

4 tablespoons (½ stick) butter, softened

2 cups heavy cream

¼ cup sugar

4 large egg yolks

1 teaspoon vanilla extract

Gummy worms, for serving (optional)

1. Combine the chocolate and the butter in a double boiler (I set a heatproof glass bowl over a saucepan of simmering water).

2. Stir it until it just barely melts (don't let it go much beyond that or it will seize). Remove it from the heat and set it aside for a few minutes to cool slightly.

3. In the bowl of a mixer fitted with a whisk attachment, whip the cream with the sugar on high speed until stiff peaks form. Set aside.

4. In a small bowl, temper the egg yolks by adding a spoonful of the warm chocolate mixture . . .

5. And whisk until it's all combined. This will bring the egg yolks to a warmer temperature so they won't set when you mix them with the rest of the warm chocolate.

6. Add the tempered eggs and vanilla to the bowl with the chocolate, and stir until it's combined.

7. Add three-quarters of the whipped cream (refrigerate the remaining whipped cream for serving), and use a rubber spatula to carefully fold it in . . .

8. Until it's combined. How irresistible does this look???

9. Spoon the mousse into serving glasses or bowls, then refrigerate for at least 1 hour. (Psst: You can make these up to a day in advance and keep them covered in plastic wrap in the fridge!)

10. Serve the mousse with dollops of whipped cream and garnish with grated chocolate.

11. And gummy worms if you want to have some fun!

DUMP CAKES

MAKES AS MANY AS YOU NEED!

Let's just get this out of the way: Dump cake is canned fruit, boxed cake mix, and butter—baked together so that it looks like a from-scratch cobbler made with fruit you grew in your orchard.

Once you accept that basic set of facts, you can relax and enjoy every bite!

Butter, for greasing the baking dishes

CHERRY-PINEAPPLE DUMP CAKE

One 21-ounce can cherry pie filling

One 15-ounce can crushed pineapple (do not drain)

1 box white cake mix

12 tablespoons (1½ sticks) butter

PEACH DUMP CAKE

One 29-ounce can sliced peaches in syrup (do not drain)

1 box white cake mix

12 tablespoons (1½ sticks) butter

Whipped cream, for serving

1. Preheat the oven to 350°F. Butter two 9 x 13-inch baking dishes.

2. For the cherry-pineapple dump cake: Dump the cherry pie filling and crushed pineapple into one baking dish . . .

3. And stir it together until combined.

4. Sprinkle the cake mix over the fruit to cover it totally.

5. Slice the butter into tablespoons and distribute it evenly over the cake mix. (Please note that the original recipe for dump cake called for 2 sticks of butter instead of 1½. I'm all about healthy choices.)

6. For the peach dump cake: Dump the peaches into the other baking dish.

7. Repeat the process of sprinkling on the cake mix and laying on the butter slices.

8. Bake the cakes until the tops are browned and bubbling, 45 to 50 minutes.

9. Serve the dump cakes nice and warm . . .

10. With plenty of whipped cream!

(Ice cream is also permitted.)

CHANGE THINGS UP!

Any combination of canned fruit and cake mix flavor can work! See how many different varieties you can come up with!

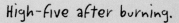

High-five after burning.

ICE CREAM PIE

MAKES 8 TO 12 SERVINGS

This ice cream pie can be kept in the freezer for several days, allowing you to sneak delicious little wedges whenever the need arises!

And boy, oh, boy . . . will the need ever arise. Trust me.

CRUST

16 graham crackers (the full sheets, with 4 sections)

⅓ cup (⅔ stick) butter, melted

FILLING

2 pints vanilla ice cream

¼ cup finely chopped pecans, plus more for serving

4 peanut butter cups, such as Reese's, roughly chopped

2 large Butterfinger bars, roughly chopped

Jarred caramel or hot fudge sauce, for serving

1. Make the crust: Preheat the oven to 350°F.

2. Place the graham crackers in a large plastic zipper bag and seal it. Smash the crackers with a rolling pin until they're crushed into fine crumbs. (Or you can use a food processor!)

3. Move the crumbs to a large bowl, then pour in the melted butter and stir them to combine.

4. Press the crumbs into a pie plate . . .

5. Slowly packing them so they're firm. Bake the crust for 5 minutes, then let it cool completely.

6. Make the filling: In a large bowl, stir the ice cream until it's smooth but still firm and somewhat frozen.

7. Add the pecans and candies . . .

8. And stir until it's all combined.

9. Pour the mixture into the cooled crust and smooth the surface, then cover the pie and place it in the freezer to harden, 2 to 3 hours minimum. (Psst: Make it up to a week in advance! It keeps well in the freezer if it's covered tightly.)

10. Use a warm knife to cut neat slices, then drizzle with your favorite jarred caramel or hot fudge sauce.

CHANGE THINGS UP!

- *Make a chocolate mint version: Use mint chocolate chip ice cream and mix in chopped peppermint patties. Pour it into a chocolate cookie crust.*

- *Use any combination of ice cream flavor and candy/nut you'd like!*

Super-quick · Kid-friendly

CHOCOLATE CAKE IN A MUG

MAKES 1 GENEROUS SERVING

Have you ever had such a wicked craving for chocolate cake that you'll simply die if you don't get a piece within 5 minutes?

Well, I have. Many, many times. Occasionally, it has affected relationships.

And that's where this little mug treat comes in! If you haven't yet discovered the joy of whipping up a 90-second chocolate cake in a mug . . . well, your life is about to change.

(Pssst. This is a rich one! Split it with a friend. Chocolate cake can build a bridge!)

3 tablespoons all-purpose flour

3 tablespoons sugar

2 tablespoons unsweetened cocoa powder

¼ teaspoon baking powder

Tiny pinch of kosher salt

3 tablespoons whole milk

3 tablespoons vegetable oil

Splash of vanilla extract

3 tablespoons semisweet chocolate chips

Whipped cream, for serving (optional)

Sprinkles, for serving (optional)

Ice cream, for serving (optional)

1. In a 12-ounce microwave-safe mug, combine the flour, sugar, cocoa powder, baking powder, and salt.

4. Stir until it just comes together . . .

7. Then let it sit for 1½ to 2 minutes, just to cool off a bit.

2. Stir with a fork . . .

5. Then add the chocolate chips and stir. Use a damp paper towel to wipe excess off the inside of the mug (just to keep things neat and tidy and picture perfect).

8. Pile in the whipped cream and sprinkles (or any flavor of ice cream!), if you like.

3. Then add the milk, vegetable oil, and vanilla.

6. Microwave for 90 seconds . . .

Will you look at that? It's chocolate cake! And it's absolutely magical.

This chocolate cake is Heaven.

Cattle Trucks

You know it's shipping season when you see the cattle trucks coming down your road before daylight, sometimes in a line eighteen to twenty trucks long. Cattle trucks have been around as long as Ladd has been alive, but there was a time when railroad cars were the only way to transport cattle for sale. This is one of many things we modern-day ranchers take for granted. Getting up at 4 a.m. to saddle horses, then gather, weigh, and load the cattle day after day for the entire month of July is difficult enough for Ladd, the cowboys, and the kids. I can't imagine if they had to drive the cattle five miles away to the train before they did the weighing and loading.

But that's exactly how it was when my father-in-law, Chuck, was a boy. They'd wake up at 3 a.m. (not 4 a.m. like we sleeper-inners do today), eat a big breakfast (isn't that a midnight snack?), then gather the cattle and make the long, slow trek (so as not to make the cattle sweat too much, since cattle are sold by weight) to the train stop miles away. They'd arrive around 1 p.m., start weighing the cattle, then finally load them on the train (sometimes up to thirty cars) at about 3 p.m. before riding their horses all the way home. They'd clean up, have dinner, and hit the hay . . . then start it all again the next morning.

As grueling as shipping season can be around here, it feels like a month at the spa compared to what the old days must have been like. (Remind me I said that when next July rolls around, okay?)

CARAMEL APPLE SUNDAES

MAKES 10 TO 12 SERVINGS

Making from-scratch sauces for ice cream is one of the best-kept secrets in quick desserts. If you can spend a few minutes dicing up some apples, you can make a caramel apple version that'll knock your dang Fruit-of-the-Loom socks—which happen to be your husband's but you don't care because you're way past the season in your life when you need to wear cute polka dots on your feet—off.

10 tablespoons (1¼ sticks) butter

4 Granny Smith apples, cored and finely diced

1 cup packed brown sugar

1 teaspoon ground cinnamon

½ cup heavy cream

2 pints vanilla ice cream, for serving

1. In a skillet, melt 2 tablespoons of the butter over medium-high heat. Add the apples . . .

4. Return the skillet to the stove and reduce the heat to medium. Add the remaining stick of butter and the brown sugar and stir until the sugar is dissolved, about 2 minutes.

8. Return the apples to the pan and stir them to coat.

2. And sauté, stirring constantly, for 3 minutes.

5. Add the cinnamon and stir, cooking the mixture for another minute. (It will start to get a little richer in color!)

9. Spoon the mixture over ice cream. You'll never be the same!

3. Remove the apples to a plate and set aside.

6. Add the cream . . .

CHANGE THINGS UP!

- *Add 1½ teaspoons (or more) kosher salt to the caramel mixture for Salted Caramel Apple Sauce.*

- *Add ¼ cup whiskey to the skillet with the butter and brown sugar. (Turn off the heat briefly as you add it if you have a gas stove.)*

- *Serve the sauce over cinnamon ice cream or dulce de leche ice cream.* Yum!

7. And stir it around, cooking it for another minute.

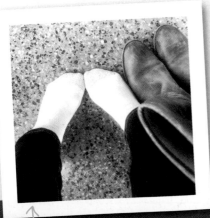

see? I told you!

NUTELLA KRISPIE TREATS

MAKES 16 TREATS

I cleaned out my pantry once—well, not just once; never mind, you know what I mean—and I found something like six giant boxes of Rice Krispies. It sparked a massive Rice Krispies Treat era in my household, and the memories of that time are very, very strong.

And very crunchy.

Needless to say, you can only make regular Rice Krispies treats for so long before you start throwing in some variations here and there. This was one of my favorite variations that came from the Great Pantry Cleanout! It has stood the test of time, and now I actually purchase the ingredients with the intention of making them instead of making them because I was inundated with Rice Krispies.

Necessity is the mother of invention.

6 tablespoons (¾ stick) butter, plus more for the pan

10 ounces large marshmallows

⅛ teaspoon kosher salt

⅓ cup Nutella

6 cups Rice Krispies cereal

1½ cups miniature marshmallows

1 cup pecans, finely chopped

5 ounces semisweet chocolate, melted

1. Generously smear the inside of a 9 x 13-inch pan with butter.

2. Melt 4 tablespoons of the butter in a large saucepan over medium-low heat.

3. Add the large marshmallows and salt . . .

4. And stir until the marshmallows are melted.

5. Add the Nutella and stir it in.

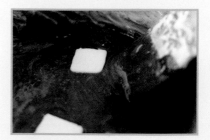

6. Add the remaining 2 tablespoons butter and stir until smooth.

7. In a large bowl, combine the Rice Krispies and Nutella mixture. Immediately start to gently fold them together . . .

8. And when it's almost all combined, add the miniature marshmallows.

9. Continue folding until everything's evenly distributed . . .

10. And immediately press the mixture into the prepared pan.

11. Sprinkle half the pecans over the treats.

12. Drizzle the melted chocolate in zigzags all over the pecans . . .

13. And sprinkle the rest of the pecans on top.

14. Let it set (place it in the fridge if you'd like to hasten this along!), then cut into squares.

GLAZED APPLE DUMPLINGS

MAKES 4 DUMPLINGS

I'll take apple dumplings in any form at all. They're comforting, scrumptious, and remind me of my childhood, especially if they're served with a scoop of vanilla ice cream. Okay, two scoops.

This is a classic (and no-fuss) way to get apple dumplings on the table without a lot of aggravation. Make one or make twenty!

DUMPLINGS

½ cup packed brown sugar

¼ cup raisins

2 tablespoons chopped pecans

½ teaspoon ground cinnamon

Zest and juice of 1 lemon

1 sheet frozen puff pastry, thawed according to the package directions

4 small tart apples, such as Granny Smith, peeled and cored

2 tablespoons butter

Egg wash: 1 large egg whisked with 1 tablespoon water

GLAZE

½ cup powdered sugar

2 tablespoons butter

1 teaspoon fresh lemon juice

Vanilla ice cream, for serving

1. Preheat the oven to 375°F. Line a baking sheet with parchment paper.

2. Make the filling for the apples: In a bowl, combine the brown sugar, raisins, pecans, cinnamon, lemon zest, and lemon juice . . .

3. And mix together until it's dark and delicious.

4. Unwrap the pastry and gently roll it into a large square . . .

5. Then cut it into four 6-inch squares.

6. Place an apple on each square of pastry.

7. Spoon the sugar–nut mixture into the hollowed-out core of each apple . . .

8. And top each with 1½ teaspoons butter.

9. Brush the egg wash around the edges of the pastry squares . . .

10. Then bring up the four corners, pressing to seal the dumplings.

11. Transfer the dumplings to the prepared baking sheet and brush them all over with the remaining egg wash. Bake until the apples are tender and the pastry is golden brown, about 30 minutes.

12. While the dumplings are baking, make the glaze: In a small pan, combine the powdered sugar, butter, lemon juice, and ¼ cup water. Cook over medium heat, stirring, until the butter has melted and the sugar has dissolved, about 5 minutes.

13. When you pull the dumplings out of the oven . . .

14. Generously brush the glaze over the baked dumplings.

15. Serve them with vanilla ice cream.

By 9 a.m., Lucy is ready for a nap! So am I, for that matter.

Kid-friendly

PEACH DUMPLINGS

MAKES 8 SERVINGS

This is a totally different kind of fruit dumpling recipe, and there's no excuse for it.

This recipe has nothing to say for itself.

This recipe has no respect for mankind.

Need I go on? No. I needn't. I shouldn't. I shan't! All I need to tell you is that this recipe, while ridiculous and (as I pointed out above) inexcusable, is beyond dreamy. The original uses apples and Mountain Dew, but I like to change it up with peaches and Sprite.

(I'm rebellious that way!)

12 tablespoons (1½ sticks) butter, plus more for the pan

2 cans refrigerated crescent rolls*

16 frozen peach slices

1¼ cups sugar

Ground cinnamon, for sprinkling

1 can Sprite

Whipped cream, for serving

This is not a paid advertisement, but I prefer Pillsbury. The flavor is better! And I repeat: This is not a paid advertisement. Pillsbury doesn't know me! Or, if they know me, they've never called me or even sent me a postcard.

1. Preheat the oven to 350°F.

2. Butter a 9 x 13-inch baking dish.

3. Unroll the crescent rolls and separate the triangles. Lay a peach slice on the larger end . . .

4. And wrap up the peach.

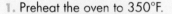

5. Lay it in the pan . . .

6. Then repeat with the rest of the crescent rolls and peach slices.

7. In a medium saucepan, melt the butter over medium heat, then add the sugar.

8. Stir it just a few times, until it's combined but still very grainy.

9. Pour the sugar mixture all over the rolls . . .

10. And sprinkle the surface with cinnamon . . .

First position

11. Then crack open a can of the hard stuff (the Sprite) and slowly pour three-quarters of the can all over the rolls, getting it around the edges and in between the cracks. (You can drink the rest!)

13. Serve up 2 dumplings per person . . .

14. Spoon some of the sauce over the top . . .

12. Bake the rolls for 40 minutes, then remove them from the oven and let them sit for 10 minutes before serving.

15. And serve with whipped cream! (And since it's a special occasion, nothing but the canned stuff will do.)

Make them soon. Because you're worth it.

BAKED ALASKA

MAKES 12 TO 15 SERVINGS

This classic dessert is *gorgeous,* and while no sane person would ever describe it as quick, I daresay one could call it easy . . . as long as you have a little time. The original Baked Alaska was served at the famed Delmonico's restaurant to celebrate the purchase of Alaska (at least that's how the story goes), and I'm sure it was slightly finer and more expertly crafted than this one. I had a very fancy version when I took a cruise with my late grandmother (love you, GaGa) when I was fifteen, and the dang thing was on fire.

But this one is nothing to shake a stick at! Use whatever kind of ice cream you want, make part of it ahead of time . . . and most of all, have fun doing it! This is a great one.

3 pints each of 3 different ice cream colors/flavors (I used cherry, chocolate, and pistachio; 9 pints total)

Cooking spray

1 store-bought round angel food cake (usually 8 or 9 ounces)

4 large egg whites

¼ teaspoon cream of tartar

3 tablespoons sugar

1 teaspoon cornstarch

Pretty!

1. Set one of the ice cream flavors (the one you want on the top) out to soften slightly.

2. Spray a 5-quart metal or glass bowl with cooking spray, then line it with plastic wrap. Make sure the piece of plastic wrap is long enough to let you fold up the edges and cover the contents of the bowl.

3. Fill it with the first ice cream flavor and smooth the surface.

4. Fold the plastic wrap up around the edges and carefully cover the ice cream. Place the bowl in the freezer for 30 to 45 minutes, or until firm on the surface. While it is freezing, take the second flavor of ice cream (the middle layer) out of the freezer to begin to soften.

5. When the first layer is firm, unfold the plastic wrap and add the second ice cream flavor . . .

6. And repeat the freezing process. Take the third flavor of ice cream out of the freezer while the second layer is freezing.

7. Meanwhile, cut the angel food cake into equal slices.

8. Add the third layer of ice cream and smooth the surface . . .

9. Then add the angel food cake in a single layer . . .

10. And keep going until the entire surface is covered, trimming pieces to fit if necessary. Bring up the edges of the plastic wrap to cover the cake and freeze for at least 2 hours—overnight is best! Or you can make it up to this point well in advance of when you want to serve it. It'll keep in the freezer for weeks!

11. When you're ready to serve, make the meringue: In the bowl of a mixer fitted with a whisk attachment, beat the egg whites on medium-high speed until frothy. Add the cream of tartar and continue beating.

12. In a separate small bowl, combine the sugar and cornstarch. With the mixer running, beat in the sugar mixture a little at a time . . .

15. Remove the plastic wrap and spread the meringue all over the surface.

18. Use a hot knife to slice and serve it up!

CHANGE THINGS UP!

- *Use chocolate cake instead of angel food for a totally different flavor and appearance.*

- *Put a layer of angel food between the ice cream layers.*

- *Use different colors of sherbet instead of ice cream.*

13. And beat it on high until the meringue is glossy and forms stiff peaks.

16. When the whole surface is covered, swirl the spatula around to create a pretty design.

14. Remove the ice cream bombe from the freezer and let it sit at room temperature for 5 minutes, then invert it onto a pretty serving plate.

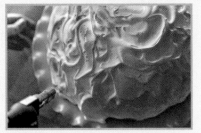

17. Use a kitchen torch to brown the surface of the meringue, moving it around to keep it from burning. (Alternatively, freeze it after the meringue is on—for up to 2 weeks—then brown it in a 500°F oven for 4 to 5 minutes. A torch is much easier!)

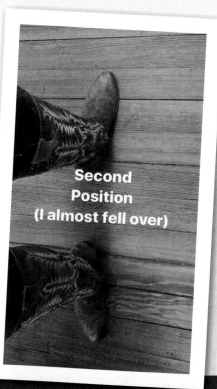

Second Position
(I almost fell over)

POTATO CHIP COOKIES

MAKES 24 COOKIES

These are good ol' basic chocolate chip cookies . . . made more perfect and delicious with a super-healthy item: crushed potato chips!

Just kidding on the super-healthy part. But I'm definitely not kidding on the perfect and delicious part!

Give 'em a try—you won't regret it.

8 ounces kettle-cooked potato chips

½ pound (2 sticks) butter, softened

¾ cup granulated sugar

½ cup packed light brown sugar

2 teaspoons vanilla extract

2 large eggs

2 cups all-purpose flour

1 teaspoon baking soda

1 teaspoon kosher salt

1 cup semisweet chocolate chips

1. Preheat the oven to 375°F. Line two baking sheets with parchment paper.

2. Place the potato chips in a large plastic zipper bag, leaving just a corner of the bag open . . .

3. And use a rolling pin to crush them. Leave the crumbs big enough to still add some crunchy texture to the cookies.

4. Pour half the potato chips into a pie plate or bowl. Set the remaining half aside in the bag.

5. In the bowl of a mixer fitted with a paddle attachment, combine the butter, granulated sugar, and brown sugar.

6. Mix on medium-high speed until light and fluffy, about 3 minutes.

7. Add the vanilla and eggs . . .

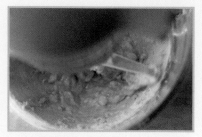

8. And beat on medium speed until just combined.

9. Add the flour, baking soda, and salt, then mix on low speed until just combined.

10. Add the potato chips from the plastic bag to the dough . . .

11. Along with the chocolate chips . . .

12. And mix it on low speed for a few revolutions, just enough to barely incorporate the potato chips and chocolate chips.

Oh my gosh, oh my goodness, oh my word. I'll just warn you . . . this is the best cookie dough in the history of doughs. Let's just put it this way: They say you can't eat just one potato chip? Well, yeah. You also can't eat just one spoonful of this dough. Consider yourself warned!

13. Use a scoop to get balls of dough . . .

14. Set them in the pie plate of potato chips . . .

15. And roll them in the chips, lightly pressing them into the surface of the dough.

16. Place the cookies 2 inches apart on the prepared baking sheets . . .

17. And bake until they're golden, 12 to 13 minutes.

They're best when they're warm!

Fourth position (In mirror)

MOCHA LAVA CAKES

MAKES 4 CAKES

This is the good ol' oozy, gooey chocolate lava cake you know and love, but with a hint of coffee flavor that will make your entire life complete! Be sure not to skip the whipped cream on top; the cake is so nice and rich, you need it to balance things out.

(I always like a little cream with my coffee anyway.)

Baking spray

4 ounces semisweet baking chocolate

8 tablespoons (1 stick) butter

1 cup powdered sugar

2 egg yolks

2 large eggs

6 tablespoons all-purpose flour

2 teaspoons instant coffee (Starbucks Via packets are good, or good ol' freeze-dried Folgers!)

Sweetened whipped cream, for serving

1. Preheat the oven to 425°F.

2. Spray four custard cups with baking spray and place them on a rimmed baking sheet.

3. In a large glass bowl, melt the chocolate and butter in the microwave in 30-second increments. Whisk until the mixture is smooth.

4. Stir in the powdered sugar until it's about three-quarters of the way mixed in.

5. Add the egg yolks and stir them in . . .

6. Then add the whole eggs and stir until combined.

7. Add the flour and the coffee . . .

8. And stir until it just comes together.

9. Divide the mixture among the prepared cups . . .

10. And bake them for about 12 minutes. Let the cakes stand for less than a minute . . .

11. Then invert them onto plates.

12. Serve with whipped cream. Sometimes the chocolate starts to ooze before you even get the cream on top!

And this is never, ever a bad thing.

Fifth.
Sort of.
Best I can do at 48.

MAKE-AHEAD NOTE: *Make these earlier in the day through step 9 and keep them in the fridge. When you're ready to bake, place them in the oven straight from the fridge. Just allow 5 to 6 minutes more baking time.*

Ladd and I don't have a lot of posed photos together through the years . . . And that's because it usually goes something like this:

He walks toward her with the moves of a jungle cat. She has a look of love in her eyes.

He makes his move and . . . and . . . we have rabbit ears.

There it is! The pose!

And a swat! Serious never lasts too long around here.

Make-ahead · Freezes well · Kid-friendly · Fancy

NO-BAKE WHITE CHOCOLATE RASPBERRY CHEESECAKE

MAKES 8 TO 10 SERVINGS

I love any cheesecake that I don't have to bake. Oh, don't get me wrong—I love to eat those regular cheesecakes. I just don't like to make them! There's so much mixing, so much baking, so much cracking on the surface! This lovely recipe eliminates the baking step, and though it does take a little time to whip up, it definitely won't give ya any headaches.

And it's just so darn pretty. Look at it!

1 pint raspberries

Juice of ½ lemon

½ cup granulated sugar

One 10-ounce package shortbread cookies, such as Lorna Doone

4 tablespoons (½ stick) butter, softened

One 12-ounce package white chocolate chips

Three 8-ounce packages cream cheese, softened

1 teaspoon vanilla extract

½ cup powdered sugar

1. Set aside 8 to 10 raspberries for garnish. Put the remaining raspberries in a saucepan with the lemon juice and ¼ cup of the granulated sugar.

3. Pour the mixture into a strainer set over a bowl and force the liquid through (discard the seeds and pulp). Let the puree cool while you make the crust.

5. Pulse until the mixture becomes coarse crumbs.

2. Bring to a boil over medium-high heat, reduce to a simmer, and cook until slightly thicker, about 2 minutes.

4. In a food processor, combine the cookies, butter, one-third of the white chocolate chips, and the remaining ¼ cup granulated sugar.

6. Press the crumbs into the bottom and up the sides of a 9-inch deep-dish pie plate. Refrigerate the crust while you make the filling.

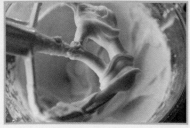

7. In the bowl of a mixer fitted with a paddle attachment, beat the cream cheese and vanilla until fluffy.

8. Add the powdered sugar and beat until smooth.

9. Melt half the remaining white chocolate chips and slowly add the melted chocolate to the mixture, beating on slow to incorporate.

10. Pour in the cooled raspberry puree and beat to incorporate until it's a beautiful shade of pink!

11. Scoop the mixture onto the crust and smooth the surface.

12. Arrange the reserved raspberries and the remaining white chocolate chips on top as a garnish, then refrigerate the cheesecake for at least 3 hours or up to overnight.

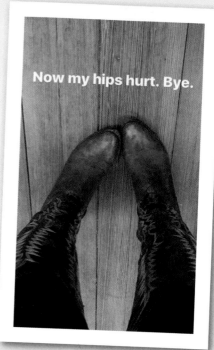

Now my hips hurt. Bye.

13. Slice and serve it up! Note that this cheesecake filling is softer than a regular cheesecake, so it definitely needs time to chill. (But at least you won't have to worry about cracks!)

(As you can tell, I've been scarred by cracking cheesecakes throughout the course of my life.)

SKILLET APPLE CRISP

MAKES 8 TO 12 SERVINGS

They serve warm apple crisp in Heaven. I'm absolutely sure of it.

Have you ever noticed that I talk about Heaven a lot, and that it's usually in the context of my thinking about what I'm going to eat when I get there someday?

I'm always thinking about what I'm going to eat wherever I go. It's a problem sometimes.

Back to the apple crisp, though: This is a recipe I use all the time! The apples are very slightly cooked before the crisp goes in the oven, and I think that makes things extra perfect. (And you don't have to go to Heaven to get it!)

CRUMB TOPPING

¾ cup all-purpose flour

½ cup packed brown sugar

¼ cup granulated sugar

½ teaspoon ground cinnamon

½ teaspoon ground nutmeg

¼ teaspoon kosher salt

8 tablespoons (1 stick) butter, cut into small pieces

APPLE FILLING

2 tablespoons butter

5 Granny Smith apples, peeled, cored, and thinly sliced

Pinch of kosher salt

2 tablespoons packed brown sugar

2 tablespoons cornstarch

1 tablespoon vanilla extract

Juice of ½ lemon

Vanilla ice cream, for serving

1. Preheat the oven to 350°F.

2. First, make the crumb topping: In a medium bowl, combine the flour, brown sugar, granulated sugar, cinnamon, nutmeg, and salt . . .

3. And whisk it together.

4. Add the butter . . .

5. And use a pastry cutter (or two knives) to mix it together until the mixture resembles coarse crumbs.

6. Make the apple filling: In an 8-inch cast-iron skillet, melt the butter over medium heat. Add the apple slices and salt . . .

7. And cook for 3 minutes, stirring gently but constantly.

8. Add the brown sugar, cornstarch, vanilla, and lemon juice . . .

9. And keep cooking the apples for another minute, until they're just slightly soft. Turn off the heat.

10. Sprinkle the crumb topping over the apples and make sure it's distributed evenly.

11. Cover the skillet with foil and bake the crisp for 15 minutes, then remove the foil and bake for 25 minutes more . . .

12. Until it's delightfully crisp (hence the name) and golden.

13. Serve it while it's still warm . . .

With vanilla ice cream.

CHANGE THINGS UP!

- *Make a mixed berry version with whole blueberries, raspberries, and blackberries. Omit the cinnamon and nutmeg and cook for only 2 minutes in the skillet before adding the crumb topping.*
- *Make a pear version around the holidays! Use the same procedure as the apple version.*

LEMON BARS

MAKES 12 TO 15 BARS

A good lemon bar is a thing of beauty, and it took me quite a few years to get mine just where I wanted them: in my mouth! Just kidding. I never had any problem with that. What I meant was that it took me many years to perfect them. They need to be slightly tangy, slightly sweet (not too much of either!), and I like a slightly thicker crust than standard lemon bars. And I pretty much put as much powdered sugar on the top as is humanly possible.

The result? Lemon bar perfection! And you can make a pan at the beginning of the week, cut them into squares (you can go smaller if you like littler quantities), and pack them in lunches as you need them.

Butter, for greasing the pan

CRUST

2 cups all-purpose flour

½ cup sugar

¼ teaspoon kosher salt

½ pound (2 sticks) butter, cut into small cubes

LEMON FILLING

1½ cups sugar

¼ cup all-purpose flour

4 large eggs

Zest and juice of 4 lemons

Powdered sugar, for sifting

1. Preheat the oven to 350°F. Grease a 9 x 13-inch pan with butter.

Looking for his lemon bars!

2. Make the crust: In a large bowl, stir together the flour, sugar, and salt.

3. Add the butter cubes . . .

4. And use a pastry cutter (or two knives) to cut it all together . . .

5. Until the mixture resembles fine crumbs.

6. Pour the crumbs into the prepared pan . . .

7. And press until slightly firm.

8. Bake until golden around the edges, about 20 minutes. Let the crust cool slightly while you make the lemon filling (leave the oven on).

11. And whisk to combine.

14. Pour the filling over the crust and bake until set, about 20 minutes.

9. Make the filling: In a large bowl, stir together the sugar and flour.

12. Add the lemon zest and juice . . .

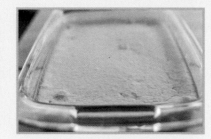

15. Let it cool on the countertop for about 15 minutes, then refrigerate, covered in plastic wrap, for a minimum of 2 hours. (It looks weird at this stage; don't worry! It'll be perfect when it's finished.)

10. Crack in the eggs . . .

13. And whisk lightly until combined.

16. Sift powdered sugar over the top, then cut into squares.

17. Serve with coffee. (Or make it part of a Cowboy Bento Box [page 34].) Delicious!

BLUEBERRY CAKE MILKSHAKE

MAKES 3 OR 4 MILKSHAKES

This is an utterly ridiculous sweet treat, and I do mean preposterous. Outrageous, even! Out of respect for common sense, it most definitely isn't something you'll want to make every day after lunch, but it's a fun, quite rebellious dose of decadence if you're in the mood for that sort of thing every now and then. (It's the perfect slumber party food!)

Overall, this starts as a pretty innocent, straightforward shake—until you get to one specific ingredient. I'll just let you see it as it unfolds.

About 7 scoops vanilla ice cream

¾ cup whole milk, plus more if needed for thinning

⅓ cup white cake mix

1 pint fresh blueberries

Whipped cream, for serving

Rainbow sprinkles, for serving

Crazytown!

1. Scoop the ice cream into the blender . . .

2. Then pour in the milk.

6. Blend it for a good 30 seconds, until it's very smooth. Add milk as needed to get the consistency you like! (I prefer milkshakes a little on the thin/pourable side.)

10. Some rainbow sprinkles are just what it needs to drive home the fun factor.

3. Grab the cake mix. (Any brand will do!)

4. Add it to the blender . . .

7. Pour it into a pretty glass . . .

8. Add the reserved blueberries on top . . .

5. Then sprinkle in the blueberries (reserve a few for garnish).

9. Then squirt on some whipped cream!

CHANGE THINGS UP!

- *For a regular "confetti" version, omit the blueberries and add a few sprinkles to the milkshake just before it finishes blending. Serve as above.*

- *Imagine the other possibilities! Spice cake mix with crumbled ginger cookies, chocolate cake mix with raspberry garnish, strawberry cake mix with fresh strawberries thrown in. Wow!*

ITTY-BITTY CAKES

MAKES AS MANY AS YOU NEED!

This is the quickest way I know of "baking" cute little individual cakes that can be served at baby showers, birthdays, or any celebration. I think the reason they're so quick has something to do with the fact that there's no baking involved at all. Ha ha. I'm so loosey-goosey with the rules sometimes!

These are so much fun to put together, and a great project for kids. And speaking of rules: There are none! Just have fun with these.

Angel food cake loaf (found in the bakery section of grocery stores)

Jarred lemon curd

Fruit jam of your choice (I used cherry)

Frozen whipped topping (such as Cool Whip), thawed in the fridge according to the package directions

1. Unwrap the cake and place it on a cutting board.

2. Slice it in half horizontally through the middle . . .

3. Then use a square cookie cutter to cut neat squares from the cake. (Use the scraps to make a trifle!)

4. Slice each square of cake horizontally in half to make two thinner layers.

Cute!

Pssst: This makes a cute little birthday cake!

5. Spread half the squares with lemon curd and half the squares with jam.

7. Add about 3 tablespoons whipped topping . . .

Or just a Wednesday cake.

Or a Tuesday cake.

Or a Friday cake.

Amen.

CHANGE THINGS UP!

- *Fill the layers with Nutella instead of curd and jam.*
- *If you have the time, make itty-bitty ice cream cakes! Fill the layers with slightly softened ice cream flavors of your choice, then freeze them for 30 minutes before spreading on the whipped topping.*
- *Substitute pound cake for the angel food cake.*
- *Add sprinkles to the top!*

6. Stack 3 squares together.

8. And spread it all over the surface, using the back of a spoon or spatula to make little peaks on top. Repeat with the remaining cake slices.

Ode to Charlie

THE DOG OF A LIFETIME

We got a pup named Charlie
One year at Christmastime.
He changed our lives completely
So I'll share this dog rhyme.

His ears were long and dangly,
His legs were short and fat,
His naps were almost constant,
'Cept when he chased the cat.

I dressed him up in outfits,
In dresses, shirts, and jeans,
In boots and leather loafers—
The dapp'rest pup I'd seen!

He started working cattle
With Ladd and all the crew.
He thought this was his purpose.
Oh, if he only knew!

That he was just a Bassett
And bred for not so much.
But Charlie rose above it
And learned that cowdog touch.

But man, that short dog syndrome . . .
He thought he was in charge
And ruled the other doggies
His bravado, always large!

But deep down, all he wanted
Were tummy rubs all day
And sausage, ham, and burgers
And bacon, I would say.

He snored just like an engine,
His breath was not so great,
His ears were always crusty
From hanging in his plate.

But Charlie Boy was perfect
And loyal through and through.
He knew what we were thinking,
He sensed what we would do.

We thought he'd live forever
But cancer came and stayed,
Then left with our dear Charles
And left us all dismayed.

And yet, we feel so lucky
He got to be our friend.
We have a million memories
Right up until the end.

We loved you, Charlie, you were the best
We never will forget you
And the very second we get to Heaven . . .
We're coming straight to get you!

ACKNOWLEDGMENTS

To my cookbook editor, the inimitable Cassie Jones Morgan. Fact: There's no way I could go through the cookbook process with anyone else. It's been such a great ride, and as Ladd and I both agreed recently, meeting you was totally a God thing. Thank you!

To the incomparable Matt Ball, the first photographer I've ever used for one of my cookbooks! You allowed me to focus on the recipes, to have more fun during the shoot . . . and to be able to show *both* my hands in my recipe photos. A first! Thanks for sharing your talent (and your wisecracks) with me. You rock. (Your mom rocks.)

To the wise and unshakable David Domedion, who kept me organized and motivated, and who made sure I never ran out of butter, flour . . . or jarred sliced mango. Ha! Thank you for your friendship, kind sir.

To Caitlyn Brown and Aleigh Thompson, for being true workhorses! From prepping to testing to marinating to styling to grilling to roasting to braising to baking, you allowed me to keep breathing (literally and figuratively) through the cookbook shoot. Well, and you made sure I got it done! You're amazing ladies, and I appreciate you.

To Kris Tobiassen, for designing this cookbook (and all my cookbooks!) and for never stopping until everything is perfect. I'll never understand where your brand of patience comes from, but I'll always appreciate it! Thank you, Kris.

To Susanna Einstein, Sharyn Rosenblum, Anwesha Basu, Liate Stehlik, and Lynn Grady, for your support with my cookbooks. So great to know you're always there for me!

To Haley Carter. Talk about the wind beneath my wings! Thank you for being my connection to the civilized world, for keeping me organized (this is a gargantuan job), and for your sweet friendship.

To Kurtess Mortensen and every single member of the amazing staff at The Merc! You kept everything running so smoothly and beautifully, which allowed me to concentrate on getting this book done. Thank you, team!

To Hyacinth, Beccus, and Connell, my BFFs. I love you more'n my luggage.

To Jenn, Jules, Sarah, and Ang, for always being there, and for making sure I never get too mature (or well behaved) for my britches.

To Ladd, Alex, Paige, Bryce, and Todd. Mama loves you so much.

To my entire family! Thank you for being there and cheerin' me on.

And to *you*. Your love and support is so tangible, and I thank you for being there through the years. I wouldn't be doing this without you!

RECIPES FOR ALL OCCASIONS!

If you are a LOL (Lover of Lists) like I am, you'll enjoy browsing these carefully curated (by yours truly) recipe collections!

Plentiful Potluck

Whether you're headed to church or the PTA meeting, these travel well and please a crowd!

Slow Cooker Glazed Ribs, 162
Slow Cooker BBQ Chicken, 167
Stuffed Bell Peppers, 189
Mini Turkey Meatloaves, 193
King Ranch Chicken, 197
Cincinnati Chili, 199
Festive Pasta Salad, 246
Edna Mae's Escalloped
    Cabbage, 272
Hominy Casserole, 286
Funeral Potatoes, 295
Dump Cakes, 324
Peach Dumplings, 339

Neat to Reheat

These go from fridge (or freezer) to oven (or microwave!) to table without compromising any flavor.

Crunchy French Toast Sticks, 2
Mini Sausage Casseroles, 20
The Merc's Queso, 89
Roasted Red Pepper Soup, 104
Slow Cooker "Pot" of Beans, 164
Slow Cooker Spaghetti Sauce, 169
Stuffed Bell Peppers, 189
Mini Turkey Meatloaves, 193
King Ranch Chicken, 197
Cincinnati Chili, 199
Meat Pies, 202
Hominy Casserole, 286

Cocktail Party

Whether you plan it ahead and send out invites, or decide to throw a party on the fly, here are some great options for cute and delicious nibbles. They all go great with wine and drinks!

Watermelon Feta Bites, 68
Tortilla Pinwheels, 76
Bacon-Wrapped Almond-Stuffed
    Dates, 79
Rosemary Skewers, 82
Zucchini Roll-Ups, 92
Cheese Lover's Crostini, 95
Milk Chocolate Mousse (spoon into
    shot glasses!), 322
Lemon Bars (cut very small!), 358
Itty-Bitty Cakes, 364

Date Night

Stay in with your sweetie and make an evening of it!

Stuffed Pizza Crust
    (fun to share), 71
Fried Shrimp, 116
Chicken Piccata, 125
Honey-Soy Salmon, 136
Steaks with Chimichurri, 146
Lamb Chops with Mint Sauce, 154
Lobster Mac and Cheese, 207
Steak and Bell Pepper Sheet Pan
    Supper, 232
Marvelous Mille-Feuille, 319
Milk Chocolate Mousse, 322
Mocha Lava Cakes, 348

Nice and dusty; just the way I like him!

Slumber Party Delights

If your kids have friends to spend the night, they will eat you out of house and home. I suggest you be prepared with this kid-friendly fare.

Crunchy French Toast Sticks, 2
Amish Baked Oatmeal, 10
Mini Sausage Casseroles, 20
Orange-Vanilla Monkey Bread, 22
The Merc's Queso, 89
Slow Cooker Beef Enchilada
    Dip, 97
Cap'n Crunch Chicken Strips, 102
Taco Quesadillas, 128
Dinner Nachos, 149
Cincinnati Chili, 199
Curly Fries, 290
Roasted Garlic Pull-Apart Cheese
    Bread, 300
Potato Chip Cookies, 345
Blueberry Cake Milkshake, 362

Delightful Ladies' Lunch

A little bit pretty, a little bit fancy . . . just like you and your friends!

Greek Feast To-Go (without the
    "to-go" component!), 57
Watermelon Feta Bites, 68
Tortilla Pinwheels, 76
Zucchini Roll-Ups, 92
Shrimp Mango Lettuce Cups, 110
Marsala Mushroom and Goat
    Cheese Flatbread, 144
Roasted Shrimp with Cherry
    Tomato Sheet Pan Supper, 212
Citrus Salad with Vinaigrette, 236
Roasted Vegetable Panzanella, 243
Quinoa and Roasted Veggie
    Salad, 260
Mango-Avocado Salad, 278
Checkerboard Rolls, 308
No-Bake White Chocolate
    Raspberry Cheesecake, 353

Picky Eaters

Every family has one. (Or two . . . or nine.) These recipes are well-loved by the more "discerning" types.

Crunchy French Toast Sticks, 2
Mini Sausage Casseroles, 20
Orange-Blueberry Muffin Tops, 30
Stuffed Pizza Crust, 71
Cap'n Crunch Chicken Strips, 102
Fried Shrimp, 116
Pepperoni Chicken, 152
Slow Cooker Spaghetti Sauce, 169
Slow Cooker Broccoli Cheese
    Soup, 176
Meat Pies, 202
Broccoli Cheese Potatoes, 240
Hasselback Potatoes, 280
Curly Fries, 290
Checkerboard Rolls, 308
Milk Chocolate Mousse, 322
Nutella Krispie Treats, 334
Lemon Bars, 358

UNIVERSAL CONVERSION CHART

OVEN TEMPERATURE EQUIVALENTS

250°F = 120°C
275°F = 135°C
300°F = 150°C
325°F = 160°C
350°F = 180°C
375°F = 190°C
400°F = 200°C
425°F = 220°C
450°F = 230°C
475°F = 240°C
500°F = 260°C

MEASUREMENT EQUIVALENTS

Measurements should always be level unless directed otherwise.

⅛ teaspoon = 0.5 ml
¼ teaspoon = 1 ml
½ teaspoon = 2 ml
1 teaspoon = 5 ml
1 tablespoon = 3 teaspoons = ½ fluid ounce = 15 ml
2 tablespoons = ⅛ cup = 1 fluid ounce = 30 ml
4 tablespoons = ¼ cup = 2 fluid ounces = 60 ml
5⅓ tablespoons = ⅓ cup = 3 fluid ounces = 80 ml
8 tablespoons = ½ cup = 4 fluid ounces = 120 ml
10⅔ tablespoons = ⅔ cup = 5 fluid ounces = 160 ml
12 tablespoons = ¾ cup = 6 fluid ounces = 180 ml
16 tablespoons = 1 cup = 8 fluid ounces = 240 ml

Glazed Apple Dumplings, page 336

INDEX

A

Almond(s)
  Granola Bars, 5–7
  -Stuffed Dates, Bacon-Wrapped,
    78–79
Appetizers and snacks
  Bacon-Wrapped Almond-Stuffed
    Dates, 78–79
  Cheese Lover's Crostini, 94–96
  Hot Corn Dip, 74–75
  The Merc's Queso, 88–91
  Pimento Cheese, 66–67
  Pretzel-Coated Fried Goat
    Cheese, 80–81
  Roasted Red Pepper
    Hummus, 58
  Rosemary Skewers, 82–83
  Slow Cooker Beef Enchilada Dip,
    97–99
  Stuffed Pizza Crust, 70–72
  Tortilla Pinwheels, 76–77
  Watermelon Feta Bites, 68–69
  Zucchini Roll-Ups, 92–93
Apple(s)
  Caramel, Sundaes, 332–33
  -Celery Slaw, 40–41
  Crisp, Skillet, 355–57
  Dumplings, Glazed, 336–38
Artichokes
  Pantry Pasta, 238–39
Asparagus
  True Pasta Primavera, 262–65
Avocado(s)
  Dinner Nachos, 148–51
  -Mango Salad, 278–79
  Shrimp Mango Lettuce Cups,
    110–12

B

Bacon
  Bean with, Soup, 178–80
  Hominy Casserole, 286–87
  The Merc's Queso, 88–91
  Spaghetti Carbonara, 140–41
  storing, xiv
  -Wrapped Almond-Stuffed
    Dates, 78–79
Baked Alaska, 342–44
Bananas
  My Mom's Muffins, 24–26
Bars
  Granola, 5–7
  Lemon, 358–61
Basil
  -Lemon Potato Salad, 38–39
  True Pasta Primavera, 262–65
  Zucchini Roll-Ups, 92–93
BBQ Chicken, Slow Cooker, 166–68
BBQ Chicken Wings, 36–37
Bean(s)
  with Bacon Soup, 178–80
  canned, x
  Cincinnati Chili, 199–201
  Dinner Nachos, 148–51
  dried, x
  green, frozen, xii
  Green, Spicy Blue Cheese,
    292–93
  Meatball Tortilla Soup, 181–83
  Slow Cooker Mexican Chicken
    Soup, 174–75
  Roasted Red Pepper
    Hummus, 58
  Slow Cooker Beef Enchilada Dip,
    97–99

  Slow Cooker "Pot" of, 164–65
  Turkey Taco Skillet, 138–39
  Tuscan Chicken Sheet Pan
    Supper, 222–23
Beef
  chuck roast, about, xvi
  Cincinnati Chili, 199–201
  Dinner Nachos, 148–51
  Enchilada Dip, Slow Cooker, 97–99
  favorite cuts, xvi–xvii
  Hamburger Steaks with
    Mushroom Gravy, 113–15
  Meatball Tortilla Soup, 181–83
  Meat Pies, 202–5
  Noodle Salad Bowls, 48–51
  short ribs, about, xvi
  Slow Cooker Spaghetti Sauce,
    169–71
  Steak and Bell Pepper Sheet Pan
    Supper, 232–33
  steaks, types of, xvi–xvii
  Steaks with Chimichurri,
    146–47
  Steaks with Wasabi Cream Sauce,
    156–57
  Stuffed Bell Peppers, 188–91
  Taco Quesadillas, 128–29
  tenderloin, about, xvi
Bento Box, Cowboy, 34–41
Berries
  Blueberry Cake Milkshake,
    362–63
  Marvelous Mille-Feuille, 319–21
  No-Bake White Chocolate
    Raspberry Cheesecake, 352–54
  Orange-Blueberry Muffin Tops,
    30–31
  storing, xv

Blueberry Cake Milkshake, 362–63
Breadcrumbs, xi
Bread dough, freezing, xiii
Breads. *See also Tortilla(s)*
    Checkerboard Rolls, 308–10
    Cheese, Roasted Garlic Pull-
        Apart, 300–302
    Confetti Cornbread, 311–13
    Crunchy French Toast Sticks,
        2–4
    dinner rolls, freezing, xiii
    Orange-Vanilla Monkey, 22–23
    Quick-and-Easy Garlic Rolls,
        314–15
    Roasted Vegetable Panzanella,
        243–45
    Shortcut Olive Focaccia, 306–7
    Zucchini, 303–5
Breakfast
    Amish Baked Oatmeal, 10–11
    Chilaquiles, 8–9
    Crunchy French Toast Sticks,
        2–4
    Granola Bars, 5–7
    Mini Sausage Casseroles, 20–21
    My Mom's Muffins, 24–26
    Orange-Blueberry Muffin Tops,
        30–31
    Orange-Vanilla Monkey Bread,
        22–23
    Overnight Muesli, 15–17
    Peachy Pancakes, 12–14
    Waffle Iron Hash Browns, 27–29
Broccoli
    Cheese Potatoes, 240–42
    Cheese Soup, Slow Cooker,
        176–77
Broccolini with Garlic and Lemon,
    282–83
Broths, x
Brussels sprouts
    Sausage and Root Vegetables
        Sheet Pan Supper, 224–25
    Veggietastic Sheet Pan Supper,
        218–21
Butter, xv

C

Cabbage
    Apple Celery Slaw, 40–41
    Edna Mae's Escalloped, 272–74
Cakes
    Chocolate, in a Mug, 328–29
    Dump, 324–25
    Itty-Bitty, 364–65
    Mocha Lava, 348–49
Cap'n Crunch Chicken Strips, 102–3
Caramel Apple Sundaes, 332–33
Carrots
    Chicken Fennel Bake, 226–27
    Doctored-Up Ramen, 132–33
    Quinoa and Roasted Veggie
        Salad, 260–61
    Roasted Vegetable Panzanella,
        243–45
    Thai Chicken Wraps, 54–56
Casseroles
    Edna Mae's Escalloped Cabbage,
        272–74
    freezing, xiii
    Funeral Potatoes, 294–96
    Hominy, 286–87
    King Ranch Chicken, 196–98
    Lobster Mac and Cheese, 206–9
    Mini Sausage, 20–21
Cauliflower
    Crust Pizza, 250–53
    Veggietastic Sheet Pan Supper,
        218–21
Celery Apple Slaw, 40–41
Checkerboard Rolls, 308–10
Cheese
    Blue, Green Beans, Spicy, 292–93
    Bread, Roasted Garlic Pull-
        Apart, 300–302
    Broccoli Potatoes, 240–42
    Broccoli Soup, Slow Cooker,
        176–77
    Cauliflower Crust Pizza,
        250–53
    Cheese Lover's Crostini, 94–96
    Cincinnati Chili, 199–201

Citrus Salad with Vinaigrette,
    236–37
Cream, and Grilled Veggie
    Sandwiches, 60–62
Dinner Nachos, 148–51
Edna Mae's Escalloped Cabbage,
    272–74
Festive Pasta Salad, 246–47
Funeral Potatoes, 294–96
Goat, Pretzel-Coated Fried,
    80–81
Greek Grilled Eggplant Steaks,
    258–59
Greek Salad, 58–59
Hominy Casserole, 286–87
Hot Corn Dip, 74–75
King Ranch Chicken, 196–98
Lobster Mac and, 206–9
Marsala Mushroom and Goat
    Cheese Flatbread, 144–45
Marvelous Mille-Feuille, 319–21
Meat Pies, 202–5
The Merc's Queso, 88–91
Mini Sausage Casseroles, 20–21
No-Bake White Chocolate
    Raspberry Cheesecake, 352–54
Parmesan-Panko Chicken, 158–59
Pasta Salad in a Jar, 42–45
Pepperoni Chicken, 152–53
Pimento, 66–67
Quinoa and Roasted Veggie
    Salad, 260–61
Roasted Vegetable Panzanella,
    243–45
Rosemary Skewers, 82–83
Salad on a Stick, 46–47
Shortcut Ravioli, 254–56
Slow Cooker Beef Enchilada Dip,
    97–99
Spaghetti Carbonara, 140–41
storing, xiv
Stuffed Bell Peppers, 188–91
Taco Quesadillas, 128–29
Tortilla Pinwheels, 76–77
True Pasta Primavera, 262–65
Waffle Iron Hash Browns, 27–29

Watermelon Feta Bites, 68–69
Zucchini Roll-Ups, 92–93
Cheesecake, No-Bake White
    Chocolate Raspberry, 352–54
Cherry-Pineapple Dump Cake,
    324–25
Chicken
    (Legs) and 40 Cloves of Garlic
        Sheet Pan Supper, 214–15
    Fennel Bake, 226–27
    Greek Feast to Go, 57–59
    King Ranch, 196–98
    Mango-Chile, 106–7
    Parmesan-Panko, 158–59
    Pepperoni, 152–53
    Piccata, 125–27
    Slow Cooker BBQ, 166–68
    Soup, Mexican, 174–75
    Strips, Cap'n Crunch, 102–3
    Thighs, Pan-Roasted, 184–87
    Tuscan, Sheet Pan Supper,
        222–23
    Wings, BBQ, 36–37
    Wraps, Thai, 54–56
Chilaquiles, 8–9
Chiles
    Hot Corn Dip, 74–75
    The Merc's Queso, 88–91
    pickled jalapeños, xi
    Slow Cooker Beef Enchilada Dip,
        97–99
Chili, Cincinnati, 199–201
Chimichurri, Steaks with, 146–47
Chocolate
    Cake in a Mug, 328–29
    Milk, Mousse, 322–23
    Mocha Lava Cakes, 348–49
    Nutella Krispie Treats, 334–35
    Potato Chip Cookies, 345–47
    White, Raspberry Cheesecake,
        No-Bake, 352–54
Cilantro
    Shrimp Mango Lettuce Cups,
        110–12
    Slow Cooker Beef Enchilada Dip,
        97–99

Steaks with Chimichurri,
    146–47
Cincinnati Chili, 199–201
Citrus Salad with Vinaigrette,
    236–37
Citrus Snap Peas, 268–69
Condiments, xi
Confetti Cornbread, 311–13
Cookies, Potato Chip, 345–47
Corn
    Confetti Cornbread, 311–13
    Dip, Hot, 74–75
    Doctored-Up Ramen, 132–33
    frozen, xii
    Meatball Tortilla Soup, 181–83
Cornbread, Confetti, 311–13
Cowboy Bento Box, 34–41
Cream, xv
Crostini, Cheese Lover's, 94–96
Cucumbers
    Greek Grilled Eggplant Steaks,
        258–59
    Greek Salad, 58–59
    Salad on a Stick, 46–47
    Thai Chicken Wraps, 54–56
Curried Rice, 276–77

D

Dates, Bacon-Wrapped Almond-
    Stuffed, 78–79
Desserts
    Baked Alaska, 342–44
    Blueberry Cake Milkshake,
        362–63
    Caramel Apple Sundaes, 332–33
    Chocolate Cake in a Mug,
        328–29
    Dump Cakes, 324–25
    Glazed Apple Dumplings,
        336–38
    Ice Cream Pie, 326–27
    Itty-Bitty Cakes, 364–65
    Lemon Bars, 358–61
    Marvelous Mille-Feuille, 319–21
    Milk Chocolate Mousse, 322–23

Mocha Lava Cakes, 348–49
No-Bake White Chocolate
    Raspberry Cheesecake, 352–54
Nutella Krispie Treats, 334–35
Peach Dumplings, 339–41
Potato Chip Cookies, 345–47
Skillet Apple Crisp, 355–57
Dinners (meatless)
    Broccoli Cheese Potatoes,
        240–42
    Cauliflower Crust Pizza, 250–53
    Citrus Salad with Vinaigrette,
        236–37
    Festive Pasta Salad, 246–47
    Greek Grilled Eggplant Steaks,
        258–59
    Pantry Pasta, 238–39
    Quinoa and Roasted Veggie
        Salad, 260–61
    Roasted Vegetable Panzanella,
        243–45
    Shortcut Ravioli, 254–56
    True Pasta Primavera, 262–65
Dinners (sheet pan suppers)
    Chicken (Legs) and 40 Cloves of
        Garlic, 214–15
    Chicken Fennel Bake, 226–27
    Roasted Shrimp with Cherry
        Tomato, 212–13
    Sausage and Root Vegetables,
        224–25
    Spanish Salmon, 230–31
    Steak and Bell Pepper, 232–33
    Teriyaki Salmon and Kale,
        216–17
    Tuscan Chicken, 222–23
    Veggietastic, 218–21
Dinners (take your time)
    Bean with Bacon Soup, 178–80
    Cincinnati Chili, 199–201
    King Ranch Chicken, 196–98
    Lobster Mac and Cheese, 206–9
    Meatball Tortilla Soup, 181–83
    Meat Pies, 202–5
    Mexican Chicken Soup, 174–75
    Mini Turkey Meatloaves, 192–95

Dinners (take your time) *continued*
 Pan-Roasted Chicken Thighs,
  184–87
 Slow Cooker BBQ Chicken,
  166–68
 Slow Cooker Broccoli Cheese
  Soup, 176–77
 Slow Cooker Glazed Ribs,
  162–63
 Slow Cooker "Pot" of Beans,
  164–65
 Slow Cooker Spaghetti Sauce,
  169–71
 Stuffed Bell Peppers, 188–91
Dinners (under 20 minutes)
 Dinner Nachos, 148–51
 Doctored-Up Ramen, 132–33
 Honey-Soy Salmon, 136–37
 Lamb Chops with Mint Sauce,
  154–55
 Marsala Mushroom and Goat
  Cheese Flatbreads, 144–45
 Parmesan-Panko Chicken,
  158–59
 Pepperoni Chicken, 152–53
 Spaghetti Carbonara, 140–41
 Steaks with Chimichurri,
  146–47
 Steaks with Wasabi Cream Sauce,
  156–57
 Turkey Taco Skillet, 138–39
 Veggie Tortellini Soup, 134–35
Dinners (under 40 minutes)
 Cap'n Crunch Chicken Strips,
  102–3
 Chicken Piccata, 125–27
 Fried Shrimp, 116–17
 Hamburger Steaks with
  Mushroom Gravy, 113–15
 Mango-Chile Chicken, 106–7
 Roasted Red Pepper Soup, 104–5
 Shrimp Mango Lettuce Cups,
  110–12
 Shrimp Po' Boys, 118–19
 Smothered Pork Chops, 122–24

Taco Quesadillas, 128–29
Tex-Mex Butternut Squash Soup,
 108–9
Dips
 Hot Corn, 74–75
 The Merc's Queso, 88–91
 Pimento Cheese, 66–67
 Roasted Red Pepper Hummus, 58
 Slow Cooker Beef Enchilada,
  97–99
Dump Cakes, 324–25
Dumplings
 Glazed Apple, 336–38
 Peach, 339–41

E

Eggplant Steaks, Greek Grilled,
 258–59
Eggs
 Chilaquiles, 8–9
 Mini Sausage Casseroles, 20–21
 Spaghetti Carbonara, 140–41
 storing, xv

F

Fennel Chicken Bake, 226–27
Fish. *See Salmon*
Focaccia, Shortcut Olive, 306–7
Freezer staples
 bread dough, xiii
 casseroles, xiii
 cooked meat "components," xiii
 dinner rolls, xiii
 freezing your own produce, xii
 frozen corn, xii
 frozen fruit, xii
 frozen green beans, xii
 frozen peas, xii
 nuts, xiii
 pie crust, xiii
 puff pastry, xiii
 raw meats, xii
 sauces, stews, and soups, xiii

French Toast Sticks, Crunchy, 2–4
Fries, Curly, 290–91
Fruit. *See also specific fruits*
 frozen, xii
Funeral Potatoes, 294–96

G

Garlic
 40 Cloves of, and Chicken (Legs)
  Sheet Pan Supper, 214–15
 and Lemon, Broccolini with,
  282–83
 Marsala Mushroom and Goat
  Cheese Flatbreads, 144–45
 peeled, xv
 Roasted, Pull-Apart Cheese
  Bread, 300–302
 Rolls, Quick-and-Easy, 314–15
 storing, x
Grains. *See also Oats; Rice*
 Quinoa and Roasted Veggie
  Salad, 260–61
Granola Bars, 5–7
Greek Feast to Go, 57–59
Greek Grilled Eggplant Steaks,
 258–59
Greek Salad, 58–59
Green Beans
 frozen, xii
 Spicy Blue Cheese, 292–93
 Tuscan Chicken Sheet Pan
  Supper, 222–23
Greens. *See also Kale; Lettuce*

H

half-and-half, xv
Ham
 Waffle Iron Hash Browns,
  27–29
Hasselback Potatoes, 280–81
Herbs. *See also Basil; Cilantro*
 Mint Sauce, 154–55
 Rosemary Skewers, 82–83

Steaks with Chimichurri, 146–47
True Pasta Primavera, 262–65
Hominy Casserole, 286–87
Honey-Soy Salmon, 136–37
Hummus, Roasted Red Pepper, 58

I

Ice Cream
Baked Alaska, 342–44
Blueberry Cake Milkshake,
362–63
Caramel Apple Sundaes, 332–33
Pie, 326–27
Itty-Bitty Cakes, 364–65

J

Jams, xi
Jellies, xi

K

Kale
Mango-Chile Chicken, 106–7
Pasta Salad in a Jar, 42–45
Spaghetti Squash and, 288–89
and Teriyaki Salmon Sheet Pan
Supper, 216–17
King Ranch Chicken, 196–98

L

Lamb Chops with Mint Sauce,
154–55
Lemon(s)
Bars, 358–61
-Basil Potato Salad, 38–39
Citrus Snap Peas, 268–69
and Garlic, Broccolini with,
282–83
storing, xv
Lettuce
Citrus Salad with Vinaigrette,
236–37

Cups, Shrimp Mango, 110–12
Festive Pasta Salad, 246–47
Salad on a Stick, 46–47
Thai Chicken Wraps, 54–56
Limes, storing, xv
Lobster Mac and Cheese, 206–9
Lunches
Apple-Celery Slaw, 40–41
BBQ Chicken Wings, 36–37
Beef Noodle Salad Bowls, 48–51
Cowboy Bento Box, 34–41
Greek Feast to Go, 57–59
Grilled Veggie and Cream Cheese
Sandwiches, 60–62
Lemon-Basil Potato Salad, 38–39
Pasta Salad in a Jar, 42–45
Salad on a Stick, 46–47
Thai Chicken Wraps, 54–56

M

Mango
-Avocado Salad, 278–79
-Chile Chicken, 106–7
Shrimp Lettuce Cups, 110–12
Meat. *See also Beef; Lamb; Pork*
cooked "components," freezing,
xiii
freezing, xii
Pies, 202–5
Meatball Tortilla Soup, 181–83
Meatloaves, Mini Turkey, 192–95
The Merc's Queso, 88–91
Mexican Chicken Soup, 174–75
Milkshake, Blueberry Cake, 362–63
Mille-Feuille, Marvelous, 319–21
Mint
Sauce, 154–55
Steaks with Chimichurri, 146–47
True Pasta Primavera, 262–65
Mocha Lava Cakes, 348–49
Mousse, Milk Chocolate, 322–23
Muesli, Overnight, 15–17
Muffins
My Mom's, 24–26

Orange-Blueberry Muffin Tops,
30–31
Mushroom(s)
Doctored-Up Ramen, 132–33
Gravy, Hamburger Steaks with,
113–15
Marsala Mushroom and Goat
Cheese Flatbread, 144–45

N

Nachos, Dinner, 148–51
Noodle(s)
Beef Salad Bowls, 48–51
Doctored-Up Ramen, 132–33
Nutella Krispie Treats, 334–35
Nuts. *See also Pecans*
Bacon-Wrapped Almond-Stuffed
Dates, 78–79
freezing, xiii
Granola Bars, 5–7
My Mom's Muffins, 24–26

O

Oats
Amish Baked Oatmeal, 10–11
Granola Bars, 5–7
My Mom's Muffins, 24–26
Overnight Muesli, 15–17
Oils, xi
Olive(s), xi
Cheese Lover's Crostini, 94–96
Festive Pasta Salad, 246–47
Focaccia, Shortcut, 306–7
Greek Feast to Go, 57–59
Pantry Pasta, 238–39
Spanish Salmon Sheet Pan
Supper, 230–31
Onions, storing, x
Orange(s)
Citrus Salad with Vinaigrette,
236–37
-Blueberry Muffin Tops, 30–31
-Vanilla Monkey Bread, 22–23

P

Pancakes, Peachy, 12–14
Pantry items
  breadcrumbs, xi
  canned beans, x
  canned tomato products, x
  condiments, xi
  dried beans, x
  jams and jellies, xi
  jarred marinara sauce, x
  jarred pesto, xi
  oils and vinegars, xi
  olives, xi
  onions and garlic, x
  pasta, x
  pickled jalapeños, xi
  potatoes, x
  rice, x
  roasted red peppers, xi
  salsas, xi
  stocks and broths, x
  syrups, x
  umami ingredients, xi
Panzanella, Roasted Vegetable,
  243–45
Parsley
  Mint Sauce, 154–55
  Steaks with Chimichurri,
  146–47
Parsnips
  Quinoa and Roasted Veggie
    Salad, 260–61
  Roasted Vegetable Panzanella,
    243–45
  Sausage and Root Vegetables
    Sheet Pan Supper, 224–25
Pasta, x. *See also Noodle(s)*
  Chicken Piccata, 125–27
  Cincinnati Chili, 199–201
  Lobster Mac and Cheese, 206–9
  Pantry, 238–39
  Primavera, True, 262–65
  Salad, Festive, 246–47
  Salad in a Jar, 42–45

Shortcut Ravioli, 254–56
Slow Cooker Spaghetti Sauce,
  169–71
Spaghetti Carbonara, 140–41
Veggie Tortellini Soup, 134–35
Peach(es)
  Dump Cake, 324–25
  Dumplings, 339–41
  Peachy Pancakes, 12–14
Peanut butter
  Peanut Sauce (for salad), 48–51
  Peanut Sauce (for wraps), 54–55
Peas
  frozen, xii
  Snap, Citrus, 268–69
  True Pasta Primavera, 262–65
Pecans
  Citrus Salad with Vinaigrette,
    236–37
  Glazed Apple Dumplings,
    336–38
  Granola Bars, 5–7
  Ice Cream Pie, 326–27
  Nutella Krispie Treats, 334–35
Pepperoni Chicken, 152–53
Pepper(s). *See also Chiles*
  Bell, and Steak Sheet Pan
    Supper, 232–33
  Bell, Stuffed, 188–91
  Grilled Veggie and Cream Cheese
    Sandwiches, 60–62
  Hominy Casserole, 286–87
  Hot Corn Dip, 74–75
  King Ranch Chicken, 196–98
  Mango-Chile Chicken, 106–7
  Meat Pies, 202–5
  Mexican Chicken Soup, 174–75
  Pimento Cheese, 66–67
  Roasted Red, Hummus, 58
  roasted red, jarred, xi
  Roasted Red, Soup, 104–5
  Smothered Pork Chops, 122–24
  Spanish Salmon Sheet Pan
    Supper, 230–31
  Tortilla Pinwheels, 76–77

Veggietastic Sheet Pan Supper,
  218–21
Pestos, jarred, xi
Pie, Ice Cream, 326–27
Pie crust, freezing, xiii
Pimento Cheese, 66–67
Pineapple-Cherry Dump Cake,
  324–25
Pizza
  Cauliflower Crust, 250–53
  Marsala Mushroom and Goat
    Cheese Flatbreads, 144–45
  Stuffed Pizza Crust, 70–72
Po' Boys, Shrimp, 118–19
Pork. *See also Bacon; Ham; Sausage*
  Chops, Smothered, 122–24
  Slow Cooker Glazed Ribs,
    162–63
Potato Chip Cookies, 345–47
Potato(es)
  Broccoli Cheese, 240–42
  Chicken Fennel Bake, 226–27
  Curly Fries, 290–91
  Funeral, 294–96
  Hasselback, 280–81
  Salad, Lemon-Basil, 38–39
  Sausage and Root Vegetables
    Sheet Pan Supper, 224–25
  storing, x
  Sweet, Baked, with Sour Cream
    and Mint, 270–71
  Waffle Iron Hash Browns, 27–29
Poultry. *See Chicken; Turkey*
Pretzel-Coated Fried Goat Cheese,
  80–81
Puff pastry
  freezing, xiii
  Glazed Apple Dumplings, 336–38
  Marvelous Mille-Feuille, 319–21

Q

Quesadillas, Taco, 128–29
Quinoa and Roasted Veggie Salad,
  260–61

R

Raisins
  Curried Rice, 276–77
  Glazed Apple Dumplings, 336–38
  My Mom's Muffins, 24–26
Ramen, Doctored-Up, 132–33
Raspberry(ies)
  Marvelous Mille-Feuille, 319–21
  White Chocolate Cheesecake, No-Bake, 352–54
Ravioli, Shortcut, 254–56
Refrigerator staples
  bacon, xiv
  berries, xv
  butter, xv
  cheese, xiv
  cream, xv
  eggs, xv
  half-and-half, xv
  lemons and limes, xv
  peeled garlic, xv
  sour cream, xv
  tortillas, xv
  yogurt, xv
Rice, x
  Curried, 276–77
  Honey-Soy Salmon, 136–37
  Stuffed Bell Peppers, 188–91
Rice cereal
  Granola Bars, 5–7
  Nutella Krispie Treats, 334–35
Rolls
  Checkerboard, 308–10
  dinner, freezing, xiii
  Garlic, Quick-and-Easy, 314–15
Rosemary Skewers, 82–83

S

Salads
  Apple-Celery Slaw, 40–41
  Beef Noodle Salad Bowls, 48–51
  Citrus, with Vinaigrette, 236–37
  Greek, 58–59
  Lemon-Basil Potato, 38–39
  Mango-Avocado, 278–79
  Pasta, Festive, 246–47
  Pasta, in a Jar, 42–45
  Quinoa and Roasted Veggie, 260–61
  Roasted Vegetable Panzanella, 243–45
  on a Stick, 46–47
Salmon
  Honey-Soy, 136–37
  Spanish, Sheet Pan Supper, 230–31
  Teriyaki, and Kale Sheet Pan Supper, 216–17
Salsas, xi
Sandwiches
  Grilled Veggie and Cream Cheese, 60–62
  Shrimp Po' Boys, 118–19
  Thai Chicken Wraps, 54–56
Sauces
  freezing, xiii
  marinara, jarred, x
  Mint, 154–55
  Peanut, 48–51
  Peanut Sauce, 54–55
  Spaghetti, Slow Cooker, 169–71
  Wasabi Cream, 156–57
Sausage
  Casseroles, Mini, 20–21
  The Merc's Queso, 88–91
  and Root Vegetables Sheet Pan Supper, 224–25
Seafood. *See Lobster; Salmon; Shrimp*
Shellfish. *See Lobster; Shrimp*
Shrimp
  Fried, 116–17
  Mango Lettuce Cups, 110–12
  Po' Boys, 118–19
  Roasted, with Cherry Tomato Sheet Pan Supper, 212–13

Sides
  Apple-Celery Slaw, 40–41
  Baked Sweet Potato with Sour Cream and Mint, 270–71
  Broccolini with Garlic and Lemon, 282–83
  Citrus Snap Peas, 268–69
  Curly Fries, 290–91
  Curried Rice, 276–77
  Edna Mae's Escalloped Cabbage, 272–74
  Funeral Potatoes, 294–96
  Hasselback Potatoes, 280–81
  Hominy Casserole, 286–87
  Lemon-Basil Potato Salad, 38–39
  Mango-Avocado Salad, 278–79
  Spaghetti Squash and Kale, 288–89
  Spicy Blue Cheese Green Beans, 292–93
Slaw, Apple Celery, 40–41
Soups
  Bean with Bacon, 178–80
  Broccoli Cheese, Slow Cooker, 176–77
  Chicken, Mexican, 174–75
  freezing, xiii
  Roasted Red Pepper, 104–5
  Tex-Mex Butternut Squash Soup, 108–9
  Tortilla, Meatball, 181–83
  Veggie Tortellini, 134–35
Sour Cream, xv
  and Mint, Baked Sweet Potatoes with, 270–71
  Steaks with Wasabi Cream Sauce, 156–57
Spanish Salmon Sheet Pan Supper, 230–31
Squash. *See also Zucchini*
  Quinoa and Roasted Veggie Salad, 260–61
  Roasted Vegetable Panzanella, 243–45

Spaghetti, and Kale, 288–89
Tex-Mex Butternut, Soup, 108–9
Stews, freezing, xiii
Stocks, x
Sweet Potatoes
    Baked, with Sour Cream and
        Mint, 270–71
    Sausage and Root Vegetables
        Sheet Pan Supper, 224–25
Syrups, x

T

Taco Quesadillas, 128–29
Teriyaki Salmon and Kale Sheet
    Pan Supper, 216–17
Tex-Mex Butternut Squash Soup,
    108–9
Thai Chicken Wraps, 54–56
Tofu
    Veggietastic Sheet Pan Supper,
        218–21
Tomato(es)
    Cheese Lover's Crostini,
        94–96
    Cherry, with Roasted Shrimp
        Sheet Pan Supper, 212–13
    Dinner Nachos, 148–51
    Festive Pasta Salad, 246–47
    Greek Grilled Eggplant Steaks,
        258–59
    Greek Salad, 58–59
    Mango-Avocado Salad, 278–79

Meatball Tortilla Soup,
    181–83
The Merc's Queso, 88–91
Mexican Chicken Soup,
    174–75
Pantry Pasta, 238–39
Pasta Salad in a Jar, 42–45
products, canned, x
Rosemary Skewers, 82–83
Salad on a Stick, 46–47
Shrimp Po' Boys, 118–19
Slow Cooker Spaghetti Sauce,
    169–71
Stuffed Bell Peppers, 188–91
Tuscan Chicken Sheet Pan
    Supper, 222–23
Tortilla(s)
    Chilaquiles, 8–9
    Dinner Nachos, 148–51
    King Ranch Chicken, 196–98
    Pinwheels, 76–77
    Soup, Meatball, 181–83
    storing, xv
    Taco Quesadillas, 128–29
    Thai Chicken Wraps, 54–56
    Turkey Taco Skillet, 138–39
Turkey
    Meatloaves, Mini, 192–95
    Taco Skillet, 138–39

U

Umami ingredients, xi

V

Vegetables. *See also specific vegetables*
    frozen, xii
    Veggie Tortellini Soup, 134–35
Veggietastic Sheet Pan Supper,
    218–21
vinegars, xi

W

Waffle Iron Hash Browns, 27–29
Walnuts
    My Mom's Muffins, 24–26
Wasabi Cream Sauce, Steaks with,
    156–57
Watermelon Feta Bites, 68–69
White Chocolate Raspberry
    Cheesecake, No-Bake, 352–54

Y

Yogurt, xv

Z

Zucchini
    Bread, 303–5
    Grilled Veggie and Cream Cheese
        Sandwiches, 60–62
    Roasted Vegetable Panzanella,
        243–45
    Roll-Ups, 92–93
    Stuffed Bell Peppers, 188–91

The End